Translation and Migration

Translation and Migration examines the ways in which the presence or absence of translation in situations of migratory movement has currently and historically shaped social, cultural, and economic relations between groups and individuals. Acts of cultural and linguistic translation are discussed through a rich variety of illustrative literary, ethnographic, visual, and historical materials, also taking in issues of multiculturalism, assimilation, and hybridity analytically re-framed. This is key reading for students undertaking translation and interpreting studies courses, and will also be of interest to researchers in sociology, cultural studies, anthropology, and migration studies.

Moira Inghilleri is currently Associate Professor in the Comparative Literature Program and Director of Translation Studies at the University of Massachusetts Amherst.

New Perspectives in Translation and Interpreting Studies

Series editors

Michael Cronin holds a Personal Chair in the Faculty of Humanities and Social Sciences at Dublin City University.

Moira Inghilleri is Director of Translation Studies in the Comparative Literature Program at the University of Massachusetts Amherst.

The *New Perspectives in Translation and Interpreting Studies* series aims to address changing needs in the fields of translation studies and interpreting studies. The series features work by leading scholars in both disciplines, on emerging and up-to-date topics. Key features of the titles in this series are accessibility, relevance, and innovation.

These lively and highly readable texts provide an exploration into various areas of translation and interpreting studies for undergraduate and postgraduate students of translation studies, interpreting studies, and cultural studies.

Cities in Translation
Sherry Simon

Translation in the Digital Age
Michael Cronin

Translation and Geography
Federico Italiano

Translation and Rewriting in the Age of Post-Translation Studies
Edwin Gentzler

Eco-Translation
Michael Cronin

Translation and Migration

Moira Inghilleri

LONDON AND NEW YORK

First published 2017
by Routledge
2 Park Square, Milton Park, Abingdon, Oxon OX14 4RN

and by Routledge
711 Third Avenue, New York, NY 10017

Routledge is an imprint of the Taylor & Francis Group, an informa business

© 2017 Moira Inghilleri

The right of Moira Inghilleri to be identified as author of this work has been asserted by her in accordance with sections 77 and 78 of the Copyright, Designs and Patents Act 1988.

All rights reserved. No part of this book may be reprinted or reproduced or utilised in any form or by any electronic, mechanical, or other means, now known or hereafter invented, including photocopying and recording, or in any information storage or retrieval system, without permission in writing from the publishers.

Trademark notice: Product or corporate names may be trademarks or registered trademarks, and are used only for identification and explanation without intent to infringe.

British Library Cataloguing in Publication Data
A catalogue record for this book is available from the British Library

Library of Congress Cataloguing in Publication Data
A catalog record has been requested for this book

ISBN: 978-0-415-82808-6 (hbk)
ISBN: 978-0-415-82811-6 (pbk)
ISBN: 978-1-3153-9982-9 (ebk)

Typeset in Sabon LT Std
by Out of House Publishing

This book is dedicated to my parents
who met at a dance in Manhattan
Eileen (O'Brien) Inghilleri,
first-generation Irish immigrant
and
L. Frank (Lorenzo Francesco) Inghilleri,
second-generation Sicilian immigrant

Contents

List of figures   viii
Acknowledgments   x

1 Migration, mobility, and culture   1

2 The multiple meanings of hospitality   39

3 Translation and labor migrants   69

4 Translating the landscape   108

5 Signs of transnationalism from above and below   149

6 Constructing and contesting young migrant identities   176

Index   208

List of figures

1.1	Moving traces. Photograph: author's own	4
1.2	Making tracks. Photograph: author's own	5
2.1	"Slovak woman and children 1902–1914." Manuscripts and Archives Division, The New York Public Library	41
2.2	"Italian woman 1902–1913." Manuscripts and Archives Division, The New York Public Library	42
2.3	"Immigrants undergoing medical examination 1902–1913." The Miriam and Ira D. Wallach Division of Art, Prints and Photographs: Photography Collection, The New York Public Library	47
2.4	"Immigrants waiting in line for processing by Immigration Bureau officials 1902–1913." The Miriam and Ira D. Wallach Division of Art, Prints and Photographs: Photography Collection, The New York Public Library	48
2.5	"A private interview between a young immigrant and an Ellis Island official. Two staff members [?] are also present 1902–1910." Manuscripts and Archives Division, The New York Public Library	49
2.6	"Pacific Chivalry: Encouragement to Chinese Immigration," *Harper's Weekly,* August 7, 1869. AP2.H3, 13:152. Courtesy of the Bancroft Library, University of California, Berkeley	51
2.7	Poem on a wall at the detention barracks, Angel Island. Courtesy of Chris Carlsson, photographer	55
3.1	Assembly lines (Ngai, 2005)	86
3.2	Mural by Banksy, Chalk Farm, London	93
3.3	'Kumjings.' Courtesy of Empower Foundation	101
3.4	'Mida Tapestry.' Courtesy of Empower Foundation	102
4.1	Moody Street feeder, Irish canal workers, circa 1896. Lowell, Massachusetts. Courtesy of The University of Massachusetts Lowell, Center for Lowell History	115
4.2	Moody Street feeder, Lowell, Massachusetts, 2016. Photograph by Roger Hewitt	116

4.3	"East and West Shaking Hands at Laying of Last Rail." Golden Spike ceremony, Promontory Summit, Utah Territory, May 10, 1869. Photograph by A.J. Russell. Collection of the Oakland Museum of California	123
4.4	"Chinese Laying Last Rail / U.P.R.R." Promontory Summit, Utah Territory, May 10, 1869, A.J. Russell's Stereoview #539 H69.459.2426. Collection of the Oakland Museum of California	126
4.5	"Does Not SUCH a Meeting Make Amends?" Wood engraving, May 29, 1869. Courtesy of the Library of Congress, Prints and Photographs Division, LC-USZC2-747	127
4.6	"The Great Fear of the Period, That Uncle Sam May Be Swallowed Up By Foreigners: The Problem Solved," White and Bauer [1860–1869]. Courtesy of the Library of Congress, Prints and Photographs Division, LC-DIG-pga-03047	130
4.7	Shiva lingam. Photo courtesy of Shastri Akella	133
4.8	Ice lingam, Amarnath Cave. Photo courtesy of Shastri Akella	133
5.1	Inter-semiotic signs at the British Museum, London. Photograph: author's own	150
5.2	Villa Fundacion, New York. Photograph by Milica Bogetic and Stephanie Kaplan	151
5.3	Burj Khaleefa Deli, New York. Photograph by Milica Bogetic and Stephanie Kaplan	152
5.4	Smog, Koreatown, Los Angeles. Photograph by Roger Hewitt	158
5.5	Streetview, Koreatown, Los Angeles. Photograph by Roger Hewitt	159
5.6	Life Medical Supply, Koreatown, Los Angeles. Photograph by Roger Hewitt	160
5.7	Jae Bu Do, Koreatown, Los Angeles. Photograph by Roger Hewitt	161
5.8	Multimodal signs, Koreatown, Los Angeles. Photograph by Roger Hewitt	162
5.9	Multimodal signs, Koreatown, Los Angeles. Photograph by Roger Hewitt	162

Acknowledgments

The visual images that appear throughout this book are an essential part of the story I wished to tell. I am very grateful to the many institutions and individuals that assisted me in this endeavor. I thank the Bancroft Library at the University of California, Berkeley; the Oakland Museum of California; the Library of Congress, Prints and Photographs Division; the New York Public Library Digital Collections; the University of Massachusetts Lowell, Center for Lowell History; and Chantawipa Apisuk ("Pi Noi") at The Empower Foundation. Thanks also to Milica Bogetic and Stephanie Kaplan for their many photos of bodegas in New York City. Thanks also to Roger Hewitt for taking the photographs of Koreatown and Lowell. I would like to thank Chris Carlsson for allowing me to use his photograph of the Angel Island poem. The poems of the Chinese immigrants on Angel Island are reprinted with permission of the University of Washington Press. The footprints and tractor marks are my responsibility alone.

I would like to thank the University of Massachusetts Amherst for granting me both funding for research support and a research-intensive semester to enable me to complete the book. I would also like to thank my colleagues at the University of Massachusetts Amherst for their support and encouragement throughout the writing of this book. I would especially like to acknowledge three of our group of talented graduate students, Shastri Akella, Hyongrae Kim, and Una Tanović for our stimulating conversations about migration and translation. Many thanks also to Jihyon Kim and Hyongrae Kim for their translations of the Korean signs in Chapter Four.

I wish to acknowledge support from the Massachusetts Society of Professors in the form of a grant for indexing and copyright and reproduction fees for some of the images in the book.

My sons, Louie and Pablo Hewitt, are a constant source of inspiration. They show me by example that their generation is way out ahead in redefining what unity in diversity can mean in the twenty-first century.

Finally, words cannot do justice to the thanks owed to my husband, Roger Hewitt. Decades ago, he, an Englishman, introduced me, an American, to the modern American poet, William Carlos Williams, and to the Black Mountain poets Charles Olson and Robert Creeley. Carlos Williams' famous line "no ideas but in things" has continued to influence both our approaches to research. This book is a product of our countless dialogues, without which it would never have come into being.

1 Migration, mobility, and culture

Migrants, like all human beings, are always simultaneously influencing and being influenced by others, perceiving the world and evolving within it even when they appear to be standing still.[1] The immediate effects of migration on individuals are mostly experienced in synchronic moments – events lived at particular points in time as a cluster of culturally, socially, and linguistically managed encounters and entanglements with others. Migration is at the same time an unfolding diachronic process: a singularly marked instantiation of social life involving movement, transformation, and continuous becoming.

In debates over migration and its local or global impact, migrants from the same nations, regions, or continents are often referred to as homogeneous categorical entities, despite vast differences among them. After their arrival, these categories and their associated characteristics often persist. Once migrants establish a more permanent residence, legal or not, designations become more varied and finely tuned – contingent on factors such as who is doing the labeling and in what context. Names themselves can take on particular significance, representing a fixed otherness or morphing opportunely, whether to fit local cultural or phonological norms or create symbolic or strategic links between departure and arrival; or as the following extract about a New York sweatshop in the 1890s shows, to respond to the very specific circumstances of the local:

> When Mrs Nelson [the boss's wife] had worked a few minutes she asked father in very imperfect Yiddish: "Well, Mr ---, have you given your daughter an American name?"
>
> "Not yet," father answered. "What would you call her? Her Yiddish name is Rahel."
>
> "Rahel, Rahel," Mrs Nelson repeated to herself, thoughtfully, winding the thread around a button, "let me see." The machines were going slowly and the men looked interested.
>
> The presser called out from the back of the room: "What is there to think about? Rahel is Rachel."
>
> [...]

2   Migration, mobility, and culture

> Mrs Nelson turned to me: "Don't let them call you Rachel. Every loafer who sees a Jewish girl shouts 'Rachel' after her. And on Cherry Street where you live there are many saloons and many loafers. How would you like Ruth for a name?"
> I said I should like to be called Ruth.
>
> (Dublin 1993: 162)

Though the experience of migration varies significantly between individuals and cultural groups and across history and geographical settings, there is also commonality. Migration can involve the maintenance of strong attachments with a particular culture or social group and/or an opportunity for reinvention – a means to create distance between a new and a prior self. Migrants often suffer social and cultural isolation due to processes of racialization, ethnicization, and/or ethnocentric attitudes from individuals, communities, or entire nations. The form of migration – whether individuals have left their homes voluntarily or under political, social, or economic duress; the socioeconomic status of migrants; whether an individual or family intends to return or not; how first-generation migrants situate themselves in relation to their identity/identities – always leaves an impress on how individuals and subsequent generations adapt to or are received in a new environment. Language has always been an active site where the contours of inclusion and exclusion become most visible. Utterances between co-ethnics can signify warmth or shame or warning, and access to new sources of knowledge in a new land can be found in translation as well as lost.

Much has been made of the fact that, unlike their predecessors, twenty-first-century migrants are able to maintain virtual if not physical contact with their past and present as a result of technological advances. The availability and greater affordability of air travel in the mid to late twentieth century and less expensive forms of telecommunication like smart phones, the internet, and satellite radio and television which link migrants culturally, linguistically, and psychologically to their countries or regions of origin, has transformed the experience of migration significantly. It has become less unidirectional, and communication between migrants and those they leave behind can be more frequent and not limited to letters delivered by surface mail with weeks or months in between. The internet provides webcasts, blogs, and access to information in national newspapers or news programs from countries of origin. For many communities, local radio and television programming, community newspapers, and supplements in local newspapers keep individuals informed about national and global events *in their own languages*. The significance of these particular media varies with personal profile. Email, instant messaging, webcam sessions, and social media sites allow many foreign overseas workers living thousands of miles away from their parents, children, wives, or husbands to sustain these relationships at a distance over years, and often decades. Music and video circuits and locally produced websites offer younger first and second-generation immigrants a way to cultivate and express their multilingual identities. Transnational media within migrant societies give greater fluidity to territorial and conceptual boundaries, fostering new sensibilies of geographic and temporal locality, intimacy and distance, community and society. Taken together, different media – and the new technologies that make them possible – play a central role in the formation of a particular migrant sensibility, a migratory 'aesthetic' created by a departure from one place and arrival in another.

Transnational media open up new 'routes' and provide different possibilities for or challenges to the concept of 'roots' in the twenty-first century. The effects of this wider range of media on issues historically associated with migration, such as acculturation and advancement within the new environments migrants inhabit and their relationships with the places and people they leave behind, remains a complex matter however. The compression of time and space that characterizes transnational communication is invariably shaped by social identities as well as geographical locations (Baldassar et al 2016).

This chapter presents aspects of the historical, social, philosophical, and geographical conditions that have shaped migration and the different forms of multi- or transcultural societies that result, framed within theoretical considerations that are, in my view, the most pertinent to an understanding of cultural translation in all its many voices. It provides the material and theoretical background for the themes explored in depth in subsequent chapters which bring substantive contexts of translation into view, seen through the diverse forms that migration has taken and continues to take across the globe.

Migration, mobility, and landscape

Migrants transform and are transformed by the communities and societies they become a part of, and translation is central to this process. With the aid of different types of translation, strangers to one another's cultures and languages glimpse their differences but also their possible overlapping values and prior experiences. These precarious moments of attempted mutual recognition establish the initial conditions for further contact. The movement of people, historically and geographically, has played a vital role in the evolution of both the social and the physical world. This evolution is not only a product of encounters between humans; it also involves humans interacting with the physical environment. Migration necessitates movement through land, sea, and/or air.

Most of the physical evidence of this mobility, the traces that individuals leave behind, is erased over time. Footprints and vehicles only temporarily leave their marks on different surfaces and modern paved roads retain little evidence of the multitudes that traverse them daily

4 *Migration, mobility, and culture*

Figure 1.1 Moving traces. Photograph: author's own

(Figures 1.1 and 1.2). It is only when bodies are washed up on a beach, lost at sea, or when remains are discovered in the desert that we are reminded of the relationship between migration and the topographical spaces that are integral to the journey. In these cases, it is almost always humans, not the chosen terrain or the mode of transportation, who are responsible for these deaths.

In his book, *Being Alive: Essays on Movement, Knowledge and Description* (2011), the anthropologist Tim Ingold makes the important observation that locomotion and cognition are inseparable. He contends that knowledge is formed as humans move across the surface of the earth, not by collecting information from observations they make about this place or that place, but from human action and lived experiences. Wayfaring, he suggests, is the fundamental mode by which living beings inhabit the earth.

> Like all other creatures, humans do not exist on the other side of materiality, but swim in the ocean of materials. Once we acknowledge our immersion, what this ocean reveals to us is not the bland homogeneity of different shades of matter, but a flux in which materials of the most diverse kinds, through processes of admixture and distillation, of

Figure 1.2 Making tracks. Photograph: author's own

> coagulation and dispersal and of evaporation and precipitation undergo continual generation and transformation.
>
> (Ingold 2011: 24)

Though migration is frequently associated, mainly in a negative sense, with words like *uprooted*, *unsettled*, *disruption*, and *displacement*, all of which represent movement as a break with an immovable foundation, throughout history humans have shown themselves to be disposed to and capable of adaptation and change. Their relationship with landscape has been an intricate part of this process. The significance of the physical environment to migration endures, while the landscape remains alive too.

> And as the environment unfolds, so the materials of which it is comprised do not *exist* – like the objects of the material – but *occur*. The properties of materials, regarded as constituents of the environment, cannot be regarded as fixed, essential attributes of things, but are rather processual and relational. They are neither objectively determined nor subjectively imagined but practically experienced. To describe the properties of materials is to tell the stories of what happens to them as they flow, mix and mutate.
>
> (ibid.: 30)

These ideas about mobility, materials, and their relation to the physical environment correspond with the view of migration and translation offered in this book. All human beings can be said to be 'migrating' to some degree. To be human entails *moving* through life in much the same way that being a fox entails "*streaking* like a flash of fire through the undergrowth" and being an owl entails "*perching* in the lower branches of spruce trees" (ibid.: 72). Like all sentient beings and other non-human entities such as stone and wood, human attributes are in a constant state of fluidity. The archaeologist Christopher Tilly has described the properties of "stoniness" as "endlessly variable in relation to light or shade, wetness or dryness, and the position, posture or movement of the observer" (Tilly qtd. in Ingold 2011: 30–31). But stones, like humans, also "have histories, *forged in ongoing relations with surroundings* that may or may not include human beings and much else besides" (ibid.: 31, my emphasis). The ability of humans to adapt to different environments – from geological and climatic to ecological and social – provides strong evidence of human malleability and connectivity.

In the era of globalization, however, despite an abundance of increasingly accessible technologies of connectivity, mobility has come to mean different things to different people. For a transnational elite it may offer the possibility of a cosmopolitan freedom, but for many migrant workers, refugees, and other persons politically, culturally, and economically displaced by the consequences of global capitalism it can signify isolation, desperation, and restricted opportunity. Indeed, the very notion of transnationalism can "obscur[e] and elid[e] different scales, networks and manifestations of connections, diminishing its clarity as a conceptual tool" (Harney and Baldassar 2007: 190).

Departures

Significant waves of global migration took place in the nineteenth and twentieth centuries. The first, from the mid-nineteenth to the first half of the twentieth century, involved millions of people leaving Europe largely for economic reasons in the direction of the Americas and Australia. In the mid-nineteenth century, Australia, a colonial outpost itself, was also a major recruiter of cheap indentured labor from India, Sri Lanka, China, and the Pacific Islands for its sugar plantations, despite otherwise exclusionary immigration policies regarding non-Whites and strong local resistance to Asian migrants (Rivett 1975). Around the same time, Chinese migrants, driven by the colonial expansion leading up to the Opium Wars and the weakening of Chinese sovereignty, departed in large numbers for Australia and the United States alongside the many others who were seeking their fortune in gold (Clarke 2006). The second wave of migration beginning in the latter half of the twentieth century was triggered by decolonization and the initial recruitment of individuals from prior colonies as laborers to fulfill the needs of the growing European economies. Western Europe also served as a destination during World War II and the Cold War for those escaping Nazi Germany and other autocratic regimes in Africa, Asia, and Latin America.[2]

A new twenty-first century wave is currently taking place as autocratic regimes in the Middle East long supported by the United States and Europe are being challenged, and in some cases, ousted by their own populations. In Iraq, Afghanistan, and Syria political and economic turmoil caused by invasion and civil war have driven millions to leave their homes to seek refuge in neighboring countries, Europe, and elsewhere. The UN Refugee Agency (UNHCR) has indicated that these and other conflicts have forced more people than at any other time since records began – surpassing World War II – to flee their homes and seek refuge elsewhere.

Departures are rarely the beginning for migrants and refugees. The final moments before their 'flight' come after many tough choices made, terrifying escapes, hopeful realizations, dangers encountered, loved-ones anguished over, and stark realities confronted. While migrations forced on people by war or sudden changes in regimes or economies are one kind of urgent pressure toward leaving their homeland, social ideals and a belief in the ability to make a new life can be quite a different impetus, sometimes prepared for by earlier generations – parents and grandparents – who forged the social and political vision of radical change, of human progress thwarted at home now translated into the hope of a promised land of possibility. Migration from Europe in the nineteenth century was often of this kind, with migrants 'setting sail,' literally or figuratively, for opportunities in the United States, Canada, Latin America, Australia, and elsewhere. This presented individuals and families with the chance to do what they had hoped to do at home – a bloodless revolution of sorts, deeply needed to make something happen elsewhere.

During this time, destinations in Europe, the Americas, and Australia became the repository of many different kinds of 'dreams' – the secularized versions of the millenarian movements of earlier centuries to create "God's kingdom on earth" that would rescue others from destitution and despair (Cohn 1970). Although for many, then and now, such dreams became quickly tarnished and early expectations qualified by so much else, the economic and political motives retain all of their urgency and then some in the present, as individuals, families, and even unaccompanied children continue to drag themselves across borders or stow away in the holds of boats, trains, and trucks out of both the profoundest need and the glimmer of hope that life elsewhere has more to offer.

To rehearse some important iconic moments in recent and relevant migration, the civil war in Syria is the latest example of the above. The exodus of refugees has created new pressures on European powers and radical reassessments of the nature of the European Union. It has also called into question the commitment of the United States and other countries to provide unconditional refuge to populations who find themselves victims of violent conflict and its consequences. Since 2011, in response to peaceful anti-government protests as part of the Arab Spring, the civil war in Syria has killed over 220,000 people, half of whom are believed to be civilians, and has produced millions of refugees. Bombs are destroying cities, and human rights violations are widespread. Basic necessities like food and medical care continue to be limited or unavailable. A 2015 joint report by UNICEF and Save the Children, *Small Hands, Heavy Burden: How the Syrian Conflict is Driving More Children into the Workforce*, revealed an increasing number of young children forced to work and deprived of education both inside Syria and in the refugee camps.[3]

> Children affected by the Syria crisis are working primarily because of poverty and their families' loss of livelihoods. Whether in Syria or in neighbouring countries, children have become main players in the survival of households as partial or even sole breadwinners. Inside Syria, some children have found themselves separated from their caregivers or have themselves become the head of the household following the death or disappearance of their parents. In other cases, families send children away to work in other areas of the country or across borders to generate income and avoid them being recruited by armed groups or getting injured in the conflict.
> (UNICEF / Save the Children 2015: 10)

According to UNHCR statistics, by the start of 2016, 11.6 million Syrians had been displaced, nearly half of Syria's entire population. Most are dispersed within Syria, though at the beginning of May 2016, 4.8 million were registered as living in Egypt, Turkey, Lebanon, Jordan, and Iraq. In the first months of 2016, 74,000 more migrants, the majority Syrian, 43 percent of them women and children, had already fled via the Mediterranean route with 391 reported dead or missing upon arrival.[4] Most had walked for hours on foot to reach the boats that precariously cross the Mediterranean and will do the same again to reach their final destinations in Europe and beyond.

The exodus from Syria has been referred to as a "modern migration,"[5] the first of its kind in a fully digital age where refugees rely on smartphones (and phone charging stations) to be able to find safe routes at different border crossings,[6] wrapping their phones in waterproof plastic or balloons to protect them during sea crossings, or once in refugee camps. The technology serves as a lifeline connecting refugees to points of departure (selfies and social media let their families back home know they have arrived safely and help them to find those from whom they have been separated on a journey), to the present (apps help them locate food and shelter, translate signs, and map out local surroundings upon arrival, giving them immediate access to 'local knowledge' that previously would have required time or the 'kindness of strangers'), and to future destinations (bus, train, and ferry schedules are posted online in translation, GPS coordinates are shared among refugees, and the conditions at particular refugee camps or borders are disseminated).[7]

Despite the clear benefits of technology, journeys undertaken by refugees – even with a presumption of eventual sanctuary – remain treacherous due to any number of inhospitable conditions presented by the proximity of physical and human threats to security along the way, including traffickers, sea pirates, border guards, and the politics and policies of nation states themselves.

Individuals fleeing their countries of origin due to war, violence, persecution, and other types of social and economic hardships have always had to rely on, and at times have been refused, temporary or permanent hospitality from the international community. In 1939, at a time when thousands of Jews had already fled, were in hiding, or had been sent to concentration camps as a consequence of the Nazi government, Hitler's regime was also attempting to rid itself of its Jewish population by terrorizing and intimidating those with the means to leave Germany. An ocean liner, the *SS St. Louis*, sailed from Germany headed for Havana, carrying 937 Jews who had paid for visas from Cuban Embassy officials in Berlin, hoping eventually to find refuge in the United States. In some cases, whole families boarded the ship; in others, men left their wives and children behind or women and children took the journey alone. Upon their arrival in Cuba, however, the Cuban government revoked the visas of all but a few of the passengers. Eventually the ship sailed toward Florida in the slim hope of being granted permission to dock in the United States where the passengers would be granted refugee status. However, the US Congress, under President Franklin Roosevelt, refused them entry citing the quota system that limited the number of immigrants from any one country per year, but also owing to increasing public backing of an isolationist stance in relation to the crisis in Europe and an open campaign of anti-Semitism that was garnering support from certain segments of the population. In the end, the *SS St. Louis* was forced to return to Europe, where the passengers were dispersed to France, Belgium, Great Britain, and the Netherlands. It has been estimated that at least 254 of them were later killed in the camps or in war-related violence (Thomas and Morgan-Witts 1974).

In the aftermath of the US defeat in Vietnam and subsequent withdrawal from South Vietnam, over 2 million refugees fled Vietnam, Laos, and Cambodia. The first waves of Southeast Asian refugees were disproportionately comprised of elites who left because of political opposition to the Communist regimes. During the fall of Saigon in 1974, it was mostly Vietnamese professionals and members of the military who were evacuated by sea or air to American bases in Guam and the Philippines, while many Hmong, an ethnic group from Laos who had been heavily recruited by the US military to fight against the North Vietnamese, were forced to flee on foot across the Mekong River into Thailand. In Vietnam and Laos hundreds of thousands were imprisoned in 're-education camps,' some 50,000 of whom would eventually be released according to an agreement signed in 1989 between the United States and Vietnam which stated that current and former detainees in the camps would be permitted to leave for the United States (Rumbaut 1996: 5–6). Prior to this arrangement, however, thousands more people would be forced to flee due to the worsening economic conditions that resulted from years of war and continuing ideological conflicts in the region. In 1978 this second large wave of refugees, some of whom became known as the 'boat people,' began to flee Vietnam, Cambodia, and Laos.

According to Rumbaut (2006: 265–266):

> Hundreds of thousands of Cambodian survivors of the Pol Pot labor camps fled to the Thai border along with increased flows of Hmong and other refugees from Laos; about 250,000 ethnic Chinese from North Vietnam moved across the border into China; and tens of thousands of Chinese and Vietnamese "boat people" attempted to cross the South China Sea packed in rickety crafts suitable only for river travel, many of whom drowned or were assaulted by Thai pirates preying on refugee boats in the Gulf of Thailand. By Spring 1979 nearly 60,000 boat people were arriving monthly in the countries of the region. These events led to an international resettlement crisis later that year when those "first asylum" countries (principally Thailand, Malaysia and Indonesia) refused to accept more refugees into their already swollen camps, often pushing boat refugees back out to sea, where many perished – Malaysia alone pushed some 40,000 out – or forcing land refugees at gun-point back across border mine fields (US Committee for Refugees, 1985, 1986, 1987). In response, under agreements reached at the Geneva Conference in July 1979, Western countries began to absorb significant numbers of the refugee camp population in Southeast Asia.

Nyguen Huu Chung, one of those who left Vietnam by boat at the age of twelve with two of his cousins, recalled his journey in an autographical essay written as a university student in the United States almost a decade later.

> We escaped in September 1978 on a small boat along with twenty-six other people. We were on the sea for three days. Then we saw another boat. At first, we thought it was a rescue boat, but it turned out to be a Thai fishing boat. When they saw us, they began to approach us. Once we were in contact with their boat all of the men, who were armed with weapons, jumped over to our boat and began to strip us to search for gold. After that they began to rape all the women on board. I will never forget seeing all the men crying when they watched their wives being raped and were unable to do anything. One man could not take

it anymore, and he jumped and tried to fight the Thai, but he was shot and killed by the Thai captain. After this they began to beat all the men and throw us overboard. My two cousins and I were hit on the head and were unconscious.

The next morning when I woke up, I saw only eighteen people left on board. Upon seeing this, I asked the captain where all the people were. He replied that seven people died of drowning, one got shot, and three girls were taken as hostages on the Thai boat. He did not know what happened to those three girls! I then asked, "Where is the Thai boat?" he said, "They left last night and I hope they will never come back." After the fifth day at sea we were rescued by the ship called The Panama which took us to the Pulau Bidong refugee camp.[8]

(Nguyen 1989: 89–90)

For those refugees who ended up in the United States after the war in Vietnam, their very presence, at least initially, carried both negative and positive connotations due to the lingering divisiveness of the war in Vietnam within the US population. In many cases, local populations categorized Laotians, Cambodians, Vietnamese, Hmong, and ethnic Chinese as 'Asian' or 'Chinese,' with little regard for their significant historical, cultural, and linguistic differences. Their shared status as refugees, however, meant that their exits from their countries of origin were traumatic escapes, not mere journeys, and their migration was, at the time at least, an exilic one which held no prospect of return.

The ongoing process of a migrant identity formation of child victims and survivors of violent conflicts across the globe is inevitably shaped by the wars that have left millions dead, often members of their own families and communities, forcing individuals and families to flee under perilous conditions, spending in some cases years in refugee camps before migrating thousands of miles from home to become part of a large, multifaceted diaspora. Fortunately, evidence suggests that for Southeast Asian refugees like Nguyen Huu Chung the intense pre-arrival trauma they suffered was reduced over time as their lives became more similar to other immigrants', that is, as "contexts of incorporation supplanted contexts of exit in their compelling psychosocial effects," particularly among those refugees who "adapted to American ways while retaining their ethnic attachments and identity" (Rumbaut 1996: 17).

Permanent displacement

While the loss of a homeland, permanent or temporary, can have these psychosocial effects, the total loss of any legal citizenship anywhere, which is the fate of those rendered stateless, can be even more profound. In 2014, the UNHCR launched a ten-year campaign to eradicate the "devastating legal limbo" of statelessness by 2024, drawing attention to one of the major challenges of the twenty-first century: the enduring situations of statelessness for an estimated more than 10 million people across the globe. According to one UNHCR website, the international legal definition of a stateless person as set out in Article 1 of the 1954 Convention relating to the Status of Stateless Persons is "a person who is not considered as a national by any State under the operation of its law." This means that a stateless person is someone who does not have a nationality of any country. Some people are born stateless, while others become stateless over the course of their lives.[9]

In his recent book-length study, *Statelessness: The Enigma of the International Community* (2014), legal scholar William E. Conklin critically evaluates the efforts of nations in the context of the 'international community' to address the pressing issue of statelessness. While it is not possible to do full justice to his argument here, he identifies a number of significant interrelated factors for the continued lack of a resolution relevant to migration more generally. Conklin notes that international legal discourse offers two very different senses of a legal bond with regard to membership in a community: one emphasizes the conferring of membership as the right of the nation over the international community, judicially recognized as the "reserved domain" of sovereign states; the other recognizes the social bonding of "natural persons," i.e. fellow human beings, that is not limited to a specific territory, judicially referred to as "effective nationality." He suggests that as long as the will of the international community is understood to be no more than the aggregate of the wills of states (Conklin 2014: 6), the choice of any one nation to exclude a natural person from its citizenry or its territory remains immune from external intervention, rendering the notion of the international community an empty signifier, too abstract and devoid of social content to be an effective tool of justice.

The enigma of statelessness can best be appreciated by juxtaposing the traditional quest for discrete rights, such as a right to nationality or a right to be recognized as a legal person, with the ethos of an international community in which such rights are nested. With the one sense of an international community, a right to nationality is read against the fundamental condition of community: namely, the reserved domain of the community. As such natural persons will be excluded as well as included into a membership, de jure and effective statelessness will remain despite treaty assertions that the right to nationality applies to 'everyone.' The quest to identify an international legal rule for the traditional Article 38[10] sources reinforces such an exclusionary international legal norm. A state must expressly (by a treaty) or impliedly (by a customary norm) consent to the discrete international rule or right. Why is any international rule or right binding against a state's authority if the state's authority trumps any such international right or rule in matters of nationality? (ibid.: 23).

Conklin argues for, among other things, a stronger recognition and enforcement of the legal bond of "effective nationality" – those socially experienced relationships of different kinds to do with birth, marriage, ancestry, and other forms of engagement to persons or places – that would be binding upon all states. Drawing a parallel to international criminal law, particularly to the ad hoc tribunals that were set up after Rwanda and Yugoslavia, he suggests that, like international criminal law, protecting stateless persons is implicit in international treaties and should be adjudicated in a similar way.

While statelessness results from a unique confluence of history, geopolitics, and culture in relation to a specific group, stateless individuals share in common high rates of poverty, unemployment, poor housing conditions, and the psychological trauma brought about by their lack of legal recognition as 'natural persons' entitled to permanent residency and nationality rights. Among the millions of stateless people, countries that currently cite figures in the hundreds of thousands are Côte d'Ivoire (in part due to changed nationality laws that exclude persons previously included from neighboring states), the Dominican Republic (children of Haitian parentage), the Gulf States and Iraq (foreign workers and ethnic Bedoons), Lebanon (long-term Palestinian and recent Syrian refugees) and Myanmar (ethnic Rohingya Muslims). A recent report in *Forced Migration Review* on stateless persons describes a typical situation for members of the ethnic Rohingya.

> Tarik is a stateless Rohingya who fled Myanmar in 1989 and was trafficked into Malaysia in 1991. He was in bonded labour in Thailand for three months until he paid off his debts. He continued to suffer discrimination in Malaysia, affecting his enjoyment of fundamental rights including liberty and security of the person and various socio-economic rights. Treated as an 'illegal immigrant' under Malaysian law, Tarik is not allowed to work, leading to his arrest for working illegally, detention and 'deportation' into the hands of traffickers on three separate occasions.[11]

Because Palestinians have long been under the mandate of the United Nations Relief and Works Agency for Palestine Refugees (UNRWA), they are not included in the 2014 mandate of the UNHCR despite the fact that, according to UNRWA, out of all registered Palestine refugees:

> nearly one third, more than 1.5 million, live in fifty-eight recognized Palestine refugee camps in Jordan, Lebanon, the Syrian Arab Republic, the Gaza Strip and the West Bank, including East Jerusalem, while the remaining two thirds live in and around the cities and towns of the host countries, and in the West Bank and the Gaza Strip, often in the environs of official camps.[12]

The motivation for leaving the Palestinians off the list according to UN refugee chief António Guterres is that the case of Palestinians is a "very specific situation" that requires a "political solution."[13] In a moving passage from *The Disinherited: Journal of a Palestinian Exile* (1972), the first of three memoirs written by the essayist and poet Fawaz Turki who grew up in the Bourj al-Barajneh camp in East Beirut having fled Palestine with his family in 1948, Turki makes clear that the millions of Palestinians who have lived in refugee camps for generations experience that trauma no differently from other stateless people, whatever the politics that informs their particular situation.

> If you live a comfortable existence where the problems of life are examined within the matrix of ideology and rationality, your world is a habitable one. If you give twenty years of your life in a refugee camp, you have paid a high price. If you are asked to sacrifice another twenty, the price becomes intolerable. If you are asked to make your yet unborn child take on your burden, you are committing an injustice. If you look around you and your existence is and has been a meaningless and tedious round of sparring with the vagaries of life for the most basic and most simplest needs of nature, when now you win, now you lose, ideology and rationality go out the mudhouse window into the courtyard, near the water pump, at the refugees camp. And because you are fatigued and dispossessed, you want to accept the part and not the whole. The Palestinian problem has never been to the Palestinian people a crisis, a crisis of political intent, but a tragedy, a tragedy they lived every day of their lives.
>
> (Turki 1972: 144–145)

The decision to exclude Palestinians among the stateless is itself, of course, a political decision as are other categorizations of migration – political refugees, economic refugees, asylum seekers, contract laborers, guest workers, temporary workers, and so on – created by nation states to serve their geopolitical interests and control residency, nationality, and labor rights within their borders. The loss of access to a public space for human beings suffering a loss of rights by virtue of their relationship or lack thereof to a nation state, as Hannah Arendt noted, excludes them to different degrees from full participation in political life, relegating them to the private sphere which she described as "unqualified, mere existence." Excluded from civil society, Arendt wrote, they are "deprived of expression within and action upon a common world." Once human beings lose the very qualities that make it possible for others to treat them as fellow human beings, they "los[e] all significance" (Arendt 1952: 302).

More than 60 million people are temporarily or permanently displaced because of violence and persecution around the world, the largest number ever recorded by the United Nations. When refugees flee their own countries, most wind up with their immediate neighbors, often some of the world's poorer nations. In terms of hosting displaced people, developed countries pale in comparison to nations bordering conflict zones. The interconnectedness of societies in the form of an international community and the erosion of national borders presumed in notions like transnationalism remain largely symbolic for the people most in need of their material realization. In a recent report, *Fatal Journeys: Tracking Lives Lost During Migration* (Brian and Laczko 2014), published by the International Organization of Migration well before Syrians began fleeing the ongoing conflict there, it was estimated that globally at least 4,077 migrants – the majority from Africa, the Middle East, Central America and Mexico – died in 2014 on attempted journeys and at least 40,000 have died since the year 2000, with the true number of fatalities likely higher given the number of deaths that are never recorded.

> For many of the 232 million people around the world who live outside their country of birth today, migration means the opportunity for a better life for themselves and their families. Yet, for many others, the search for such an opportunity comes at an extremely high cost, as they face unimaginable and often fatal dangers along their journeys. Some are ready to spend their lifetime savings or take on massive debts and risk their lives and the lives of their families for a new start. Death is a risk worth taking in desperate situations of violence, persecution, famine or even absence of prospects of a decent life.
>
> [...]
>
> The paradox is that at a time when one in seven people around the world are migrants in one form or another, we are seeing a harsh response to migration in the developed world. Limited opportunities for safe and regular migration drives would-be migrants into the hands of smugglers, feeding an unscrupulous trade that threatens the lives of desperate people. We need to put an end to this cycle. Undocumented migrants are not criminals, but human beings in need of protection and assistance, entitled to legal assistance, and deserving respect.
>
> (Brian and Laczko 2014: 5)

For many would-be migrants, the significance of their international legal recognition as 'natural persons' is crucial to their short- and long-term security. Both symbolic and material capital, far from diminishing in significance, continues to legitimize individual identity and access to material goods, enabling the very *mobility* between nation states and across continents that remains the primary means to claim as well as enact a transnational identity. Global hospitality remains elusive for many of the world's citizens despite globalization and the economic and political interdependence among all members of the global community it entails. Efforts to identify or create new forms of global transnational citizenry or global cosmopolitanism freed from the constraints of nationalism, political allegiance, or territorial borders must take note of the millions for whom nationality, citizenship, permanent residence, and a valid passport remain well outside their grasp.

Arrivals, multiculturalism, and critique

Those fortunate enough to gain legal permanent status in a place of their choosing can still be perceived as a potential threat to the cultural and national identity of established residents, including previous migrants. Migrants can also be embraced and understood as setting in motion the kind of diversification within families and communities to which multicultural societies are hospitable. Migration as a phenomenon is understood both positively as promoting diversity, creating economic opportunity, social integration, or cosmopolitanism, and negatively when associated with invasion, unwanted competition, dependence, or unchecked forms of exclusion. Although tensions can and do emerge between the embrace and intolerance of diversity, especially triggered by changes in local economic conditions or geo-political events, the norm within established and even emergent multicultural societies has tended toward acceptance of diversity over the long term.

The 'transnational' perspective of migrants maintaining links with their own cultural traditions has historically been a part of this acceptance, though normally on the condition that new migrants embrace to a greater or lesser extent the core cultural values and linguistic practices of the destination culture, the latter view commonly associated with assimilation. In practice, this has taken on different forms in different contexts. Within the United States, for example, 'hyphenated' identities – e.g. Italian American, Irish American, Polish American, Jewish American (shifting to White), Chinese American, Korean American (shifting to Asian American), Mexican American, Cuban American (shifting to Latin American, Latino or Hispanic) – historically have indicated an acceptance of a private–public distinction, however problematic these titular ethnic or racial representations.

The notion of multiculturalism has tended to mean different things depending on the national or regional setting. In Canada, for example, multiculturalism has been most associated with the territorial claims of the Native Peoples and the Québécois and their respective struggles for territorial autonomy and separate political representation. With regard to new migrants in Canada, multiculturalism has been more about their official rights to full and equal participation in the country's political life, including those specifically related to migrant and minority issues or sensibilities (Kymlicka 1995).

In contrast, in the Australian context, state policy deemed multiculturalist was developed initially to help promote the smooth and gradual integration of new immigrants, and did not include the territorial claims of

Aboriginal Australians. When multiculturalism was officially formalized as a policy for all Australians at the end of the 1980s, the leaders of the Aboriginal peoples argued against their inclusion as it diminished the force of their unique status as First Australians (Levey 2008; see also Dunn et al 2010). In the United States, the term multiculturalism is not restricted to ethnic inclusiveness, but has served more as a reference to liberal pluralism and diversity with the issue of rights more broadly applied and addressed through anti-discrimination legislation.

In Europe, as immigration has increased since the second half of the twentieth century, references to multiculturalism have tended to refer to public policy promoting respect for cultural difference – including former colonial subjects – within presumptively homogeneous populations. After an uphill struggle during this period, multiculturalism in Europe enjoyed a period of acceptance until events, including the World Trade Center bombing and especially the wars in Iraq and Afghanistan, ushered in a new era of contraction. There as elsewhere attention on Islam intensified, which before, in the context of multiculturalism, had largely been viewed as only one component of certain minority ethnic cultures. The issues of national identity and immigration were also central factors in the outcome of the 2016 UK referendum vote ('Brexit') in which a majority of the voters opted to leave the European Union. The 'leave' vote has been understood by many as a backlash against globalization policies that supported the free movement of capital, people, and goods; trickle-down economics; and a diminished role for nation states. Many voting to leave, however, including some of the UK's more established immigrant communities, placed the blame squarely on the influx of migrants from European Union countries, particularly Central and Eastern Europeans.

Migration has thus once again come under scrutiny and the politics of multiculturalism has become less interested in the question of recognition of and across difference than in social cohesion and common values, in the belief that communities had become divided and their differences entrenched. For many, multiculturalism, when it includes Muslims and their communities, has become more than obliquely linked with terrorism. In this way the rise of a refreshed image of unified and cohesive societies in which values remain stable, unchallenged, and non-contradictory, has re-emerged. The cultivation of relationships of mutual respect between the sensibilities of established residents and those of migrants and newer minority cultures, however, remains crucial to the very idea of a multiculture. This idea – the proposal of mutual respect within a multiculture – is a big one and rests on a number of assumptions that have naturally attracted much elaboration, comment, and critique from within cultural, political, and social discourses, parts of which are not only relevant but in my view central to the issue of translation, cultural and linguistic. These I address in some detail in the following three sections, each of which serves as a different lens combining to intersect and illuminate migration and translation in its broadest sense.

Lens 1: Fluidity, hybridity, identity

The emergence of the postcolonial critique in the 1980s embraced the idea of diasporic and non-originary locations of identity unencumbered by territorial boundaries or ethnic absolutism, both of which had indiscriminately served a central role in the creation and reification of the nation state. These ideas were given particular voice in the work of Homi Bhabha, who advanced the notion of the space of identity as hybrid, interstitial, and resistant to any imposed attempts at universality or other totalizing concepts. What has been most significant about the recognition of the transnational and transcultural nature of migration in postcolonial re-readings of modern imperialist and colonialist history is the explicit challenge to Eurocentric hegemonic binarisms (here/there, center/periphery, us/them) through which individuals from once-colonized countries were historically narrated. Anti-essentialism and deterritorialism were important components of the postcolonial project's task to "disrupt the settled relations of domination and resistance inscribed in other ways of telling these stories ... [and] reposition and displace difference without, in the Hegelian sense, 'overcoming' it" (Hall 1996: 251). The adoption of the term 'hybridity' – a term Bhabha has recently claimed as a "resistant minoritarian term of art" (Bhabha 2015: x) – was a means of describing both the state of being an un-synthesized person (in the Hegelian sense) as a consequence of colonialism, as well as the positive strength of identity one could derive from that state, including the right to define that identity on one's own terms (see Chakrabarty 2000, Friedman 2012).

The term hybridity is more often used these days as a superordinate term covering a multiplicity of cultural conjunctions. This has clearly weakened its reputed instrumental value as resistance in the postcolonial sense where it originated. The contrast between cultural hybridity and cultural homogeneity that some writers make has also led to problematic and, in many ways, unhelpful distinctions between different migrant groups and different historical contexts of migration. These unfortunate dichotomies have given durability to another flawed binary – between transnationalism and assimilation. When considering migration in the context of two of the largest multicultures, the United States and Australia, for example, first, second, and even third-generation migrants from the latter half of the twentieth century onwards are often understood and described by drawing on postcolonial and postmodern discourses of hybridity where migrant identity is defined as diasporic and transnational, fragmented, and flexible. In contrast, the identities of first, second, or third-generation migrants from the nineteenth and early twentieth century are associated with cultural and territorial fixity and homogeneity, often conflated with hegemony, as a consequence of a presumed universal and unproblematic assimilation. This notion, however, that transnationalism and assimilation are historically distinct practices or sensibilities ignores the historical reality that migrant sensibilities are rarely lived as a one-way process of assimilation even where socioeconomic, political, or geographical factors prevent regular contact or back and forth travel.

Where migration is concerned, hybridity as a term of description that has applicability beyond its origins in postcolonial discourse seems most useful as a way of describing those moments in the life of all migrants, lived in the present or through memory, that illuminate the inevitable transformations of identity that migration precipitates, and less informative about the stages of evolution of this identity over time. As Nicholas Harney's study of Bangladeshi street vendors in Naples suggests, the stated links between hybridity, transnationalism, and the maintenance of connections with migrants' countries of origin can ignore the significance of the personal and pragmatic bonds that develop between migrants, locals, and migrants from different countries which often benefit them far more than the frequently alluded to "vertically integrated group connections linking migration chains, distributors and street-vendors" (Harney 2007: 229). Speaking of these Bangladeshi migrants, Harney notes:

> [T]he more remarkable capacity I observed was their willingness and skill at developing new networks with non-Bangladeshis to sustain their livelihood, share information, organise their daily affairs – ties with Italian small-shop owners, and Pakistani, Chinese and Senegalese street-vendors. In this sense, the transnational practices that emphasise the ongoing connections with 'home' imprison and caricature these migrants within the assumption of a territorially-based ethnic identity formation.
>
> (ibid.: 230)

Although globalization may have altered the trajectories of present day migrants compared to previous generations in certain ways, the experience of arriving, of inserting oneself into a new place, of becoming someone different while retaining what remains the same, is not altogether different from one wave of migration to another for the vast majority of migrants. Many of the same factors that have always shaped identities in migrant societies continue to do so, including: specific forms of socialization that individuals from the first, second, and third generations undergo which redefine them in relation to their past, their present, and their future; the longitudinal effects of multiple encounters with different others in workplaces, schools, and communities; the effects of exogamy and endogamy, and so on. Differences in social class, race, gender, and religion continue to be factors that are as likely to establish different perspectives among members of the same cultural group as between diverse cultural groups in this regard. These factors may also be less likely than ethnicity to be experienced as transient, fluid, and flexible signifiers of identity. Paradoxically, their very stability can make them important resources for building solidarity among members of different cultural groups in the workplace or around social policies that target or discriminate against religious, racial, or social groups, or the economically disadvantaged.

These forms of solidarity contribute to what the philosopher Jacques Ranciere (2004: 43) has referred to as the "redistribution of the sensible" in relation to stratified societies, and which can usefully be applied to the specific forms of disruption and reorganization that migration initiates. This redistribution is inevitably political; it gives new expression to the past and present and to 'us' and 'them'; in this way it operates as a positive destabilizing force. The specific transnational nature of twenty-first-century migration has created the potential for such a redistribution of power and influence at the global and the local level that affects not only those migrating, but the people they leave behind and the places they enter, both virtually and proximally. It has directed attention to the ambivalence present in multicultural societies, or societies wishing to be so, that celebrate and encourage diversity while maintaining conditions that allow some members and their views more visibility and audibility, hence greater legitimacy, than others. Where such restrictions are placed on the redistribution of new codes or practices entering the existing social order, the positive process of disruption and reorganization that deterritorialization and reterritorialization precipitates is curtailed (Deleuze and Guattari 1987: 11). Migration has always involved movement away from some established state toward something newly configured for all those involved. Deterritorialization (the breaking of habits) and reterritorialization (the forming of habits) are relational and inherently political concepts, and ones that presume a degree of reciprocity. The association of deterritorialization merely with ease of movement and the freedom to select and appropriate cultures and ways of life elides this political function, limiting it to a politics of identity. This association more often than not assumes a privileged social group (a transnational elite) as its normative subject unencumbered by territorial boundaries and it understates the differential power of both nation states and their citizens in relation to global market forces and geopolitics.

If in the end the term hybridity is simply a claim about diasporic identity or diversity as opposed to unity as the condition of cultural change, these are not particularly novel views. At the cultural level, the formation of multicultural societies has long been recognized as involving the juxtaposition of diverse subjectivities or worldviews, individuals operating in different places – and on different planes – in which past, present, and future subjectivities are continually registered, reconfigured, contested, and reproduced by social actors engaged in the complicated and never-ending task of building different forms of community. The history of migration makes it very clear that locations, cultures, and the social relations that these facilitate are not fixed in time or place.

Some though, including Bhabha himself, continue to identify hybridity as an ethical and political force originating in the liminal spaces within society, a force that allows alternative voices and visions to emerge that counter attempts at universalizing hegemonic discourses. Recently in his Foreword to a new edition of Pnina Werbner and Tariq Modood's influential book, *Debating Cultural Hybridity* (2015), Bhabha decries the appropriation of the concept of hybridity in the discourse of "neoliberal globalistas" where it has been transformed into a "monster of hegemony" itself, used in the service of promoting global homogeneity over alterity.

> Large scale hybridity – the medium of the 'multi' – replicates the logic of national cohesion on a grand scale. Despite the heavy play of 'diversity', the global dream of hybridity is at heart the familiar national creed of *E pluribus unum*, dressed up in the motley mix-and-match garments of different cultural traditions and practices.
> (Bhabha 2015: x–xi)

Bhabha is right to want to resist the use of hybridity in the service of a homogenizing pluralism that serves national and corporate interests while ignoring systematic misrepresentation and insensitivity to salient cultural issues. He cites the Marxist philosopher Antonio Gramsci, in particular his analysis of the "relations of force" operating in societies, comparing hybridity to the "dialectical nexus" between organic and conjunctural power, the space, according to Gramsci, where opposing ideological orientations and political hegemonies confront one another (ibid.: xii).[14] What remains unclear in Bhabha's use of the term, however, is precisely how hybridity can function dialectically in the Gramscian sense, given its resistance to operating as a unifying force. For Marxists like Gramsci and Lenin, the seeds of a different social and cultural order resided within the conditions and contradictions of the existing one. Dialectics involved a synthesizing unity of opposites, as this passage from Lenin suggests:

> Dialectics is the teaching which shows how Opposites can be and how they happen to be (how they become) identical, – under what conditions they are identical, becoming transformed into one another – why the human mind should grasp these opposites not as dead, rigid, but living, conditional, mobile, becoming transformed into one another.
> (Lenin qtd. in Gogol 2012: 252)

This observation indicates a paradox in Bhabha's embrace of Gramsci's utilization of dialectics in the service of his argument about hybridity, a term Bhabha opposes to any synergy of opposites, seemingly ignoring the "living, conditional," or "mobile" state of the opposites themselves. Whatever its rhetorical or ideological uses in particular contexts, the phrase *E pluribus unum* is a descriptive term, implying nothing about how the many or the one are constituted. What it can assume though is the reasonable expectation of members of multicultural societies that their diverse individual or collective beliefs and values find not only political legitimacy but are perceived over time as beliefs and values, stable and coherent enough to be recognized as commensurable with those of others within the same society. Liminality can accurately and effectively be used to affect a state of transition from one condition to another, but it is misapplied – and loses its power as a revitalizing tool for change – when understood as a permanent state from which to build relationships with others.

Lens 2: Reconfiguring 'us' and 'them'

In the history and context of migration, policies and practices that are either directed at recognizing and embracing migrant cultures or at making their legitimate inclusion in society conditional on their adoption of dominant cultural values and linguistic practices are both traceable to a view of cultures as relatively holistic. The idea of cultures as articulated wholes served as an argument for the European nativist view of cultures as biologically transmitted, fixed complexes of behavior where this was used to assign inferior cognitive traits to particular groups of immigrants based on their race or ethnicity (Jacobson 1999). The nativist idea also served as an important strategic defense against calls for cultural consensus or the broad application of democratic standards. In the field of cultural anthropology there were methodological and political reasons for viewing cultures as semantic 'monads' which developed according to their own constitution as far as they could toward the reflection of a presumed whole – the incommensurability paradigm.

The uptake of the idea of cultures and languages as 'incommensurable' can be traced to the German-born anthropologist Franz Boas who, working in the United States, argued against the evolutionist tradition prevalent throughout the West in the nineteenth century (Stocking 1974). Boas disavowed the idea of physical or biological causality with respect to cultural phenomena that was being used in the West to support racist attitudes toward 'primitive' cultures. He maintained that cultures were integrated wholes comprised of 'almost accidental' accretions of elements – the products of "the history of the people, the influence of the regions through which it passed in its migrations, and the people with whom it came into contact" (Boas qtd. in Stocking 1974: 5). He viewed the formation of cultures and of languages as both a conscious and an unconscious process, one in which the "genius of a people" acted to mold the accumulated elements of its history into traditional patterns of behavior or meaningful wholes. Boas' ideas on culture were taken up by his student, Ruth Benedict, whose book, *Patterns of Culture*, published in 1935, reiterated his belief in cultures as historically constituted articulated wholes and not as biologically transmitted complexes of behavior. Against the prevailing Western ethnocentrism toward 'primitive' cultures, Benedict argued for the 'incommensurability' of cultures, echoing Boas in her emphasis on cultures as demonstrations of distinctive 'patterns,' not simply varied assortments of incoherent acts and beliefs. In her study of three 'primitive' cultures, for example, she wrote:

> They differ from one another not only because one trait is present here and absent there, and because another trait is found in two regions in two different forms. They differ still more because they are oriented as wholes in different directions. They are travelling along different roads in pursuit of different ends, and these ends and these means in one society cannot be judged in terms of those of another, because essentially they are incommensurable.
> (Benedict 1935: 161)

Both Boas and Benedict downplayed the universal aspects of human behavior, although Boas did view human beings' tendency to classify phenomena as common to all cultures (Stocking 1974: 8). Although they acknowledged the historical fact of cultural interpenetration, they were primarily concerned with documenting and describing local processes of integration and classification. For Benedict, 'primitive' cultures were the best sources for studying the diversity of coherent patterns of behavior precisely because they had been less affected by historical contact with others (Benedict 1935: 12).

In certain multiculturalist discourses aimed at recognizing cultures and languages that have gone unnoticed or been undervalued, the priority is commonly deemed to be not dialogue across difference but dialogue about difference. To this end, the emphasis is on what makes individuals or cultures distinctive, not what makes them similar. But while what makes one culture distinct from another is an important issue in its own right, or as a strategy in struggles over social justice generally, it can also serve to close down rather than open up the question of how individuals critically understand or alter their perceptions of themselves and others; thus, it promotes an extreme form of relativism.

A similar understanding of cultures as objects or end products – for the anthropologist, ethnographic texts – is implied in Clifford Geertz's proposed response to the moral challenge of living in what he refers to as the "collage" of contemporary multicultural societies (Geertz 2000: 87). With respect to the diversity of the multiculture, Geertz suggests that we must "learn to grasp what we cannot embrace" by strengthening the capacity of our imaginations to 'see' and to 'judge' individuals and their cultures that are "alien to us and likely to remain so." A problem with this 'us' and 'them' view of diversity, however, is that it is far from clear exactly which individuals or groups, out of the whole population, are understood to constitute the 'us' and what factors – historical, cultural, economic, geographical – set them apart from the 'them'. Geertz sees the solution to this problem as a matter of "learning" the "skill" of "grasping what is in front of us" (ibid.):

> To live in a collage one must in the first place render oneself capable of sorting out its elements, determining what they are (which usually involves determining where they come from and what they amounted to when they were there) and how, practically, they relate to one another, without at the same time blurring one's own sense of one's own location and one's own identity within it. Less figuratively, "understanding" in the sense of comprehension, perception, and insight needs to be distinguished from "understanding" in the sense of agreement of opinion, union of sentiment, or commonality of commitment; the *je vous ai compris* that DeGaulle uttered from the *je vous ai compris* the *pieds noirs* heard. We must learn to grasp what we cannot embrace.

In the above passage, Geertz elucidates his view by way of example. The ability to distinguish between the meaning of "je vous ai compris" as uttered by French president Charles de Gaulle from the "je vous ai compris" as heard by the *pieds noirs* is a reference to de Gaulle's famous speech of March 1958 in Algeria in which, while addressing a crowd made up of large numbers of the European minority population (*pieds noirs*), de Gaulle famously proclaimed, "I have understood you," which the *pieds noirs* took to mean he supported their desire that Algeria remain a French colony. Four years later, when Algeria gained its independence from France with de Gaulle's support, these words appeared deceptive. With the benefit of hindsight, modern historians suggest that de Gaulle's utterance "je vous ai compris" was used strategically, particularly as his intentions with respect to the political situation in Algeria were not clear at the time of the speech (Buchanan 2012: 94). The ambiguity of the utterance allowed de Gaulle to signal simultaneously to the *pieds noirs*, the Algerian independence movement, as well as the French and Algerian public, that he grasped their respective concerns. In contrast, the interpretation by the *pieds noirs* that he supported their wish to remain a French colony reflected their own calculated understanding that they were the 'you' to his 'I', that he considered them as an 'us'. The fact that de Gaulle uttered "Vive l'Algérie française" in the same speech further supported this particular interpretation.

Geertz's view that to live in a diverse society one must render oneself capable of "sorting out its elements" implies that inhabitants relate to one another in a similar way that anthropologists in the field relate to their objects of study. He suggests that diverse cultures can at best "understand" one another based on "comprehension" and "insight" and not on a "union of sentiment," for the latter would require a more proximal, interactive relationship, not one based primarily on observation. What Geertz is doing in this passage is essentially repackaging his notion of thick description in ethnographic fieldwork and applying it to modern multicultural societies. He seems to be suggesting that, in order to better understand one other, inhabitants must sort out the structures of signification and established codes of the diverse cultures among them. And just as Geertz deemed anthropologists' ethnographic texts to be a representative product of their imaginative grasp of the publically available meanings of the cultures they studied, so he views the 'insights' gathered by members of multicultural societies as a product of their imaginative grasp of the diverse 'others' among them.

There are several problems with this analogy. First, although Geertz is not forthcoming in his comments about who is doing the 'sorting' or 'understanding' of whom, his reference to 'one' and 'they' suggests an observer and an observed. The 'us' in this passage appears to be the established members within the multicultural societies and the 'they' the migrants and minorities whose cultures are not sufficiently recognized or regarded. While Geertz is right to be concerned about the misrecognition of minority cultures within these societies, the problem with this view is that inhabitants of multicultural communities do not necessarily function in the same way as anthropologists and their subjects in the field. His analogy reduces social relations in multicultural societies to a dualistic 'understanding' on the part of one group (established inhabitants) with respect to others (the historically or currently marginalized). As a matter of social policy, a focus on the disenfranchised members of society serves as an important starting point toward greater equality of opportunity and outcome. In terms of the wider social function of diversity, however, one-sided attempts at understanding tend to reproduce a hierarchical and distant relationship between observer and observed which disregards the active participation of presumed cultural 'others,' their observations of and impact on the dominant culture, and the possibility of an extended dialogue between the two. By viewing minorities and migrants individually or collectively as observed and not as observers in their own right, no consideration is given to their diverse insights with respect to the dominant culture, nor are they, or anyone for that matter, presumed to be working toward greater inclusion, a "commonality of commitment," within the society of which they are a part. Although Geertz would maintain that the form of distant comprehension he has in mind can potentially change the self-image of established inhabitants, the kind of observation he has in mind does not have dynamic social or cultural change as its goal.

Geertz seems to be suggesting that the *pieds noirs*' reading of the situation was in fact a misperception on their part, based on a presumed "commonality of commitment" that turned out to be false. They failed to properly distinguish between one form of understanding and another and did not "grasp what was in front of them" as reflected in de Gaulle's utterance. But the meaning of any utterance is not given in language via some form of direct correspondence; it is an outcome of the relationship between utterances in specific contexts where language is but one of many tools used to communicate. Geertz uses the example of de Gaulle's speech to support his view of the difficulty of getting our self-perceptions and our perceptions of others right. But the problem for the *pieds noirs* was not that they did not grasp the intended meaning of de Gaulle's utterance. They may have fully comprehended the ambiguity of the utterance, and like him sought to use it to their advantage by filling in the referents as themselves.

What the French Algerians failed to recognize fully, however, was their lack of real power and influence over the workings of French colonial politics at the time and the geopolitical stage on which it was being played out. This would become even clearer in the aftermath of Algeria's independence when their desire to enter France as refugees after the war was met with resistance from the French metropole. A majority of the French public opposed the right of the Algerian-born *pieds noirs* to be considered French due to their involvement with violent fascist and colonialist agendas before and during the war. The question of which Algerians should be categorized as French became part of the reconstruction of France's self-perception as a colonial power after the war. The previously colonized Arabs, for example, were duly recognized as 'not French' in recognition of their independence from French colonial rule. The *pieds noirs*, however, were considered not French for very different ideological and cultural reasons (Shepard 2006). Eventually, succumbing to pressure after nearly 1 million *pieds noirs* arrived in France after the war, the French government admitted them as French citizens where they were allowed to settle among the French. The same, however, cannot be said for the hundreds of thousands of Algerian Muslims or *harkis* who served as auxiliaries in the French army during the war. In the aftermath, the many *harkis* who were blocked from repatriating to France by the French government were tortured and killed for their perceived betrayal, and those who entered France illegally were segregated in internment camps or housed in public housing far outside the metropolitan French population (Cohen 2006: 170).

What is clear from this example is that both self- and other's perceptions of the *pieds noirs* and the *harkis* in relation to French culture cannot be comprehended outside of the context in which these were constructed and contested. In response to questions about their cultural identity in 1981, a group of children of the *harkis* said: "We were never liked, I am always an Arab"; "From all points of view I am French, but we are kept out of the system"; "We have no rights, we are called Algerians"; "He who says I am French is a liar"; and "Look at what being French has brought us" (ibid.:171). On a different occasion, an older *harki*, however, declared, "I am French; my grandfather fought for France, and in the Algerian War my brothers did. I have always thought I am French" (ibid.: 173).

Geertz has elsewhere stated that "[o]ne of the most significant facts about humanity may finally be that we all begin with the natural equipment to a live a thousand kinds of life but end in the end having lived only one" (Geertz 1973: 45), a view that suggests stasis over change as a chief characteristic of human life. But what the different statements above reflect is that whether an individual identifies consciously as a member of a particular cultural group is often more a matter of context than content, or a relation between the two. Culture, like language itself, is not something 'out there': the surface reflection of an objective world. To belong to a cultural group is to feel and to be recognized as a possible participant in the shaping of that group's self-image. The fracturing of cultural and linguistic practices throughout history is often most evident in instances where friction over mutual recognition occurs between the dominant and dominated, between dominant groups, or among the dominated. Culture is lived in and through experience: the degree of unity or fragmentation that is felt both within and between different cultural practices and forms of belonging is largely determined by specific circumstances. To be a part of any society, and of any culture, is to be part of a continuous evolution and synthesis of continuously altering social-cognitive orientations, worldviews so to speak, structured in and by language understood in the broadest sense.

Lens 3: Translation and hospitality – Khan and Kant speak

In recent decades a renewed emphasis has been placed on a means of fostering relationships of mutual recognition and inclusion through both official macro-level policies and through micro-interactions at the local community level. Situated communicative encounters that take place in private/ everyday and public/procedural contexts – where individual agency and authority compete – are recognized as important contexts for attaining cultural and political legitimacy for newly arrived migrants, minorities engaged in long-term struggles, and any member of a society at odds with its dominant values. Although there can be no complete agreement about what constitutes the common ground on which individuals and cultures recognize their presumed inter-subjectivity, it is generally agreed that reasoned deliberation is present in all cultures to varying degrees. The very act of address, of directing conversation toward another individual or group, establishes an interactive space where designations of meaning and understanding become possible. Dialogue can also happen indirectly, through different forms of communication seen and not seen, heard and not heard in both public and private places within societies. These communicative events, large or small, reflect the awareness of its members to the presence of difference among them, mobilizing certain ways of 'seeing' and 'hearing' each other.

The task of creating and expanding dialogues across difference is of fundamental importance within communities seeking to develop and sustain a politics of inclusion. This does not assume a juxtaposition of several intact cultures or their assimilation into one common culture, in which the particularities of individual cultures are dissolved. The principal aim of such dialogues is not to eradicate difference but to promote a healthy tolerance toward diversity through which to extend the quotidian discourse and pragmatic nature of social and cultural life: what is sometimes referred to as 'cosmopolitanism from below,' which supports "an ethos of cultural openness that actively seeks out and tries to understand and appreciate ways of thinking and acting found in different cultures" (Kurasawa 2004: 240). The way that power and domination work to silence and subjugate some individuals and cultures, however, means that it may not always be or be seen as strategically beneficial for participants from one community to engage in a process that threatens to dilute or subsume their particular beliefs and practices into a universalizing discourse. Such strategic disengagement is a very different matter, however, to the stance taken by proponents of an identity politics that promotes cultural essentialism and a commitment to a strong form of incommensurability of cultures. This latter position ends up being less a defense against conditions of inequality and more an embrace of irreconcilable and uncompromising difference for its own sake.

Cross-cultural and linguistic interactions within societies have historically either been shaped by custom or by edict, or by some confluence of the two. Remarkable among the examples in history was Kublai Khan's insightful and benign approach to the several religions, and their scriptural languages, present in the vast domain of his Mongolian empire over which he ruled from 1260 to 1294. His combination of pragmatism and wisdom placed him far in advance of his grandfather Genghis Khan and the other Mongol lords. From his mother, Sorkaktani, Kublai had learned never to let one religion dominate so as to not alienate the others. Sorkaktani had been a member of the heretical Nestorian Christian sect. She was not a Mongol but a member of the Turkic-speaking Kerait tribe, yet was one of the most influential people of her time, being the mother of Genghis' son Tolui and of two emperors (Weatherford 2010). Kublai was extremely reserved when it came to passing judgment on the religions practiced in his Empire – Judaism, Christianity, and Islam. When a young regional commander named Nayan decided to challenge Khan's control in the field of battle and rode out under a Christian flag, his forces were easily defeated by those of Khan. When Nayan was finally caught and executed, the Jews and Muslims taunted the Christian inhabitants of their community, saying in effect – that is what following the cross of Jesus gets you. The Christians complained to Kublai Khan about this derision, and, as Marco Polo reports, Khan berated the Jews and Muslims with the following words:

> If the cross of Christ, he said, has not proved advantageous to the party of Nayan, the effect has been consistent with reason and justice, inasmuch as he was a rebel and a traitor to his lord, and to such wretches it could not afford its protection. Let none therefore presume to charge

with injustice the God of the Christians, who is Himself the perfection of goodness and of justice.

(Polo 1818: 166–167)

Khan's generous good sense was also evidenced by his displays of respect for all four of the major religions under his purview, as Marco Polo (ibid.: 167–168) went on to report:

> The grand khan, having obtained this signal victory, returned with great pomp and triumph to the capital city of Kanbalu. This took place in the month of November, and he continued to reside there during the months of February and March, in which latter was our festival of Easter. Being aware that this was one of our principal solemnities, he commanded all the Christians to attend him, and to bring with them their Book, which contains the four Gospels of the Evangelists. After causing it to be repeatedly perfumed with incense, in a ceremonious manner, he devoutly kissed it, and directed the same should be done by all his nobles who were present. This was his usual practice upon each of the principal Christian festivals, such as Easter and Christmas; and he observed the same at the festivals of the Saracens, Jews, and idolaters [the local Mongolian religion]. Upon being asked his motive for this conduct, he said: "There are four great Prophets who are reverenced and worshipped by the different classes of mankind. The Christians regard Jesus Christ as their divinity; the Saracens, Mahomet; the Jews, Moses; and the idolaters, Solomombar-kan, the most eminent amongst their idols. I do honour and show respect to all the four, and invoke to my aid whichever amongst them is in truth supreme in heaven".

The delicate balancing of religious interests in which Kublai was engaged – in China he was also involved in addressing the conflicting demands of Daoists, Buddhists, and Christian Nestorians – the 'translating' of religious imperatives into a faith-transcending diplomacy of wisdom, was, in a sense, the construction of a non-contentious cosmopolitan framework that permitted each religion its own space and due respect.

Kublai Khan was exceptional in a number of ways but in the substitution of a governance of religious tolerance and freedom for a governance of constriction and imposed conformity – the old familiar practice – his example demonstrates the significance of legal and political contexts to cultural practices of many kinds.

Several hundreds of years later, in his *Critique of Judgment* (1790/1914), Kant set down "three Maxims of common human Understanding": first, to think for oneself (unprejudiced thought), second, to put ourselves in thought in the place of everyone else (enlarged thought), and third, always to think consistently (consecutive thought)." He suggested that a crucial starting point for common human understanding was the attainment of a universal standpoint of judgment:

> However small may be the area or the degree to which a man's natural gifts reach, yet it indicates a man of *enlarged thought* if he disregards the subjective private conditions of his own judgement, by which so many others are confined, and reflects upon it from a *universal standpoint* (which he can only determine by placing himself at the standpoint of others).
> (Kant 1790/1914: 171–172, emphasis in original)

Although Kant makes a clear distinction between the "faculty of cognition" and "mode of thought" – anyone could have an enlarged (or restricted) mode of thought relative to their individual cognitive ability – the universalist perspective he had in mind was in fact highly subjective and defined by an inherent exclusivity. The extent of "man's natural gifts" was determined by his place in a gendered, racial, and geographic hierarchy with White, male, and Europe at the top. But the idea of aiming for some agreed upon standpoint to achieve a particular end in a particular context remains a worthwhile and constructive exercise whereby individuals compare their judgments by attempting to put themselves in the place of one another. Any such efforts to expand perceptions where both recognition and inclusion are the stated goals, as the anthropologist Johannes Fabian has noted, require a more "substantive" ethics, however, that is "grounded in knowledge of the ways of life that often are other than those shared by the inventors of the ethical systems" (Fabian 2001: 174). This challenge has been taken up as a principal aim of postcolonial and cosmopolitan projects, including ones that take as their starting point the Kantian ideal. These have in different ways contributed to a shift in focus – away from universalist and hegemonic notions of truth and toward more contextualist and subaltern ones. The actual substance of a more 'global' ethics beyond these binarisms, however, remains unclear and uncertain.

More recently, the possibility of a twenty-first-century reiteration of Kant's notion of hospitality – at heart, the right of a stranger not to be treated as an enemy when he arrives in the land of another – has been put forward as a possible candidate for a critical cosmopolitanism that extends beyond the universalism/particularism dichotomy. The question of hospitality as a means of sanctuary for foreigners based on their universal right to hospitality rooted in human reason was notably explored in Kant's defense of cosmopolitan values in his 1795 essay, "Toward Perpetual Peace," in which he argued for a set of common principles in the treatment of strangers, shared by individuals as well as states (Kant 1795/1957: 20–21). Hospitality has more recently been suggested as a principle that captures the substantive core of cosmopolitanism in the world in ways that facilitate cultural translation even in the face of different cosmopolitan traditions criss-crossing place and time.[15] Since its inception, practically speaking, hospitality has remained tethered to the strong desire of different regimes of power to maintain tight control over their sovereignty, despite often being the ones to blame for the forced and voluntary migrations that make the search for sanctuary necessary. Given its historical and global reach, however, the notion of hospitality may yet work as a guiding principle of migration and globalization for an 'international community' operating less as an abstract notion or a politically expedient instrument of global power brokers, and more as an entity that can effectively confront shared global problems while prioritizing the guaranteed provision of safety and security for all its citizens.

Translation and the goal of mutual understanding

Translators[16] play a major role in helping to implement the *substantive* core of cosmopolitanism by facilitating access to cultural texts (e.g. literary, legal, journalistic, scientific) and local forms of knowledge written or spoken in another language. In these transactions, translators facilitate types of encounters and exchanges that are distinct from the translations that occur regularly between individuals and groups in multicultural and multilingual encounters without recourse to mediation. Translators serve the important additional function of protecting the social, linguistic, political, economic, and legal rights of individuals and communities, particularly where a clear bias, injustice, or imbalance of power reveals itself. In these instances, translators are called upon not only to clarify linguistic or cultural issues, but to help ensure that all parties' interests and points of view are adequately understood. Re-voicing a refugee or asylum seeker's motivation to flee famine, war, or persecution, for example, often requires more than linguistic or cultural skills, as deliberations regarding whether universal hospitality should be denied or granted are habitually fused with social, political, and discursive instruments of power (Inghilleri 2012: 72–98).

The embrace and reception of refugees and asylum seekers in a given nation or region is an important test of the viability of the hospitality principle envisioned in the cosmopolitan model. The willingness of members of one community to recognize outsiders as fellow human beings or global citizens needing and entitled to seek sanctuary and temporary or permanent residence on their land has been fraught with conflict and contradiction historically and remains so despite more globalized perspectives. Migration is a crucial site where the local meets/confronts the global, and translation is a critical component of this encounter. It is through translation that people demonstrate different degrees of what Paul Ricoeur termed "linguistic hospitality" or the willingness to reside in more than one language and play host to another's culture (2006: 23), an ethical as well as a communicative task, requiring both responsibility and sympathy for listening to and interpreting others' stories. Linguistic hospitality, according to

Ricoeur, is grounded in a commitment to the belief in the translatability of all languages:

> Certainly everything does not come out in a translation, but something always does. There is no reason or probability that a linguistic sign is untranslatable. The belief that the translation is feasible up to a certain point is the affirmation that the foreigner is a man, the belief, in short, that communication is possible.
>
> (Ricoeur 1965: 282)

For newcomers to a particular sociocultural order, translation is an important means of entry into the dominant discourses of a society or alternative voices within a society, from dialogues taking place about local cultural issues to political and ideological debates. In these types of situations, translators can become key players in influencing the degree to which linguistic hospitality is extended, the measure of which is whether or not the communicative objectives of all participants involved are equally considered, if not met. Where conditions are in place for the extension or exchange of linguistic hospitality, this communicative task is managed with relative ease. However, in inhospitable social or communicative environments where the participatory rights of some individuals or groups are constrained or require some form of negotiation, the communicative and ethical demand on translation becomes far greater.

Over the past several decades, communities of activist translators have begun to organize a public ethical response to injustice, inequality, and human security by volunteering their skills in different contexts across the globe (see Baker 2009, 2016, Boéri and de Manuel Jerez 2011, Boéri and Maier 2011). A number of larger organizations have acquired prominence internationally, particularly since the rise of the internet. The oldest organization, ECOS (*Traductores e Intérpretes por la Solidaridad*), was established by students and faculty at the University of Granada, Spain, in 1998, though volunteers from outside the university also participate.[17] Its mission is to "provide translation and interpretation services to disadvantaged sectors in need and raise awareness of the injustices of the world [that] do not find much ECO [echo] in the mainstream media." ECOS has worked with humanitarian agencies and NGOs, focusing on individuals or groups who require translation and interpreting services but cannot afford to pay for professional translators.

Babels,[18] the organization with the biggest membership, was developed in 2002 to meet the translation and interpreting needs of the social forums taking place across the globe, which are an:

> open meeting place where social movements, networks, NGOs and other civil society organizations opposed to neo-liberalism and a world

dominated by capital or by any form of imperialism come together to pursue their thinking, to debate ideas democratically, to formulate proposals, share their experiences freely and network for effective action.[19]

In addition to these organizations that require more mobility from the translators who volunteer their services, there is a strong virtual online presence of volunteer translators on websites dedicated to ongoing conflicts and struggles affecting persons across the globe. The anti-war organization *Traduttori per la Pace*[20] was established in 1999 "to publish, as far as possible in every language and by whatever channel, every message against: war in general; and in particular, against the use of war as a means of resolving international disputes." *Tlaxcala*[21] appeared in 2005 with the aim of countering the political and discursive power of the English language globally through translation. Its members currently represent around thirteen languages who select texts for translation based on whether they "reflect[s] the core values of the Universal Declaration of Human Rights, aiming for full respect for the rights and dignity of the human person." Other online groups include *Global Voices*, which according to its website has been "leading the conversation on citizen media reporting since 2005," curating, verifying, and translating trending news and stories from the internet, blogs, the independent press, and social media in 167 countries. *Project Lingua* is its translation division.[22] *Translations for Progress*[23] lists itself as a community for non-professional volunteer translators from all skill levels. Its mission is "to provide translations to organizations working for the public good that wouldn't be able to pay for them otherwise and to help students get involved in social issues early on."

Though each of these organizations has a unique set of aims and functions, they share recognition of the important role of translation in helping to establish and maintain rights-respecting economic, social, cultural, and political institutions and practices. Their focused interventions on relaying the message of human and global economic diversity and equality pinpoint specific ways for translators to exercise their ethical responsibility at a transnational level, often in ways that challenge established professional translation practices and principles. They provide both an actual and virtual forum for different linguistic communities and groups to be represented who might otherwise have remained silent and marginalized.

Wherever and whenever cultural or linguistic translation occurs, the presence of diversity and the potential for a unity of purpose are in evidence. Within societies seeking to enlarge shared attitudes and interests among their co-lingual inhabitants, the attempted or achieved interactions that take place between individuals or groups, individuals, and texts, and through inter-textual relationships, influence the evolution of all societies in novel ways. The iterative nature of all forms of language allows new words, texts, and images to impact established contexts, making it possible for established forms of communication to enter into new relationships, creating and circulating new understandings. The momentary or sustained shifts in identity such exchanges provoke provide glimpses of belonging or not belonging, and also trigger a sense of the contingency of place.

Just as relevant and ubiquitous is the experience of translating and being translated within a new place through different forms of migration. Migration has never been a simple matter of reproduction in a single direction: it has always involved a combination of diffusion, appropriation, assimilation, resistance, and enduring ambivalence; and translation, as a particular form of interaction, functions as and within crucial discursive spaces where alternative modes of perception are negotiated, challenged, and configured. Acts of translation are simultaneously reflective and directive; they contribute to both the strengthening and the weakening of prior understandings. The forms of migration and translation explored in this book cover a wide range of activities and contexts. These include examples of 'linguistic' translation as practiced by translators for the benefit of migrant communities, 'cultural' translation as migrants translate themselves into the local terrain through a variety of means, and, finally, translation in the 'social' sense, in the frequent acts of translation embedded in ongoing systems of social relations performed by all members of a society as they go about their daily lives, moving, perceiving, and attempting to understand the diversity of the social and physical environments of which they are a part.

Notes

1 In popular usage the terms migrant and immigrant are used, sometimes interchangeably, to refer to individuals and families without much thought given to the many distinct categories of migration that exist, all of which are socially, legally, historically, and politically constructed. These include permanent residents/citizens who once were migrants, long or short term undocumented residents, temporary guest workers, and contract labor migrants and domestic workers. The same lack of clear reference is true for refugees and asylum seekers, whose migration trajectories (and legal status) are normally very different. An additional issue is the more complex question of at what point an individual or community is described, should no longer be described, or no longer define *themselves* by these terms. These are some of the issues that are explored through examples throughout the book.
2 Latin America and Asia have also served and continue to serve as receiving countries for significant numbers of migrants. A full account of this history is beyond the scope of this book, however.
3 http://childrenofsyria.info/wp-content/uploads/2015/07/CHILD-LABOUR.pdf (Accessed April 2016).
4 http://data.unhcr.org/mediterranean/regional.php#_ga=1.226695645.15974230 36.1454959549 (Accessed April 2016).
5 www.wired.com/2015/12/smartphone-syrian-refugee-crisis/ (Accessed April 2016).
6 The Office of the United Nations High Commissioner for Refugees has distributed 33,000 SIM cards to Syrian refugees in Jordan and 85,704 solar lanterns that can also be used to charge cellphones. www.nytimes.com/2015/08/26/world/europe/a-21st-century-migrants-checklist-water-shelter-smartphone.html (Accessed May 2016).

7 http://time.com/4064988/refugee-crisis-selfies/?xid=emailshare (Accessed May 2016).
8 Pulau Bidong, a small island in Terrenganu, Malaysia, situated off the coast in the South China Sea, served as a refugee camp between 1978–1991 for Vietnamese refugees. Set up by the Malaysian government and UNHCR, 250,000 refugees were processed through this camp, the majority of whom were accepted by third countries, principally the United States, Canada, Australia, and France. www.youtube.com/watch?v=7F_xNVu_vww (Accessed April 2016).
9 www.unhcr.org/pages/49c3646c158.html; see also www.unhcr.org/545797f06.html (Accessed April 2016).
10 Article 38 (1) of the Statute of the International Court of Justice is generally recognized as the definitive statement on sources of international law and is consistently adopted by the international criminal courts and tribunals in their judgments.
11 www.fmreview.org/afghanistan/dechickera-whiteman (*FMR 46*, 2014). The *Forced Migration Review* publishes reports on the situation for stateless people in English, Arabic, French, and Spanish. It invites translations into additional languages for their publication. See www.fmreview.org/issues/additional-languages (Accessed April 2016).
12 www.unrwa.org/palestine-refugees (Accessed April 2016).
13 www.unhcr.org/cgi-bin/texis/vtx/refdaily?pass=52fc6fbd5&id=54586eaa8 (Accessed April 2016).
14 Gramsci argued in "Prison Writings" (1919–1935) for the importance of linking the organic base (of relatively stable structures) and the conjunctural superstructure (where opposition to these structures could emerge and organize) within a political system. Unlike those Marxists who perceived them as distinct entities and either overestimated the mechanical causes of the (economic) base or exaggerated the voluntarist and individual elements of the (ideological) superstructure, Gramsci stressed their dialectical relationship (Gramsci 2000: 201–202).
15 See Dallmayr (1998), de Sousa Santos (1999), Derrida (2000), Nederveen Pieterse (2006), Sayyid (2006), Zhao (2006), and Delanty (2014) for examples of the evolution of this idea. See Inghilleri (2007) and (2012: 72–98) for its applicability to decisions about refugee admission and requests for asylum across the globe.
16 Throughout the book, for general reference *translators* and *translation* are used to refer to spoken, written, or audiovisual texts unless otherwise specified.
17 https://ecosteis.wordpress.com/about/ (Accessed April 2016).
18 http://www.babels.org/ (Accessed April 2016).
19 https://fsm2016.org/en/ (Accessed April 2016).
20 web.tiscali.it/traduttoriperlapace (Accessed April 2016).
21 www.tlaxcala.es/entree.asp?lg=en (Accessed April 2016).
22 https://globalvoicesonline.org/lingua/ (Accessed April 2016).
23 www.translationsforprogress.org/main.php (Accessed April 2016).

References

Arendt, Hannah 1952 *The Origins of Totalitarianism*. New York: Harcourt Brace.
Baker, Mona 2009 "Resisting State Terror: Theorizing Communities of Activist Translators and Interpreters," in Esperanca Bielsa and Christopher Hughes (eds) *Globalization, Political Violence and Translation*. Houndmills: Palgrave Macmillan, 222–242.

—— 2016 "The Prefigurative Politics of Translation in Place-based Movements of Protest: Subtitling in the Egyptian Revolution," *The Translator* 22(1): 1–21.

Baldassar, Loretta, Mihaela Nedelcu, Laura Merla, and Raelene Wilding (eds) 2016 "ICT-based Co-presence in Transnational Families and Communities: Challenging the Premise of Face-to-Face Proximity in Sustaining Relationships," *Global Networks* 16(2): 133–144.

Benedict, Ruth 1935 *Patterns of Culture*. London: George Routledge and Sons, Ltd.

Bhabha, Homi K. 2015 "Foreword," in Pnina Werbner and Tariq Modood (eds) *Debating Cultural Hybridity*. London: Zed Books, ix–xiii.

Boéri, Julie and Carol Maier (eds) 2011 *Compromiso Social y Traducción/ Interpretación – Translation/Interpreting and Social Activism*. Granada: ECOS.

Boéri, Julie and Jesús de Manuel Jerez 2011 "From Training Skilled Conference Interpreters to Educating Reflective Citizens: A Case Study of the Marius Action Research Project," *The Interpreter and Translator Trainer* 5(1): 41–64.

Brian, Tara and Frank Laczko (eds) 2014 *Fatal Journeys: Tracking Lives Lost During Migration*. Geneva: International Organization of Migration.

Buchanan, Thomas 2012 *Europe's Troubled Peace: 1945 to the Present*. Second edition. Chichester: Wiley-Blackwell.

Chakrabarty, Dipesh 2000 *Provincializing Europe*. Princeton, NJ: Princeton University Press.

Clarke, Manning 2006 *A Short History of Australia*. Fourth revised edition. Camberwell: Penguin Group Australia.

Cohen, William B. 2006 "The Harkis: History and Memory," in Patricia M.E. Lorcin (ed) *Algeria and France 1800–2000: Identity, Memory and Nostalgia*. Syracuse, NY: Syracuse University Press, 170–180.

Cohn, Norman 1970 *The Pursuit of the Millennium*. Oxford: Oxford University Press.

Conklin, William E. 2014 *Statelessness: The Enigma of the International Community*. Oxford: Hart Publishing.

Dallmayr, Fred 1998 *Alternative Visions: Paths in the Global Village*. Lanham, MD: Rowman & Littlefield.

de Sousa Santos, Boaventura 1999 "Towards a Multicultural Conception of Human Rights," in Michael Featherstone and Scott Lash (eds) *Spaces of Culture: City, Nation, World*. London: Sage, 214–222.

Delanty, Gerard 2014 "Not All Is Lost In Translation: World Varieties of Cosmopolitanism," *Cultural Sociology* 8(4): 374–391.

Deleuze, Gilles and Felix Guattari 1987 *A Thousand Plateaus*. Trans. Brian Massumi. Minneapolis, MN: University of Minnesota Press.

Derrida, Jacques 2000 *Of Hospitality*. Trans. Rachel Bowlby. Stanford: Stanford University Press.

Dublin, Thomas (ed) 1993 *Immigrant Voices*. Urbana, IL: University of Illinois Press.

Dunn, Keven M., Alanna Kamp, Wendy S. Shaw, James Forrest, and Yin Paradies 2010 "Indigenous Australians' Attitudes towards Multiculturalism, Cultural Diversity, 'Race' and Racism," *Journal of Australian Indigenous Issues* 13(4): 19–31.

Fabian, Johannes 2001 *Anthropology with an Attitude*. Stanford: Stanford University Press.

Friedman, Susan Stanford 2012 "World Modernisms, World Literature, and Comparativity," in Mark Wollaeger (ed) *The Oxford Handbook of Global Modernisms*. New York: Oxford University Press, 499–525.

Geertz, Clifford 1973 "The Impact of the Concept of Culture on the Concept of Man," in *The Interpretation of Cultures*. New York: Basic Books, 33–54.

—— 2000 *Available Light*. Princeton: Princeton University Press.

Gogol, Eugene 2012 *Towards a Dialectic of Philosophy and Organization*. Leiden: Brill.

Gramsci, Antonio 2000 "Prison Writings," in David Forgacs (ed) *The Gramsci Reader: Selected Writings 1916-1935* [IV: Hegemony, Relations of Force, Historical Bloc]. New York: New York University Press, 187–221. http://ouleft.org/wp-content/uploads/gramsci-reader.pdf (Accessed April 2016).

Hall, Stuart 1996 "When Was 'the Post-colonial'? Thinking at the Limit," in Iain Chambers and Lidia Curti (eds) *The Postcolonial Question: Common Skies, Divided Horizons*. London: Routledge, 242–260.

Harney, Nicholas DeMaria 2007 "Transnationalism and Entrepreneurial Migrancy in Naples, Italy," *Journal of Ethnic and Migration Studies* 33(2): 219–232.

Harney, Nicholas DeMaria and Loretta Baldassar 2007 "Tracking Transnationalism: Migrancy and its Futures," *Journal of Ethnic and Migration Studies* 33(2): 189–198.

Ingold, Tim 2011 *Being Alive: Essays on Movement, Knowledge and Description*. London: Routledge.

Inghilleri, Moira 2007 "National Sovereignty vs. Universal Rights: Interpreting Justice in a Global Context," *Social Semiotics* 17(2): 195–212. Reprinted, with editorial apparatus, in Mona Baker (ed) 2009 *Critical Readings in Translation Studies*. London and New York: Routledge, 229–244.

—— 2012 *Interpreting Justice: Ethics, Language and Politics*. London: Routledge.

Jacobson, Matthew Frye 1999 *Whiteness of a Different Color: European Immigrants and the Alchemy of Race*. Cambridge, MA: Harvard University Press.

Kant, Immanuel 1790/1914 *Critique of Judgment*. Second revised edition. Translated with Introduction and Notes by J. H. Bernard. London: Macmillan and Co. Ltd.

—— 1795/1957 Lewis White Beck (ed) *Perpetual Peace*. New York: The Bobbs-Merrill Company, Inc.

Kurasawa, Fuyuki 2004 "A Cosmopolitanism from Below: Alternative Globalization and the Creation of Solidarity without Bounds," *European Journal of Sociology* 45(2): 233–255.

Kymlicka, Will 1995 *Multicultural Citizenship*. Oxford: Oxford University Press.

Levey, Geoffrey Brahm (ed) 2008 *Political Theory and Australian Multiculturalism*. New York: Berghahn Books.

Nederveen Pieterse, Jan 2006 "Emancipatory Cosmopolitanism: Towards an Agenda," *Development and Change* 37(6): 1247–1257.

Nguyen, Huu Chung 1989 "Separation and Reunion," in Lucy Nguyen-Hong-Nhiem and Joel Martin Halpern (eds) *The Far East Comes Near*. Amherst, MA: The University of Massachusetts Press, 86–91.

Polo, Marco 1818 *The Travels of Marco Polo: The Venetian*. Revised translation with Notes by William Marsden. London: Cox and Baylis.

Ranciere, Jacques 2004 *The Politics of Aesthetics*. Trans. Gabriel Rockhill. London: Continuum.

Ricoeur, Paul 1965 *History and Truth*. Translated with an Introduction by Charles A. Kelbley. Evanston: Northwestern University Press.

—— 2006 On Translation. Trans. Eileen Brennan, Introduction by Richard Kearney. London: Routledge.

Rivett, Kenneth 1975 *Australia and the Non-White Migrant*. Melbourne: Melbourne University Press.

Rumbaut, Rubén G. 1996 "A Legacy of War: Refugees from Vietnam, Laos and Cambodia," in Silvia Pedraza and Rubén G. Rumbaut (eds) *Origins and Destinies: Immigration, Race, and Ethnicity in America*. Belmont, CA: Wadsworth, 1–24. E-copy available at: http://ssrn.com/abstract=2146972 (Accessed May 2016).

—— 2006 "Vietnamese, Laotian and Cambodian Americans," in Pyong Gap Min (ed) Asian-Americans: Contemporary Trends and Issues. Second edition. Thousand Oaks, CA: Pine Forge Press, 262–289.

Sayyid, Salman 2006 "After Babel: Dialogue, Difference and Demons," *Social Identities* 12(1): 5–15.

Shepard, Todd 2006 "Pied-Noirs, Betes Noirs Anti-"European of Algeria" Racism and the Close of the French Empire," in Patricia M. E. Lorcin (ed) *Algeria and France 1800–2000: Identity, Memory and Nostalgia*. Syracuse, NY: Syracuse University Press, 150–163.

Stocking, George W. 1974 *The Shaping of American Anthropology 1883–1911: A Franz Boas Reader*. New York: Basic Books, Inc.

Thomas, Gordon and Max Morgan-Witts 1974 *Voyage of the Damned*. New York: Skyhorse Publishing Inc.

Turki, Fawaz 1972 *The Disinherited: Journal of a Palestinian Exile*. New York: Monthly Review Press.

Weatherford, Jack 2010 *The Secret History of the Mongol Queens: How the Daughters of Genghis Khan Rescued His Empire*. New York: Random House.

Zhao, Tingyang 2006 "Rethinking Empire from a Chinese Concept 'All-under-Heaven' (Tian- xia)," *Social Identities* 12(1): 29–41.

2 The multiple meanings of hospitality

All forms of translation are implicated in the reproduction of existing ideologies; they are also opportunities for resisting, challenging, and creating alternatives to prevailing beliefs and attitudes about similarity and difference. Whether communicative acts are interrogated as micro- or macro-level phenomena, the visible and audible presence of the processes and products of translation in the social and cultural life of multicultural societies, and in other contact zones created by globalization, re-opens the issue of hospitality publically and politically. Acts of translation are an important outward, visible sign that the principles of recognition and inclusion are valued within and across communities, societies, and nations when formulating frameworks of social and economic justice; they play a vital role in accommodating the uniqueness of particular cultures and diffusing the psychological impact of recognition denied in multicultural contexts. Resistance to the maintenance or expansion of provisions for translation services in the public sphere spurred on by popular movements or government policies clearly works against such objectives. The foundations of this resistance may result from the fear that translation encourages too much transnationalism at the expense of assimilation or, more bluntly, from the xenophobic impulse to suppress diversity and promote exclusion.

Issues of these kinds seen in contemporary multicultural societies have been evident in all expansionist populations or incorporating regimes throughout history, with Egyptians, Romans, and Greeks being the obvious examples. In the east, China, Japan, and Mongolia have also faced those practicalities of population management that can make multilingualism and translation a pragmatic, non-ideological issue as well, something that the Rosetta Stone program by its very existence makes clear. Wherever societies experience sudden accelerated change, for whatever reason, movements of peoples and new configurations of cultural interactions give rise to many complex contours and social and political challenges.

Shifting promises

The writer Mary Antin arrived in the United States from Russia at the age of thirteen with her mother, brother, and sisters. Her father had preceded them three years earlier in 1891. Two years after the publication in 1912 (after excerpts had appeared in the *Atlantic Monthly*) of her widely read memoir entitled *The Promised Land,* which presented a portrait of Jewish village life in tsarist Russia, Antin published a second book, *They Who Knock at Our Gates* (1914), subtitled *A Complete Gospel of Immigration.* This publication presented a vigorous polemic in support of immigrants and against the rise of the nativist and xenophobic sentiment in the United States that would eventually lead to the Immigration Acts of 1917 (also known as the Asiatic Barred Zone Act), 1921, and 1924, the latter of which explicitly set out to control the composition of immigrant flow into the United States, primarily by stopping immigration from Southern and Eastern Europe, and also included Arabs and Africans.[1] The photos below, taken by August Sherman, a clerk on Ellis Island from 1892 to 1925, of a Slavic woman and her children (Figure 2.1) and an Italian woman (Figure 2.2) represent just some of the immigrant groups who were seen as among the least desirable at that time, with evidence from psychologists, social scientists, medical doctors, and politicians providing support for this view.[2]

Antin, no doubt aware that many held similar views about Jews, wrote forcefully against the idea of migrant exclusion on racial or ethnic grounds, emphatically reminding her readers of the rights and values expressed in the Declaration of Independence, as in this passage from *They Who Knock at Our Gates*:

> But what is there in all this that bears on the right of free men to choose their place of residency? Granted that Sicilians are not Scotchmen, how does that affect the right of a Sicilian to travel in pursuit of happiness? Strip the alien down to his anatomy, you still find a *man*, a creature made in the image of God; and concerning such a one we have definite instructions from the founders of the Republic.
> (Antin 1914: 10)

> [...]

> Has then the newest arrival the same rights as established citizens? According to the Declaration, yes; the same right to live, to move, to try his luck. More than this he does not claim at the gate of entrance; with less than this we are not authorized to put him off. We do not question the right of an individual foreigner to enter our country on any peaceable errand; why, then, question the rights of a shipload of foreigners?
> (ibid.: 13)

There can be little doubt that her target audience was the rich and influential. She almost directly places responsibility on the "favored classes" to help enable migrants to fully participate in what she determines to be the mission of the nation: the "elevation of humanity":

Figure 2.1 "Slovak woman and children 1902–1914." Manuscripts and Archives Division, The New York Public Library

[...] in which every citizen should have a share, or he is not an American citizen in the spiritual sense. The poor must give of their little – the workingman must not seek to monopolize the labor market; and the rich must give of their plenty – their time, their culture, their wealth. [...] We know what schools and lectures and neighborhood activities can do to promote assimilation. We cannot fail if we multiply these agencies as fast as the social workers call for them. The means for such extension of service are in the hands of the rich. Whoever doubts our ability to assimilate immigration doubts the devotion of our favored classes to the country's cause.

(ibid.: 126–127)

42 *The multiple meanings of hospitality*

Figure 2.2 "Italian woman 1902–1913." Manuscripts and Archives Division, The New York Public Library

Antin's unquestioning embrace of assimilation in this and other statements – though here she clearly uses the term to mean *uncompromised* integration – has been strongly criticized by some. As Jules Chametzky has rightly pointed out however, her stance on assimilation must be understood together with her belief that all immigrants had the right to become "fully American" at a time when nativism was once again on the rise and it was widely felt that many immigrants, particularly those from southern and eastern Europe, were "unassimilable to American life and a danger to the country" (Chametzky 2001: xi). Without denying or denigrating immigrants' origins, Antin repeatedly makes the point that all immigrants, past and present, have much in common, as she claims in the resonant line, "The ghost of the Mayflower pilots every immigrant ship and Ellis Island is another name for Plymouth Rock" (Antin 1914: 98), a sentiment that caused her trouble with those who drew a clear line between individuals whose roots stretched back to the earliest days of the colony and more recent arrivals. Perhaps this is why, in her references to the earliest New England immigrants, the Puritans, though she is careful to characterize them as the settler colonists they were in relation to the land they occupied, she is not explicitly critical about their exchanges with Native Americans.

The work that the Declaration of Independence performs in her argument throughout *They Who Knock at Our Gates* is interwoven repeatedly with references to the Puritans who are praised for their love of liberty in the face of persecution in England. She suggests affinities between them and the Jews persecuted in tsarist Russia, though, she insists, the latter faced an even greater challenge: "It takes a hundred times as much steadfastness and endurance for a Russian Jew of today to remain a Jew as it took an English Protestant in the seventeenth century to defy the established church" (ibid.: 37). Appealing again primarily to the most influential in American social and political opinion, she declares that idealism was the predominant virtue of the Pilgrims (ibid.: 36) while cannily forestalling criticisms of all immigrants based on the faults of the few.

> No doubt the austere ambitions of the voyagers of the Mayflower made them stern recruiting masters, but our knowledge of men in the mass forbids the assumption that they were all heroes of the first rank who stepped ashore on Plymouth Rock. I have little sympathy with declaimers about the Pilgrim Fathers who look upon them all as men of grand conceptions and superhuman foresight. An entire ship's company of Columbuses is what the world never saw.
>
> (ibid.: 69)

Antin's use of the early Puritan settlers is reminiscent of certain other dimensions to inter-ethnic relations at that earlier time that remain relevant to any discussion of the politics of migration, and the role of translation.

Sassamon's dilemma

With their Geneva Bibles in hand, and from their position of weakness in relation to the local Wampanoag, the Puritans extended a short-lived instrumental friendliness, remembered in celebration of the real or imaginary 'First Thanksgiving' feast between the English and the Indians. At the same time, in need of support against neighboring tribes and following the decimation of their numbers through illness, the Wampanoag extended their hospitality to the English ensuring their survival through the initial cruel winter and beyond. That moment of mutuality, lasting from 1620 until 1630 when larger waves of Puritan migrants started to arrive from England, became reflected a few years later in a translating partnership established between one remarkable Wampanoag named John Sassamon, who had been orphaned in his teens and brought up in an English family to speak English, and John Eliot, a uniquely gifted Englishman who unlike almost all of his fellow countrymen painstakingly managed to learn Massachusett, the Algonquian language spoken in eastern New England, with the purpose of converting the Indians to Christianity. As historian Jill Lepore reports (1998: 29):

> From the time of their arrival, English settlers were baffled by the native languages they heard spoken, but few bothered to learn them, relying instead on Indian interpreters such as the famous Squanto. In 1634 William Wood observed that "the language is hard to learn, few of the English being able to speak any of it, or capable of the right pronunciation, which is the chief grace of their tongue." Although Wood had noticed that the Indians "love any man that can utter his mind in their words," few colonists were willing to learn even the most basic Algonquian vocabulary. Consistent with European attitudes about native cultures, most colonists considered the local languages barbaric, even satanic, and found the Indians' lack of a writing system powerful evidence of the primitiveness of their culture.

During the late 1640s John Sassamon became Eliot's interpreter and gradually each became the teacher of the other. John Eliot's purpose was both to bring the Indians to Christianity and to establish a number of 'praying towns' where Christian Indians would live following conversion and become Anglicized. In 1650 he established the first of these in Natick, Massachusetts, physically built by – among others – Sassamon, who later became one of its schoolteachers. By 1653 Eliot had arranged for Sassamon to attend Harvard College along with his own son. Despite his high level of assimilation Sassamon remained ambivalent about Puritan society, "alternately embracing and rejecting it" (ibid.: 30). Their reciprocal relationship, however, flourished long enough for Eliot to launch a printing press with Sassamon and two others as his assistants, and to commence an ambitious program of publications in what was called the "Indian Library," including the first Bible to be printed in America together with books and pamphlets in the Massachusett language.

This same period had seen the steady growth of English immigration with a simultaneous erosion of native land and power. With the death of the Wampanoag sachem Massasoit and the succession of his son Philip (also known as Metacom), Sassamon chose to leave Eliot's employ to work as translator and interpreter for the new sachem, translating and acting as scribe and witness for Philip on a large number of land deeds and transactions. By the early 1670s, Eliot's eagerness to convert Philip to Christianity to influence a larger number of Indians drew Sassamon into acting as a go-between. Philip, however, was presciently suspicious of the establishment of the 'praying towns' and, like his father before him, had no intention of entertaining Christianity. Though he had grown up in a world where Puritans and Indians existed side by side with much shared experience, tensions between the two sides had gradually deepened. Frustration at the increased military strength and assertiveness of the English moved Philip toward making secret alliances with other Indian tribes with the intention of driving the English out. Just before the outbreak of the two-year-long bloody war between the Algonquians and the English settlers – one of the bloodiest wars in US history – Sassamon, blamed by Eliot for Philip's refusal to convert and blamed by Philip for his troubles with the English and for traveling to betray his plans to the English – was murdered by some of Philip's men.

Sassamon was probably not the first and certainly not the last translator to suffer such a fate, trapped between two worlds and a new emerging political reality. Such contradictory realities are inevitable in any instance of migration as much today as early in the American colonies when Sassamon struggled. Potentially inhospitable communicative environments, where the rights of some are limited or require negotiation, bring translation – the only mode of access to new social, cultural, and economic knowledge – to the fore where it plays a crucial role in projecting linguistic hospitality and inclusive communication.

If moving between realities is a dangerous occupation under any circumstances, moving into a terrain that is forming and inventing itself by trial and error is doubly so. By the late nineteenth century, immigration to the United States was shifting both ideological boundaries and economic possibilities. Labor was demanded by a vigorous capitalism buoyed up by the steady sophistication of mass production and returns on wealth that had never before been so unrestrainedly realized. New ideas about labor organization, leaving old European class structures and other constraints on human potential behind, combined to make hope and expectation part of the migrant experience, yet still framed by cautionary tales. When Mary Antin was writing and lecturing about immigration, industries employing hundreds and thousands of immigrant workers, many speaking little or no English, were discovering and inventing ways to get the most out of their workforce. Cities expanded to (barely) accommodate these workers and their families, as the glow of the gilded age, which from across the Atlantic was the only visible thing, obscured the daily realities of poverty.

Ellis Island and the uncertain presence of hospitality

The first attempts to occupy a new environment, bodily, linguistically, and cognitively are a rite of passage of sorts, a ritual event that marks a person's transition from one 'state' to another. The oral histories of immigrants who passed through New York's Ellis Island overwhelmingly recall the communicative demands they faced upon their arrival, including officers shouting instructions in a language they did not understand, gesturing the passengers to walk down the gangplank to the main building, passing out identity tags, and the noise of the multitudes of other immigrants. They remember the drawings and puzzles of the doctors who determined whether they were mentally fit to be allowed entry, the immigration inspectors' questions, and the sounds of a host of unintelligible languages. They also recollect iconic signs like the Statue of Liberty, the American flag, the oppressive heat of an August summer, the smells of the harbor and of their fellow travelers who, like them, had spent a week or more crossing the ocean in steerage class. They also recall the strangeness, the anxiety of the unknown, the fragility of their position in seeking admittance to this new place, and the uncertainty of their acceptance. The panoply of new signs that accompanies this transition is often remembered decades later. The American actor and director Mike Nichols (born Mikhail Igor Peschkowsky), who arrived at Ellis Island in 1939 from Germany with his brother at the age of seven, is famously quoted as saying "American society to me and my brother was thrilling because, first of all, the food made noise. We were so excited about Rice Krispies and Coca-Cola. We had only silent food in our country, and we loved listening to our lunch and breakfast." He remembers being met by his father who had fled Nazi Germany a few months earlier:

> When we got off the boat in New York, there was a delicatessen right near the dock and it had a neon sign with some Hebrew letters in it, and I said, 'Is that allowed?' So at seven, I had some sense of what that would have meant back in Germany.
>
> (Pogrebin 2005: 78)

Immigrants arriving at Ellis Island in the late nineteenth and early twentieth century faced a series of economic and communicative challenges, which, if not met, threatened immediate exclusion from permanent entry to the United States. All underwent a series of trials to ascertain their physical and mental suitability. While some immigrants were prepared for the series of tests and questions they would be required to undergo based on information from individuals from home who had succeeded or failed in their attempts, others arrived unprepared for which aspects of themselves they would need to present.

In addition to an initial medical inspection (Figure 2.3) to rule out infectious disease (an almost certain guarantee of being turned back), immigrants were required to undergo standard intelligence tests in which they were asked to solve basic math problems, count backward from twenty, or complete a puzzle. Those who had some schooling and were used to holding a pencil might be required to copy geometric shapes; for others, doctors developed tests to do with problem solving and the person's ability to

The multiple meanings of hospitality 47

Figure 2.3 "Immigrants undergoing medical examination 1902–1913." The Miriam and Ira D. Wallach Division of Art, Prints and Photographs: Photography Collection, The New York Public Library

acquire knowledge. For individuals who it was determined did not know how to read and write, they used visual tests involving comparison or mimicry that did not require an interpreter.

Fiorello LaGuardia, the son of Italian immigrants who went on to have a highly regarded career in politics, serving in the Congress and, most famously, as Mayor of New York City from 1934 to 1945, worked as an interpreter on Ellis Island from 1907 to 1910 while studying for a law degree. At the time, it was necessary to pass a Civil Service exam to qualify to work on the island as an interpreter. In his autobiography, LaGuardia recalls his time there and reports that the classification of an immigrant as mentally incompetent, which comprised over half of those deported, was largely due to the "ignorance on the part of the immigrants or the doctors and the inability of the doctors to understand the particular immigrant's norm, or standard."

> One case haunted me for years. A young girl in her teens from the mountains of northern Italy turned up at Ellis Island. No one understood her particular dialect very well, and because of her hesitancy

48 The multiple meanings of hospitality

in replying to questions she did not understand, she was sent to the hospital for observation. I could imagine the effect on this girl, who had always been carefully sheltered and had never been permitted to be in the company of a man alone, when a doctor suddenly rapped her on the knees, looked into her eyes, turned her on her back and tickled her spine to ascertain her reflexes. The child rebelled—and how! It was the cruelest case I ever witnessed on the Island. In two weeks' time that child was a raving maniac, although she had been sound and normal when she arrive at Ellis Island.

(LaGuardia 1948: 65)

Once the series of tests was completed, new arrivals would proceed to the Registry Room where they waited for immigration inspectors to verify the information contained on the ships' manifests (Figure 2.4).

For some interactions, interpreters were provided to assist in the creation of a written record. In these exchanges, the immigrants' names were recorded and information was collected about their ages, occupations, marital status, and intended destinations. Where any complications arose,

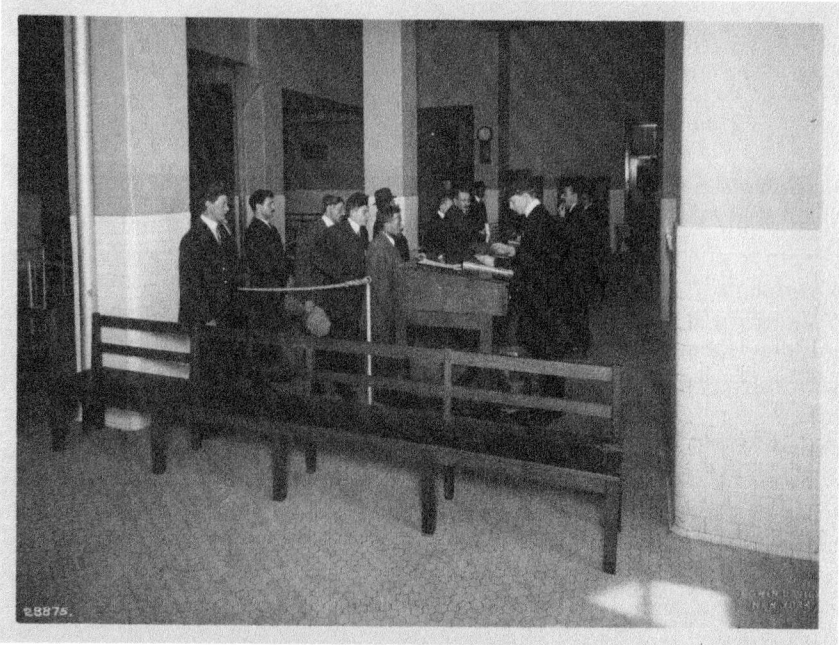

Figure 2.4 "Immigrants waiting in line for processing by Immigration Bureau officials 1902–1913." The Miriam and Ira D. Wallach Division of Art, Prints and Photographs: Photography Collection, The New York Public Library

The multiple meanings of hospitality 49

Figure 2.5 "A private interview between a young immigrant and an Ellis Island official. Two staff members [?] are also present 1902–1910." Manuscripts and Archives Division, The New York Public Library

they would be taken for further questioning to further assess their social, economic, and moral fitness. In Figure 2.5, the man in the suit to the left is most likely an unidentified interpreter.

With the passage of the Immigration Act of 1917, a further test was added which required all immigrants sixteen years or older to read a passage of between twenty and eighty words in their native language. To test for literacy, inspectors used two types of dual-language cards: either cards with printed excerpts from the Bible or instructional cards. For the instructional cards, immigrants had to follow a series of printed commands such as picking up a pencil and handing it to the immigration inspector. The inspector would observe them as they read the passage. If the person mouthed the words and followed directions correctly he or she could move on to the next phase of the inspection process. Immigrants who failed to follow the instructions or were otherwise unable to prove that they were "clearly and beyond a doubt entitled to land" were detained and had to appear before a "Board of Special Inquiry" for further evaluation (Tuttle 2004).

The Bible excerpts were written in two languages, presumably so that the inspectors who did not know the immigrants' native language could follow along with what they were reading. In these cases, the test would have involved attention to the aural qualities of a person's language competence. An excerpt on one such card written in Hebrew with the English translation below is taken from the King James version of Proverbs 12, verses 16–20. Proverbs are intended as concentrated, practical truths to be followed as rules for living. Biblical Proverbs normally prescribe certain values and forms of behavior as right or wrong, good or evil. Though there may be different ways of realizing these values, they are viewed as incontestable universal truths, with little place for cultural or contextual interpretation:

- A fool's wrath is presently known: but a prudent man covereth shame.
- He that speaketh truth sheweth forth righteousness: but a false witness deceit.
- There is that speaketh like the piercings of a sword: but the tongue of the wise is health.
- The lip of truth shall be established forever: but a lying tongue is but for a moment.
- Deceit is in the heart of them that imagine evil: but to the counsellors of peace is joy.

It is interesting that the five proverbs for this particular card repeatedly compare the desirability of speaking the truth with the evil of deceit. This directly speaks to certain widely held presumptions about immigrants: that individuals seeking to immigrate, whatever the factors compelling them to do so, may be hiding some truth or actively trying to deceive immigration inspectors or abuse the system in some way. The tone of immigration inspections is often one of doubt or incredulity aimed at the 'foreigner' whose accounts and explanations are interpreted through the worldviews of inspectors who believe their own values and expectations – of the workings of bureaucracies, democratic processes, political organizations, family ties, and social values – to be universal. Records indicate that the addition of these literacy tests at Ellis Island actually succeeded in excluding only a very small additional number of individuals, and there is nothing to suggest they were used as anything other than bureaucratic exercises. However, in this environment, even an innocuous procedural exercise can become a tacit examination or explicit rejection of the beliefs and values of one or a whole nation of immigrants, including refugees or asylum seekers – and a powerful reminder of the moral, cultural, and legal codes of the 'host' country that determine their fate.

Angel Island and the certain absence of hospitality

The misuse of entry procedures was certainly the case in San Francisco where in 1910 a prison-like detention center was established right off the coast at Angel Island, sometimes referred to as the Ellis Island of the West. The experiences of many of the mostly Asian immigrants who arrived there were radically different from most of those landing at Ellis Island. A series of inhumane laws had been passed banning the Chinese from immigrating to the United States, beginning with the Chinese Exclusion Act of 1882, extended with the Geary Act in 1892, and again with the Extension Act of 1904. The laws emanated from racist sentiments formed during the 1850s, around the time of the Gold Rush, when tens of thousands of mostly single men from all over the world headed to California in search of fortune. Out of all these migrants, internal and external, the Chinese were singled out for verbal and physical abuse due to their distinct, i.e. non-Western, cultural practices and physical appearance which prompted accusations that they were prospecting more than their fair share of gold, sending it all back to China, and stealing jobs because they were willing to work for low wages (Lee and Yung 2010).[3] Ironically, the success of Chinese laborers on the West Coast in establishing small laundry businesses, contributing to the growth of the fishing and mining industries, and building the transcontinental railroad (see Chapter Four), incited other immigrants-turned-nativists to despise them and to make them scapegoats for the wide-scale unemployment facing the country by the late nineteenth century. The caption under the Thomas Nast cartoon (Figure 2.6) says "Pacific Chivalry: Encouragement

Figure 2.6 "Pacific Chivalry: Encouragement to Chinese Immigration," *Harper's Weekly*, August 7, 1869. AP2.H3, 13:152. Courtesy of the Bancroft Library, University of California, Berkeley

to Chinese Immigration." The man wears a hat with 'California' written around the band and the wall behind him reads "Courts of Justice Closed to Chinese. Extra Taxes to Yellowjack."

The exclusion laws were particularly unjust toward the Chinese with a legal claim to reside in or return to the United States based on their own or their relatives' status as US-born Chinese Americans or legal permanent residents. The Exclusion Act was finally repealed in 1943, though largely for political reasons, as China became an important ally of the United States during World War II. In contrast to the (mostly European) migrants who arrived on the East Coast, though the entry procedures were similar, the Chinese were treated with a greater deal of hostility and suspicion, underwent much harsher inspections, and were more often than not held for weeks and months in detention before their cases were decided (Schrag 2010).

At Ellis Island, one-third of the inspectors had themselves been born outside the United States. Edward Ferro, an inspector at Ellis Island who had emigrated from Italy in 1906 at the age of twelve, remembers the positive role that interpreters played on the island:

> The language was a problem of course, but it was overcome by the use of interpreters. We had interpreters on the island who spoke practically every language. It would happen sometimes that these interpreters – some of them – were really softhearted people and hated seeing people being deported, and they would, at times, help the aliens by interpreting in such a manner as to benefit the alien and not the government. Unless you saw it, you couldn't visualize the misery of these people who came to the United States from Europe… They were tired; they had gone through an awful lot of hardships. It's impossible for anyone who had not gone through the experience to imagine what it was.
>
> (Bial 2009: 35)

In contrast, at Angel Island very few of the inspectors spoke a language other than English and there was a culture of distrust and discrimination toward Chinese employees within the Immigration Service, including the interpreters (Lee and Yung 2010: 43). Chinese who applied for interpreter positions on Angel Island, in addition to providing proof of their qualifications and prior experience, also had to obtain "letters of recommendation from a reputable white person who could vouch for their characters" (Lee 2003: 72). Once hired, they were not permitted to be alone with immigrants for long periods of time and were required to take shifts during interrogations. According to one of these interpreters, Edwar Lee, the justification for this was that:

> They were afraid of collusion between the interpreters and the applicant coming in. So in order to play it safe, one case may have two to

three. You hear a portion of the testimony, say, from the father. All right when it come to the applicant, they ask for change in interpreter.

(ibid.: 73)

Though many of the immigration inspectors disliked the disruption of their interrogations caused by this requirement, the policy remained in place. One of the inspectors, John Birge Sawyer, who served as an inspector of the Chinese division between 1916 and 1918, kept a diary of his two years on Angel Island in which he wrote unfavorably about the distrust shown toward the interpreters and the unfair treatment of the Chinese migrants (Sawyer 1917).

Sawyer's period as an inspector on Angel Island coincided with Anthony Caminetti's tenure as the US Commissioner General of Immigration between 1913 and 1920. Caminetti, like LaGuardia, was the son of Italian immigrants, a lawyer and a public servant. Caminetti, however, who was born and raised in California, expressed little sympathy for the challenges immigrants faced, and expressed a great deal of prejudice, particularly toward the Chinese, during his years as Commissioner. His views are clearly evident in his 1916 Annual Report to the Secretary of Labor under the subject heading "Oriental Immigration." In addition to the unabashed anti-Asian sentiments he expresses within the report, in one particular passage, Caminetti contrasts native-born or naturalized parents "belonging to races that are eligible to become citizens by naturalization" with native-born Chinese to argue for a ban on the children of Chinese Americans immigrating to the United States. He appeals to fairness, safety, and equality of voice "in the conduct of this Nation's affairs" while making invidious and faulty comparisons between "naturalized" or "substantial" citizens on the one hand and "accidental" citizens and their offspring on the other (United States Department of Labor, *Annual Report* 1916: xvi, my emphasis).

> A child born in this country of native-born or *naturalized* parents belonging to races that are eligible to become citizens by naturalization, who continues to live throughout childhood, who is trained in our schools and thoroughly imbued with American ideas and ideals, upon attaining his majority may exercise the franchise to the extent of casting one ballot in each political contest. Is it fair or safe that a person born to and reared abroad by parents who are *"accidental"* American citizens and nothing more, who has no training in American customs and aspirations, who has no knowledge and love for our institutions, should be permitted to remain in the foreign country of his birth and bear allegiance in every practical sense to that country and to come here only when it suits some selfish purpose of his own or his father's for him to do so, and immediately on stepping ashore enter a condition where he can have an equal voice in the conduct of this Nation's affairs with the *substantial* citizen described above?[4]

In making these statements, Caminetti elides the many realities that contribute to different patterns of immigration and settlement among ethnic groups. In the case of the Chinese, Asian immigrants were not entitled to pursue naturalization under the terms of the Exclusion Act, and the difficulties that Chinese American citizens and their families faced at US ports of entry discouraged attempts at family unification. Caminetti's lifelong nativist attitudes and policies were in sharp contrast to LaGuardia's continuous championing of immigrants and ethnic minorities, reflecting a general contrast of experience and outlook between nineteenth-century European immigrants and their descendants who went west and who tended to fare better economically and suffer less discrimination, and those who remained in East Coast cities. Both were well-educated sons of immigrants who entered public office around the same time; they are a useful reminder that the experiences of migrants from the same ethnic group are as individual as they are collective, and their attitudes toward their own communities or other migrants develop both autonomously and within specific social and historical contexts.

Chinese migrants arrived at Angel Island under the shadow of the exclusion acts. Upon their arrival, guards 'escorted' all new and some returning Chinese immigrants into the inspection station where the individuals and families were separated by gender, a separation that remained in place for the duration of their detention in barracks specifically set aside for 'Orientals' (Lee and Yung 2010: 56). They then underwent thorough, sometimes humiliating, medical inspections followed by interrogations where, compared to the thirty or so questions asked on Ellis Island, the Chinese, in particular, were expected to answer over one hundred detailed and exhaustive questions, mostly designed to entrap them in some inconsistency. Many of the immigrants prepared themselves for these lengthy interrogations with books written by 'coaching specialists' in San Francisco either sent to them by relatives before they left China or passed through the Chinese kitchen staff on the island. The primary purpose of these books was not to facilitate deception, but to help immigrants who merited legal entry to be better prepared for the intimidating questions they might be asked that were designed to draw out discrepancies between family members who were interviewed separately, sometimes for hours. In her oral history account, Law Shee Low relates how she became scared to learn that a fellow detainee (who was later deported) had been asked about the direction her house faced back in China. Not knowing the answer to that question herself, she recalled:

> When the interpreter asked me whether I had visited my husband's ancestral home during the wedding I said no because I was afraid he was going to ask me which direction the house faced like the woman told me and I wouldn't know. Evidently my husband had said yes. So when they asked me again (this time in the presence of my husband)

and I said no again, my husband said, "*Choi* [for fortune's sake]! You went; why don't you say so?" The immigration officer hit the table with his hand [in objection] and scared me to death. So I quickly said, "Oh I forgot. I did pass in the wedding sedan chair, but I didn't go in."

(ibid.: 88)

Incidents like these and the emotional impact they had on the detainees are confirmed repeatedly in the oral histories of Chinese immigrants who passed through Angel Island (ibid.).

Some of the earliest literary expressions of these individuals' experiences can be found in poems inked or carved into the walls of the detention barracks at Angel Island (Figure 2.7). One hundred and thirty-five of these calligraphic poems survived.

The poems provide an interesting snapshot of the collectively constructed consciousness of the migration experience in real time. The poems on the walls, for example, display liberal borrowing from one poem to another; they also contain internal revisions added by different people at a later date (ibid.: 24). In addition to poems, drawings of birds, fish, horses, ships, and flags were also carved into the walls, the only signs of life during long periods of detention seen outside the windows or on brief outdoor breaks. Taken together, they express the isolation, grief, despair, and anger experienced

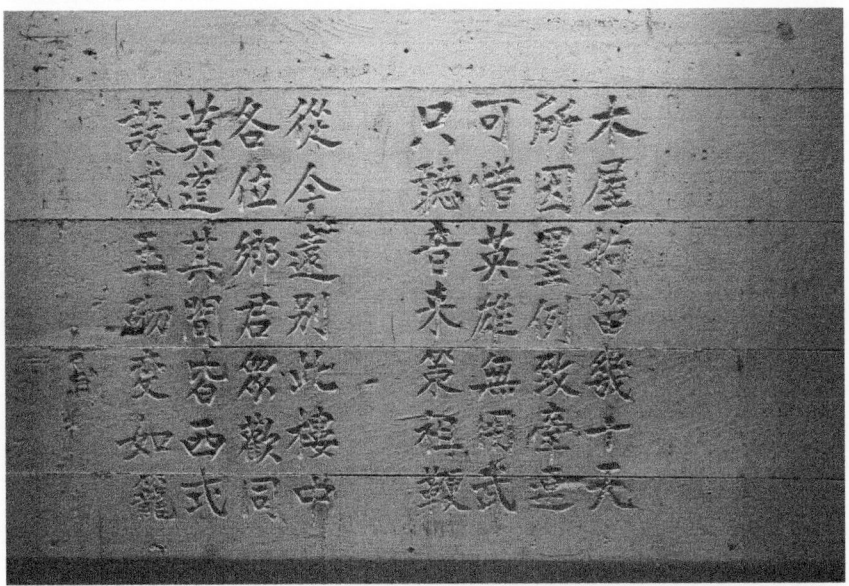

Figure 2.7 Poem on a wall at the detention barracks, Angel Island. Courtesy of Chris Carlsson, photographer

56 *The multiple meanings of hospitality*

due to prolonged confinement or imminent deportation, as illustrated in the examples below.

> 22
> America has power, but not justice.
> In prison, we were victimized as if we were guilty.
> Given no opportunity to explain, it was really brutal.
> I bow my head in reflection but there is nothing I can do
> (Lai et al 1991: 58)
>
> 46
> The low building with three beams merely shelters the body.
> It is unbearable to relate the stories accumulated on the Island slopes.
> Wait til the day I become successful and fulfil my wish.
> I will not speak of love when I level the immigration station.
> (ibid.: 94)

The original texts of the poems also provide interesting information about the social background of the detainees. Many violate the rules of rhymes and of tone required in Chinese poetry and contain incorrect characters and usages, indicating a lack of formal education beyond primary school. There is also frequent inclusion of Cantonese vernacular expressions as well as Chinese American colloquialisms (ibid.: 25). Interestingly, the sociolinguistic features that provide this knowledge in the originals were not retained in the English translations. The rationale for doing so is described in the translators' notes.

> The act of interpretation itself implies creation and the readers should bear in mind that the process of poetic translation must involve a certain compromise. While these poems express the thoughts of the individuals who wrote them, they are not reiterations of their original literal forms. The form is oftentimes compromised in order to retain the content, which we for historic reasons feel is our first priority. We do not claim adherence to the poets' original meters or rhyme-schemes. By imitating the poetic structure, we feel an injustice to the meaning of the poem would have been committed.
> (ibid.: 31)

The translators' decision to omit relevant biographical details in order to foreground the depth of the emotional impact of the carceral experience is an interesting strategic use of translation. In this case, the translators' participation in what might be considered an act of 'misrecognition' is weighed against their desire to protect the meanings of the poems against the 'injustice' of retaining form over content. The translations thus become a vehicle for a particular construction of the texts as historical records, foregrounding the aesthetic dimension of the Chinese migrant sensibility and infusing it with a political dimension. The impact of these early experiences would have an enduring effect on the trust of many members of the Chinese community in the political and social institutions of the United States and their sense of belonging to its citizenry. The contents of the poems provide clear evidence for why this was so.

This brief sketch of different early migration experiences in the United States illustrates the central role of intra-lingual, inter-lingual and inter-semiotic communication, together with the social and historical contexts in which this occurs, in the earliest formations of migrant sensibility. In the liminal moments of transition and transformation, when individuals are precariously positioned between their departure from one place and their arrival at another, language becomes significant in a heightened way. Previously taken-for-granted intra-lingual communication becomes a vital stabilizing resource, inter-lingual interactions provide migrants a voice within small-scale encounters or become sites for the realization of system-wide exclusionary practices, while inter-semiotic sign spaces can create opportunities for the exercise of greater communicative autonomy.

The constraints of role

As was the case in Angel Island and Ellis Island, translators often act only as ethically as the systems they work within or the individuals they work for encourage or permit. Conventionally, translators' ostensive invisibility and impartiality have been used as a pretext to allow translators in their professional role to remain morally blameless in the event of an injustice. But even some of the simplest decisions translators make in their professional lives involve unavoidable complex moral and ethical dilemmas. Under these circumstances, tensions can emerge, as in any profession, between the moral 'person' and the ethical 'professional,' a distinction moral philosophers sometimes make between 'ordinary' morality, the moral obligations that bind individuals (whether these are understood to be based in rights-based liberal individualism, communitarian, or universalist ethics) and 'role' morality, the duties and loyalties that go along with various social roles. Whereas ordinary morality assumes an evolving moral code that is shaped within one or more cultures and societies, role morality applies to standards or codes of behavior expected by the professional group to which an individual belongs. This becomes particularly salient when these issues arise in the context of national boundaries and judgments about who should and should not be admitted.

Role morality presupposes two core beliefs: that particular actions taken in the name of an institutional practice are justified and can be evaluated only by standards internal to the practice; and that personal judgments are too subjective to ensure the proper execution of a professional role. The legal philosopher David Luban (1988) has argued with respect to the law that creating a distinction between ordinary morality and role morality deflects ethical judgment away from personal responsibility and too often excuses individuals from considering their personal moral obligation in a conflict within an institution. He argues for what he terms a "morality of acknowledgment," which grants occupiers of a role the freedom to respond to the specific moral demands of others regardless of the normative ethical demands of the role (ibid.: 127). This does not mean that professional roles or the policies that inform them are irrelevant or without force, only that no role should demand that its occupant be blind to the moral worth of others regardless of the situation. A weaker contrast between a role and a person acknowledges that professionals operate in a world of situated human practices, not abstract de-contextualized policies, where the benefits of a morality of acknowledgment would seem to far outweigh those of a morality of non-accountability. It is not always a simple matter for individuals to act reflectively in relation to the official policies that guide their occupation, particularly where such actions challenge or resist the official codes of practice. A major function of 'role morality' is to uphold structural hierarchies of power and knowledge and maintain moral closure. This is why the principles, norms, and habitual actions associated with or prescribed by roles require constant scrutiny as well as innovative and creative interpretation from within and without.

All translators are in a unique position with regard to this function; they inhabit their own professional role from 'the inside out' and the roles of others from 'the outside in,' which invites a form of double consciousness – not in the invidious sense identified by Du Bois as a direct result of racism, but in the sense that their obligation to re-voice or re-write others' experiences and inhabit others' lives compels them to confront the boundaries of their own understandings, beliefs, and prior experiences. In order to translate others, they have to locate themselves, as persons, within the translation process, and do their best to recognize the real or fictional individuals they represent. This involves identifying any relevant cultural, linguistic, social, or historical factors that may be influencing the actions of individuals, and trying to capture the complex meanings behind their communication, whatever their form of expression.

Translators of the written and spoken word often talk about their role as involving trying to find the right voice for a character or an individual, to inhabit their feelings, to imagine themselves in the same situation (Inghilleri 2016). In a discussion of these issues, the literary translator and scholar Nicolas de Lange recalled his efforts to find the right words to reveal small details about the character in a novel he was translating of a young married woman about whom at the time he felt he knew very little.

> The first book that I translated has a female narrator living in Jerusalem in the 1950s and speaking Hebrew in her real life. I remember working very hard trying to find a voice for this young married woman. To pick up a character, a narrator from another book, from another language,

and put them into your book in your language is very difficult, isn't it? I remember thinking, 'What sort of words does she use, does she say wireless or radio, does she say frock or dress'? Little things, which make an enormous difference to the way it reads.

(Schwartz and de Lange 2006: 9)

In these comments, it is not clear whether de Lange's concern about his choice of words making "an enormous difference to the way it reads" refers to what the words might convey about the woman herself, how they might situate her character socially and historically, or if he was thinking about how they would be understood by his imagined readers. The terms 'frock' and 'wireless' for dress and radio are not commonly used throughout the English-reading world, for example, and they are not necessarily familiar across generations. To younger readers, they could appear strange or, given the modern use of the term 'wireless,' even confusing.

Elsewhere in his discussion, de Lange talks about how when he translates poetry or fiction his aim is to create a mood, transmit an emotion, make people feel rather than act; he questions whether his choices result in meanings that are beautiful enough or not tough enough, too romantic or too harsh (ibid.: 2). Whether decisions like these are taken with the characters or the readers in mind, and most often it is both, these are not merely aesthetic choices; they are ethical ones, designed to embed individuals, whether real or fictional, in a semantic-symbolic environment that optimizes their capacity for self-interpretation, and hence their recognition.

Translation as heresy

The idea of translation as an ethical act is not new or unique to contemporary contexts of migration and globalization. What occurs in diverse societies with respect to cultural and linguistic self-determinations comes already embedded in and influenced by the prevailing political order – for better or worse. Insofar as translation frequently occurs in domains closely constrained by legal, ethical, and political interests, its practice also can be a site where power and conflict become plainly visible. Because religion has both a private aspect relating to individuals and their consciences as well as a collective social and sometimes political presence, this embeddedness can, under certain circumstances – as in the positive case of Kublai and his religious factions – be clearly exposed. Negative cases, however, are easier to come by.

Some of the most graphic demonstrations of the influence of societal and cultural norms and the power of discursive and hierarchical structures on translation are found in responses to Bible translations going back centuries, with dire consequences for their translators. Two exemplary figures are John Wycliffe (ca. 1330–1384) and William Tyndale (1492–1536), Bible translators who wished to widen the circles of recognition by extending access to the Holy Scriptures beyond the wealthy and powerful to include 'ordinary' men and women. Their influence on the translation scholar and Bible translator Eugene Nida is well known; not only did they inspire his faith and his work as a linguist and translator, he saw them as models for translators more generally.

> Tyndale knew the risks he was running. He knew that the ecclesiastical hierarchy had denounced Wyclif and had even exhumed his body, burned it, and cast the ashes into the river Swift in order that the body of such a man might not pollute the holy ground of England. But just as the physical remains of Wyclif were borne out to the open sea, so the influence of both the man and his translation has been carried from the confines of England to the ends of the earth. Perils did not thwart the greatest of early missionaries, Paul. The modern translator cannot afford to falter, with need and example to spur him on.
>
> (Nida 1947: 7–8)

Wycliffe sought to turn the Church away from its involvement with secular concerns and the pursuit of wealth and corrupt practices, envisioning instead itinerant barefoot preachers teaching the gospels to the people for no material reward. To this end, Wycliffe and his followers initiated the first translation of the whole Bible since the eleventh century, handwritten and in English, so that people could read or hear the Scriptures directly in their own language (Burridge 2013: 196; and see Lechler 1904). Through his secondary translation, i.e. not from the original Hebrew or Greek but from the Latin Vulgate into English, Wycliffe wished to strengthen mutual recognition between the priests and the poor. At the time, Latin was the language of scholarship, a lingua franca limited to Europe's elite. The Oxford-educated Wycliffe, however, believed that God's ministers should live humble lives. This concern stemmed from a commitment to the idea that the Church was not in Rome but had its only existence in the totality of believers, alive, dead, and unborn. That was the Church and God was its only head.

Wycliffe's actions took him right into a major political arena of his day – the rights of the papacy against those of the king. The revenue collected by the Church and dispatched to Rome was vast and the Papal Receivers who made the collection did not attempt to hide the luxury they themselves enjoyed at the expense of the populace. Corruption and profligacy were rife. Furthermore, these practices diverted funds that otherwise would have flowed to the state for national purposes. Wycliffe's emphasis on the limited religious significance of the Church in Rome, that the people's access to the Bible should not be regulated by the Church but free, and his belief that God's ministers should live in poverty and humility did not escape the notice of the Church, which relentlessly attacked him. He and his followers were fiercely vilified until his death in 1384.

Forty-four years later, formally accused by the Church of heresy, it was ordered that Wycliffe's body be exhumed, burned, and his ashes cast into the river that ran through the town where he had lived and preached.

Some one hundred years later, Tyndale produced the first primary translation of the Bible in English based on the Erasmus Greek edition; his translation of the New Testament appeared in 1526. Banned in England for being written in the vernacular, it was printed and published on the Continent and distributed in England illegally. Living in virtual exile at the time of its appearance, Tyndale was already under scrutiny for promoting heresy by attacking Church authorities for their long-held clerical monopoly and manipulation of the Bible and for forbidding ordinary men and women to read and hear the Bible in their local language (Wright 2013: 312–313). The formal charge of heresy, however, for which he would be strangled and burned at the stake in 1536, according to his biographer and modern editor, David Daniell, was ultimately fueled by decisions he made within the translation itself. For example, he translated the Greek word *ekklesia* as 'congregation,' as written in the passage *te ekklesia, hetis estin to soma autou* (the 'congregation, which is the body of Christ'), which is correct from a philological and theological standpoint. Daniell points out, however, that though Tyndale's translation was in line with the New Testament's understanding of the "gathering of believers as a congregation of equals with no distinctions of rank," it threatened the social position and political power of the Catholic hierarchy for him to imply with this translation that their status was equal to that of the people in relationship to Christ.

> If Tyndale is saying in print that the body of Christ is everyone, without distinction – no laity, no priests, no bishops, no pope, if everyone is equal in Christ – then the gathering of Christians together is a congregation of equals, not a church of divisions and hierarchies, where priest and bishop and pope are essential.
>
> (Daniell 1994: 122)

There is little doubt that Tyndale was "translating with radical intent" (Wright 2013: 313). In addition to decisions he made regarding specific words and phrases, the prefaces, prologues, and marginal notes contain occasional comments clearly intended to send a political message. For example, in a marginal note in 1 Thess 4:11, on a line where Paul encourages his readers to "study to be quiet, to meddle with your own business, and to work with your own hands," Tyndale writes "A good lesson for monks and idle friars" (ibid.: 317) and a note in Num 6:22–27 reads: "hereof ye see that Aaron (where he lift up his hand and bless the people) was not as dumb as our bishops be" (Burke 2013: xix, n. 18). Importantly, however, marginal notes are used more often to explore theological issues directly with his readers and most often to acknowledge the craft of translation itself – and to demonstrate his awareness that the translation of the Bible will and should never end (Daniell 1994: 319).

At his execution, Tyndale's final words were, "Lord, open the king of England's eyes" (ibid.: 383). The cruel irony is that only three years later, Henry VIII, who ordered the execution, arranged to have himself declared the supreme head of the Church of England and ordered an English Bible to be placed in every English parish, though not without restrictions on who among the laity should have access (Ferrell 2013: 33). Though the Bible that was created carried the name of Miles Coverdale, a former Tyndale colleague, it was effectively Tyndale's translation. And Tyndale, though translating from a different source text from Wycliffe, had relied on Wycliffe to guide his choice of words. It was Wycliffe's translation that Thomas More, Chancellor to Henry VIII and strong supporter of the Catholic Church in Rome, had in mind in his pursuit and suppression of Tyndale's Bible when he wrote that Wycliffe had "purposely corrupted that holy text, malycyously planting therein suche wordys as might in the reders erys serue to the profe of suche heresyes as he went about to sow" (Burke 2013: xvii).

A much more recent example of how different traditions arrive at disparate readings of the Bible, and the link between translation and the politics of religion, is Aviya Kushner's *The Grammar of God* (2015). Kushner describes a scene in her book where she is carrying around the Oxford Annotated Bible (in a brown paper bag) in a Jewish Center in Iowa City. Noticing this, an older man tells her, "It is not a good book for you," according to Kushner, "echoing the Talmud's warning about reading the Torah in a language other than Hebrew" for fear that any such translation would be used to convert Jews to Christianity or to interpret the Old Testament in a negative light (ibid.: 106). She cites as an example of the source of this distrust the conflicting image of Moses in St. Jerome's fourth-century translation of the Hebrew Bible into Latin where he is described as "horned," versus the Hebrew Bible description of Moses coming down from Mt. Sinai as "beaming." Kushner reads horned as "devilish," and contends that the Christian interpretation of it as "an expression of authority and power" can be traced to an incorrect reading of the verb *karan* (meaning beamed) as the noun *karen* (meaning ray of light or the horn of an animal). In Hebrew, according to Kushner, though the two words shared the same root *krn*, the placement of lines and dots beneath certain letters make them completely different words (ibid.: 28). Hers is the latest interpretation in a longstanding debate on the translation of this Hebrew expression in both word and image. (For additional commentary see Melinkoff 1970, Medjuck 1998, Sonsino 2009.)

Words undressed

In a stirring collection of modern poems entitled *Burning Wycliffe* (2006), the poet Thom Satterlee set out to chronicle Wycliffe's spiritual journey. The volume is loosely biographical; the poet imagines a series of episodes

The multiple meanings of hospitality 63

from Wycliffe's life beginning with his childhood, to his time at Oxford, then as a writer and preacher, and ending with the posthumous exhumation that the Catholic Church inflicted on his corpse. In several poems, Satterlee addresses the significance of language for Wycliffe, most importantly as a form of expression of the Word of God, "that language before languages." The poet also suggests, however, that for Wycliffe words never provided the clear essence he sought. Ultimately, they became entangled in meanings given to them by others. In the poem, "Purvey Translates: *In ipso enim vivimus et movemur et sumus*," Satterlee alludes to the sense that Wycliffe, like other Bible translators, had of himself as essentially an instrument of God's hand.

> [...]
> I felt myself placed
> as a word on the page,
> and suddenly I saw
> the whole of who we are
> and how we're bound together -
> in the Word of God,
> and our life's goal as simple
> as remembering the lines
> He first drew us with,
> the sound and sense
> we made in that language
> before languages.

Wycliffe's aim to serve as a scribe of God's word and to achieve simplicity for himself and others in and through preaching the Scriptures was ultimately frustrated, however, as he found himself forced into the predetermined roles that history and geography imposed. In another poem, "Habitus," Satterlee expresses Wycliffe's unfulfilled desire to see words "undressed," to go toward them with the enthusiasm of a child to a fair, open to their truth and unencumbered by others' intentions.

> [...]
> But no: Wycliffe had got it all wrong.
> He was not going to see the words.
> They were coming to him
> with their arms loaded with robes
> stacked so high he couldn't see their faces,
> and before he knew it, invisible hands
> began measuring him with ropes
> stretched between his wrist and his chest,
> from his hip down to the ground,
> around his waist and around his neck.
> [...]

Wycliffe and Tyndale had absolute certainty in the ultimate Truth of the Bible as the Word of God and in their translations as faithful representations of this Truth. Both in the end felt the weight of power over the force of justice, both felt "victimized as if [they] were guilty." Following his arrest, Tyndale testified, "I call God to record that I never altered one syllable of God's word against my conscience" (Wright 2013: 314). Neither ever questioned the idea of universal truths, only the languages in which these truths could and should be expressed. In their era, human language was perceived unquestionably as given directly by God. Reading the Bible was thus considered a principal means by which humans maintained a close and direct relationship to God.

Wycliffe and Tyndale became enmeshed in a conflict over the right of the people to receive the universal Truth of the Word of God in their own language against what the Church, backed by the monarchy, determined to be the most socially and politically expedient means to express that truth, led by the desire to protect their own interests and maintain social stability. There was no disagreement over the universality of Biblical meaning, only the language used to represent it, yet both sides were clearly also aware of the relationship between the two. Satterlee's poems attempt to capture Wycliffe's coming to terms with the weight of words and the authority they gain or lose in relation to sanctioned forms of power. He experienced first hand the negative force of what Bourdieu has referred to as "authorized discourse" (Bourdieu 1991: 109), the idea that the social worth of language derives not from language itself, but from the institutional conditions of its production and reception. In contexts where an individual or group's language has no prior authorization, it cannot participate equally in the production of new forms of legitimacy. Language cannot perform a break with context. The power of language cannot be invoked linguistically alone; authority comes to language from the outside. Interestingly, at the same time Wycliffe fought for the right to translate and preach the Word of God in the English language, he condemned and sought to censor preachers of his day for "not preaching God's Word, but reciting stories, fables, or poems that were altogether foreign to the Bible" (Lechler 1904: 178).

Within the highly ritualized institution of the Christian Church, the exercise of control over official discourses was clearly a complex matter, and starkly different from the religious flexibility seen under Kublai. This is in large part due to the fact that unlike some other societies across the globe and throughout history there was no powerful priestly class connected to secular authority in Kublai's domain. The absence of any high-priestly caste in the Mongolian political order to compete with the authority of the Khan meant not only that there was plenty of space for the diversity of faiths to exist and be welcomed – Kublai was not alone in his religious tolerance – but also that censorship of matters of individual conscience did not arise. Because no single religion achieved any authority from the ruling dynasty, no one language was authorized more than another, and there was no politically salient connection between the sacred texts of the religions supported under the Khan's rule and the languages or forms of languages in which they were expressed.

The issues that emerged in fourteenth-century Europe gained their importance because, as Tyndale's politics later made apparent, for a believer to have God's word *in his own language* was a form of spiritual empowerment of the individual beyond the authority of the Church. Luther's notion of 'every man his own priest before God' when secularized could thus imply a threat to the civil authority and institutions of the state and, as the Puritan revolution in England demonstrated, to the very notion of the monarchy itself. These apparently religious controversies ultimately were about the individual and society and about sources of earthly authority. A century later, it was these tensions that precipitated the migration of the often despised and persecuted Puritans to the eastern shores of North America, escaping both the crown and the bishops of the established church.

Just as the embeddedness of linguistic acts in specific political, social, and ethical contexts shapes their form and meaning, translators and translating are also situated at the crossroads of powerful, sometimes dangerous forces. Religious hospitality of the kind that Kublai practiced vanishes where religion and political power combine and closes down the possibility for 'heretical' translation to form a bridge to common understandings. Power then becomes silence, the withdrawal of linguistic hospitality.

Wycliffe, Tyndale, and Sassamon were all, in a sense, translatorial activists. Not only did they endeavor to work within politically and ethically tense environments, they were each attempting to effect social and political change. In this they could not have been more removed from one of the most persistent tenets of current professional ethics – impartiality – which seeks to distance translators from the realm of politics and social commitments and position them where their ethics are constructed by their degree of disinterest. To translate is to assume that different systems of beliefs exist which, in order to be incorporated into or rejected by others, must be interpreted through some form of communication. Translation in whatever form is the means by which individuals determine in what ways they diverge or are the same in relation to the beliefs they experience as meaningful and as true. The possibility of agreement or disagreement with others rests on the assumption of and about beliefs. The refusal to translate, or be translated, is in this way a social or political matter, and not a question of translatability itself. It is a refusal to embrace or succumb to the possibility, indeed inevitability, that translation alters meanings in ways that are unpredictable and sometimes beyond our control or that make available meanings and understandings capable of disrupting the status quo.

Notes

1 In addition to anyone from the Asian Pacific region, the act also named "homosexuals," "idiots," "feebleminded persons," "criminals," "epileptics," "insane persons," alcoholics, "professional beggars," "mentally or physically defective" persons, polygamists, anarchists, and any immigrants over the age of sixteen who were illiterate as undesirable.
2 Sherman took over 200 photographs between 1905 and 1925. He mostly photographed immigrants who were detained briefly and used plain backgrounds so the immigrants themselves were the main focus. These were unofficial photographs based on his personal interest in recording the different cultures of the people processed at Ellis Island. His photos were collected by William Williams, Commissioner of Immigration for the Port of New York at Ellis Island from 1902 to 1905 and 1909 to 1913.
3 The Chinese were given a similar reception in Australia during the Gold Rush there in this same period. Brian Castro's novel *Birds of Passage* (1983) reconstructs the brutal racial hatred and xenophobia experienced by the Chinese diggers. Upon their arrival they were told, "… you must not have bare heads. Or bare feet. Dress like the white man. Do not wear your Chinese trousers. See how I am dressed" (ibid.: 77). The novel describes how the Chinese were routinely denied access to running water, violently slaughtered and ejected from the gold fields, and had their graves urinated on by drunken diggers. These events would lead to the White Australia Policy on immigration, which was finally completely dismantled in 1966.
4 *Annual Report of the Commissioner of Naturalization to the Secretary of Labor* January 1, 1916, US Government Printing Office https://babel.hathitrust.org/cgi/pt?id=uiug.30112004053416;view=1up;seq=9 (Accessed May 2016).

References

Antin, Mary [1912] 2012 *The Promised Land*. Introduction and Notes by Werner Sollers. New York: Penguin Classics.
—— 1914 They Who Knock at Our Gates. Boston: Houghton Mifflin.
Bial, Raymond 2009 *Ellis Island: Coming to the Land of Liberty*. New York: Houghton Mifflin.
Bourdieu, Pierre 1991 *Language and Symbolic Power*. Trans. Gino Raymond and Matthew Adamson. Cambridge: Polity Press.
Burke, David G. 2013 "Foreword: Vital Aspects of the KJV Genius," in David G. Burke, John F. Kutsho, and Philip H. Towner (eds) *The King James Version at 400*. Atlanta: Society of Biblical Literature, ix–xix.
Burridge, Richard A. 2013 "Priorities, Principles and Prefaces: From the KJV to Today (1611–2011)", in David G. Burke, John F. Kutsho, and Philip H. Towner (eds) *The King James Version at 400*. Atlanta: Society of Biblical Literature, 195–226.
Castro, Brian 1983 *Birds of Passage*. St. Leonards, NSW, Australia: Allen & Unwin.
Chametzky, Jules 2001 "Introduction and Notes," in *The Promised Land*. New York: The Modern Library.
Daniell, David 1994 *William Tyndale: A Biography*. New Haven: Yale University Press.

Ferrell, Lori Anne 2013 "The King James Bible in Early Modern Political Context," in David G. Burke, John F. Kutsho, and Philip H. Towner (eds) *The King James Version at 400*. Atlanta: Society of Biblical Literature, 31–42.
Inghilleri, Moira 2016 "'What is Red?': The Art of Interpreting Trauma," in Francoise Massardier-Kenney, Brian Baer, and Maria Tymockzo (eds) *Translators Writing, Writing Translators*. Kent, OH: Kent University Press, 77–96.
Kushner, Aviya 2015 *The Grammar of God*. New York: Spiegel & Grau.
LaGuardia, Fiorello H. 1948 *The Making of an Insurgent: An Autobiography 1882–1919*. Philadelphia and New York: J.B. Lippincott.
Lai, Him Mark, Genny Lim, and Judy Yung (eds) (1991) *Island: Poetry and History of Chinese Immigrants on Angel Island, 1910–1940*. Seattle: University of Washington Press.
Lechler, Gotthard 1904 *John Wycliffe and his English Precursors*. London: The Religious Tract Society.
Lee, Erica 2003 *At America's Gates: Chinese Immigration during the Exclusion Era, 1882–1943*. Chapel Hill: University of North Carolina Press.
Lee, Erica and Judy Yung 2010 *Angel Island: Immigrant Gateway to America*. Oxford: Oxford University Press.
Lepore, Jill 1998 *The Name of War: King Philip's War and the Origins of American Identity*. New York: Vintage Books.
Luban, David 1988 *Lawyers and Justice: An Ethical Study*. Princeton, NJ: Princeton University Press.
Medjuck, Bena Elisha 1998 *Exodus 34: 29–35: Moses' 'Horns' in Early Bible Translation and Interpretation*. PhD dissertation, McGill University, Department of Jewish Studies. www.nlc-bnc.ca/obj/s4/f2/dsk1/tape11/PQDD_0002/MQ43918.pdf (Accessed May 2016).
Melinkoff, Ruth 1970 *The Horned Moses in Medieval Art and Thought*. Los Angeles: University of California Press.
Nida, Eugene 1947 *Bible Translating: An Analysis of Principles and Procedures, with Special Reference to Aboriginal Languages*. New York: American Bible Society.
Pogrebin, Abigail 2005 *Stars of David: Prominent Jews Talk About Being Jewish*. New York: Broadway Books, 75–83.
Satterlee, Thom 2006 *Burning Wycliffe*. Lubbock: Texas Tech University Press.
Sawyer, John Birge 1917 *Diaries of John Birge Sawyer, vol. 2*. Bancroft Library, Berkeley: University of California.
Schrag, Peter 2010 *Not Fit For Our Society*. Oakland, CA: University of California Press.
Schwartz, Ros and Nicolas de Lange 2006 "A Dialogue: On a Translator's Interventions," in Peter Bush and Susan Bassnett (eds) *The Translator as Writer*. London: Continuum, 9–19.
Sonsino, Rifat 2009 *Did Moses Really Have Horns?* New York: Union for Reform Judaism Press.
Tuttle, Brad R. 2004 *The Ellis Island Collection: Artifacts from the Immigrant Experience*. San Francisco: Chronicle Books.
US Department of Labor, Bureau of Immigration. 1916 *Annual Report of the Commissioner of Naturalization to the Secretary of Labor*, January 1, 1916.

Washington, D.C.: U.S. Government Printing Office. https://babel.hathitrust.org/cgi/pt?id=uiug.30112004053416;view=1up;seq=9 (Accessed April 2016).

Wright, N. T. 2013 "The Monarchs and the Message: Reflections on Bible Translation from the Sixteenth to the Twenty-First Century," in David G. Burke, John F. Kutsho, and Philip H. Towner (eds) *The King James Version at 400*. Atlanta: Society of Biblical Literature, 309–327.

3 Translation and labor migrants

While individuals may make their own decisions to leave their countries of origin to seek out opportunities elsewhere, many among them have little choice. It can be the only way to provide for their families due to persistent poverty, chronic unemployment, or to escape political turmoil or targeted persecution. National and ethnic relations are played out in the behaviors of the many groups caught up in the migratory processes generated by the macro conditions that initiate and shape migration – the Industrial Revolution, colonialism, post-coloniality, global capitalism. The circular, fluctuating, and sustained long-distance, border-crossing character of contemporary migration is an outcome of macro-economic and geopolitical forces involving the flow of people and capital across the globe. For the many migrants who perform vital services – the unskilled laborers, factory 'sweatshop' workers and domestic workers – translation services are rare or non-existent both at the time the decision to migrate is made and later when work is undertaken in the destination country.

It is impossible to consider translation and labor migration without first examining the nature and implications of the relationship between migration and globalization. Throughout the twentieth century the greatest numbers of labor migrants and guest workers typically headed to Western Europe and the United States. Many migrant workers in Northwestern Europe came from former colonies: West Indians, Pakistanis, and Indians in the UK; Algerians in France; Surinamese in Holland. For the Irish, Eastern and Southern Europeans and, more recently, Latin Americans, the United States has been their destination. Much of late twentieth and early twenty-first century transnational migration has become directly tied to features of economic globalization and the demand for high and low-skilled labor in a growing number of advanced economies, as well as the persistence of violent conflict across the globe. The growing dependence on foreign labor in countries like Singapore reflects sustained rapid economic growth and consequent high demand for labor as well as the slow increase in domestic labor supply due to the declining fertility rate. In the wealthy Gulf oil countries, contract labor systems have effectively created dual labor markets, with well-paid public employment for the local population and heavy labor or badly paid work in the private sector for foreigners. Currently, Kuwait, Qatar, and the United Arab Emirates (UAE) have the world's highest proportion of guest workers per population. According to a recent report in *National Geographic* (Gorney 2014: 80–81), 89 percent of the total population of the UAE and Qatar are non-citizen migrants. In Singapore, 36 percent of a population of 5.2 million is made up of foreign-born workers, not including permanent residents; of these, 15 percent are highly skilled and 85 percent are semi- or unskilled (Rubdy and McKay 2013: 158).

While the term 'globalization' has entered the public discourse as a means to describe or explain such recent social and economic phenomena, similar conditions have existed historically. As Hoerder (2011: 35, emphasis in original) notes:

> The seventeenth century fur trade was global, extending from Alaska via Labrador and Scandinavia to Siberia and capitalized from London, Paris, Amsterdam and Moscow. It involved migration of traders and producers. Its gendered work processes involved men and women. Nineteenth century colonialism and imperialism were global, as was the plantation regime in subtropical and tropical zones. In a transpolity and transociety, people easily marked by color of skin or other outward physical traits became classified as inferior, segregated, and force-migrated as slaves or indentured servants and later found themselves in industrial agriculture or in low-wage industries. Scholars never conceptualized this globalization, which affected people *outside* the North Atlantic core, in the same frame as they have its more recent form affecting the *inside* of the industrialized world.

The indentured servitude of the seventeenth century served a role similar to the labor contracts widely used in certain regions today. Indenture was a legal mechanism for securing and binding voluntary labor; the indenture contract was "a legal commitment for full time labor for four, five, seven, or more years in exchange for maintenance, protection, and at termination some form of 'freedom dues'" (Bailyn 2012: 165). In the seventeenth century approximately 100,000 mostly English unskilled laborers and tradesmen and craftsmen facing high unemployment migrated to the United States colonies to work on tobacco farms in the Chesapeake Bay area, 85 percent of whom were or became indentured servants on arrival. In addition to these unemployed men, servants were comprised of vagrants, beggars, convicts, young boys, and occasionally women, many of whom were kidnapped and trafficked to the colonies to provide cheap labor for small and large tobacco farmers in Maryland and Virginia. In 1668, 45 percent of the populations of the counties in the region were servants (ibid.). Work and living conditions were harsh; between 15 and 30 percent of male immigrants to Maryland, for example, died within the first year (ibid.: 169–170).

The overlaps between the indentured servants of the seventeenth century and contract labor migrants in the twenty-first century expose an interminable and universal disregard for the rights of individuals in search of opportunities to provide for themselves and their families. Although international migration in the twentieth century and beyond differs in terms of the size and scope of modern states and their greater interdependence in multilayered global economic networks, the need of certain individuals or groups for a safe haven, a place of temporary or permanent refuge, has remained constant. The loss of employment opportunities, including that associated with ethnic conflict and war, different forms of discrimination and human rights violations, chronic unemployment and poverty, or environmental degradation have been and will continue to be significant factors behind people's motivation to migrate.

Migration and human security

There has been a push within international migration debates, partly derived from developments within the field of international relations over several decades (see Booth 1991), toward framing migration in terms of human security, advancing the perspective that the root cause of international migration be understood as the avoidance of human insecurity (Sirkeci 2007: 33). *Human security* refers to the absence of a threat to one's well-being, the recognition of the reciprocity of human rights for all, and a belief that with globalized communication, no individual or group should feel entirely helpless. It is an appeal to view people as ends not means, and a call for nation states – as part of a global community – to function as means and not ends. The concept of human security is not an utopian ideal but a way of foregrounding 'security' as the primary motivational aspect of migration, despite an awareness of the potential conflicts associated with uprooting oneself or one's family (Sirkeci 2007).

The macro-level conflicts that can impede a migrant's trajectory highlight the continued force and influence of nation states in the migration process. The relationship – too often flouted or perceived as a conflict – between the moral and legal requirement of sovereign states to offer temporary or permanent security to individuals seeking to migrate and the right of states to control the type and extent of their stay continues to inform twenty-first-century immigration policies. Current controls on international migration flows call into question whether globalization has indeed led to the erosion of the independent political authority claimed in the name of state sovereignty. While there is little debate over the fact of global interconnectedness, new patterns of social and economic stratification at the state, society, and community level throughout the developed and developing world have emerged, contributing to increased marginalization in some cases and greater opportunities for incorporation in others. While such opportunities have allowed certain individuals, poor and privileged alike, to take advantage of transnational capital and diasporic connectivity, sometimes without the need to relocate, for many unskilled or low-skilled individuals, the same processes of globalization have led to their decreased ability to find gainful work in their national economies, forcing them to migrate.

The motivation for greater human security is always accompanied by the important decision about where to migrate. Both are based on at least three inter-related determining factors: a) perceived economic opportunities; b) ethnic, community, or interpersonal ties; and c) specific organizational networks, some of which serve as recruiters for high or low-skilled laborers and foreign students, and others like NGOs, charities, and humanitarian associations that assist refugees. There are multiple transnational components to each one of these factors, with both positive and negative consequences for migrants. The ease with which communication can be maintained between families and communities in two countries can assist migrants in contracting work before leaving home or acquiring it quickly upon arrival. Yet the movement of capital away from their countries of origin means that the great majority of migrant workers are 'remittance' workers; they are responsible for redirecting massive flows of capital from the developed to the developing world, providing not only for their own and extended families back home, but also supporting their national economies which depend heavily on remittances to provide services to their domestic populations. As a result, their governments are often hesitant or feel unable to intervene on their behalf when they experience abuse or exploitation because of the enormous benefits their employment brings to their countries' GDPs.

The Bangladeshi writer Tahmima Anam has noted that given the billions of dollars' worth of remittances Bangladeshi workers send home (13 million in 2013), making it the single-largest source of foreign exchange earnings for that economy, the government "often acts less like a supplier than a supplicant" with respect to its citizens and toward other countries (Anam 2014). Similarly, in an effort to maximize women's employability as foreign domestic workers, the Philippine government has even established facilities to teach women the art of making beds, while private agencies there help prepare them to work with children by using plastic dolls (Gorney 2014: 91). For semi- or unskilled migrants working under temporary contracts, there is no path to social integration or economic mobility; for workers who continually renew short-term contracts there is no right or means toward naturalization in the countries they reside in, often for decades and sometimes permanently.

The factors determining labor migrants' decisions about why and where to migrate are also significant ones for refugee and asylum seekers. Poverty and chronic unemployment cause insecurity for labor migrants, compelling them to migrate, often without their families. For refugees and asylum seekers, similar conditions may exist as a consequence of war, political turmoil, and/or specific practices of discrimination targeted against them. There are important differences between refugees and asylum seekers, however.

Refugees generally secure their immigration status outside of the 'host' countries whose governments sponsor their applications on humanitarian grounds and based on pre-established resettlement quotas, often while in refugee camps or in transit. Foreign governments generally pre-approve refugee applications en masse, based on the general circumstances and conditions in the country they are fleeing, though certain refugees might only be offered temporary protection.

Asylum seekers must apply for protection from inside a country, either immediately upon arrival or after they have entered and resided in the country, legally or illegally, for a period of time. Asylum seekers for whom there is no pre-authorized recognition of their refugee status must demonstrate their fear of persecution based on an individual claim and provide ample supporting documentary evidence. Thus the bar for asylum seekers is often set higher, and particularly for those whose claims are predetermined to be 'bogus' based on their region or country of origin. For example, when immigration officials hear the same 'overfamiliar' accounts of persecution from individuals from the same area there is a tendency to assume they are all lying and that their motivations for leaving are economic rather than political (Inghilleri 2007, 2012).

Asylum seekers are increasingly being viewed and treated the same as other undocumented migrants, i.e. as a category of uncontrolled immigration. Upon making a claim, many are held, sometimes for months or even years, in makeshift detention centers under dehumanizing conditions while awaiting a decision on their case. This is in large part due to the persistence of the separation of the economic and political motivations of migration in many governments' immigration policies. This is a highly problematic distinction given the increasing reliance of nations throughout the global economy on the managed recruitment of highly skilled and unskilled workers beyond their borders. Many asylum seekers and refugees *are* those highly skilled and unskilled workers in another guise. As Khalid Koser has aptly observed:

> This separation might, it needs to be recognized, result in a situation where aeroplanes flying in one direction into the industrialised world carry economic migrants, while aeroplanes flying in the opposite direction carry asylum seekers rejected on the grounds that they are economic migrants.
>
> (Koser 2007: 251)

Translation and globalization

For many migrants, translation services function as an initial tool, not against, but as a means *toward* some degree of linguistic, if not cultural, assimilation. By and large, after one or two generations, many migrant families no longer depend on their first languages to navigate the public institutional contexts of their new home. Many stop using their 'native' languages in all but local or extended familial or cultural settings during that same period. Public displays of translations play a minimal role in most migrants' adjustment to their new environment. Bilingual signs or instructions in city centers, public service announcements, or telephone customer care options help with certain social transactions, but in large diverse multicultural communities, these tend to target only a few select groups of migrants, overlooking smaller less visible groups. In local migrant communities, public displays of language in the migrant language may or may not be translated into the dominant language. Translation services play the greatest role at the institutional level when they are put in place to help ensure that individuals' needs are properly communicated and understood, though these types of provision often serve the more perfunctory purpose of fulfilling the legal obligation of an institution (Davidson 2000, Inghilleri 2003). Many institutions only require that spoken interactions and written documents are translated, without regard for the suitability of the translator or the quality of the translation. Nevertheless, translation is *the* crucial means to maximize mutual understanding in situations where the psychological, spiritual, and/or physical well-being of individuals is concerned. It plays a pivotal role in acknowledging and attempting to safeguard the right of all persons to express and defend themselves.

Investigations into the function or availability of translation in the lives of particular migrants or migrant groups usually focus on individuals' interactions with educational, medical, legal, or other public institutions. From the point of view of the government and members of the public in multicultural societies, migrants' need for translation services is understood most positively when linked to their arrival and an initial period of adjustment to their new environment. The longer they reside in a particular place, however, the continued need for translation services can come to be viewed more negatively, as an indication that migrants do not intend to assimilate within the new environment or accommodate to the local language. Such criticism, though sometimes directed at wealthy expatriate communities and transnational cosmopolitans, is most often reserved for migrants who, paradoxically, are or attempt to be more fully integrated in the everyday workings of society than their cosmopolitan counterparts.

Negative valuations of migrants' reliance on translation are a result of a tendency to perceive migration synchronically, that is, to evaluate different phenomena associated with a migrant group without reference to the temporal aspects of migration. This perspective is just as likely to be held by people whose own families have migrated in the not so distant past. This is in part, perhaps, due to the long-held view that early nineteenth and twentieth-century migration from Europe mainly went in one direction and involved a permanent withdrawal from the rural countryside or the migrant's country of origin, despite the consensus among historians that there was a high incidence of transnational mobility among European immigrants during the period of 1899–1952. According to Hoerder, for example, a third of all immigrants to the United States either returned or moved on in the first half of the century, including almost two-fifths between 1925 and 1943 (Hoerder 1985: 353–354). The multidirectional nature of migration, or 'circular migration,' associated with the late twentieth and early twenty-first centuries – involving internal and external migrants – has altered some of the distinguishing features of previous large-scale migrations. For some 'circular' migrants, integration is not a priority as long as they see their stay as temporary; others are purposely excluded from participation or integration in the local civil society due to the terms of their labor contracts, residency status, or because they are undocumented. Even for permanent migrants, factors such as gender, age, language, culture, religion, and particular immigration status can also play a significant role in the probabilities of, opportunities for, and even utility of integration in a new country.

Within workplaces there can be a range of different capacities with the host language, and generalizations about the role of translation in any individual case can be very wide of the mark. Differences in the age at which migrants enter a country are of great significance. Young people may learn the new language quickly, middle-aged and older migrants are more likely to struggle and many never achieve fluency, which can significantly impact their earning power and limit their capacity to participate fully in civil society without the help of translation. Thus the uptake of translation services may be extremely diverse.

The ethnic structure of workplaces is also significant. Mutually unintelligible languages may exist side by side, with the host language being the primary lingua franca. Alternatively, it is frequently the case that many co-linguals will find work in the same business, which creates a different kind of configuration. Goldstein's investigation of the linguistic practices of Portuguese immigrant women in a Canadian factory, for example, showed how workplace practices unintentionally discouraged women working on the line from using English, as Portuguese became the language of workplace solidarity and greater efficiency among the mainly Portuguese co-workers (Goldstein 2001: 85). Though some of these workers spoke varying degrees of English, the younger female migrants who had arrived in Canada past school age and who either worked part time in the factory or stayed at home reported their fathers' objections to them attending formal instruction in English because there were boys in attendance (ibid.: 87). Circumstances like these suggest the reasons why working women and girls of a certain age, who are culturally obliged to stay at home to care for parents or children and remain within the bounds of their community, may come to depend on translation. While Goldstein's study highlighted the economic sense of women speaking Portuguese on the line at work, she nevertheless notes how the need for translation also put the women at a disadvantage.

At Stone Specialties, the people who assumed the role of language brokers were often in supervisory or management positions. As Tony – one of the bilingual Portuguese-English supervisors in the Production Department – explained, supervisors who assumed the role of language broker were expected to support the authority of management when translating messages between Portuguese workers and English-speaking managers and supervisors. As a result, they would sometimes rephrase and dilute the force of a worker's concern when passing it on to management.

(ibid.: 93)

All forms of migration involve a complex trajectory that connects the past to the present, the future, and back again, where language plays different roles and serves distinct purposes. Synchronic views of migration can distort this reality, especially where they fail to acknowledge different categories of migrants and the distinct social and cultural ties and economic and informational resources that are available to them, all of which can determine which destinations, occupations, and degrees of integration are possible or even useful.

Overseas contract laborers

It is a common practice for migrant contract laborers to sign contracts in unfamiliar languages, often English, without fully understanding their contents; few can rely on representatives of their own governments to scrutinize the agreements they sign; and often private company middlemen or local sources get involved solely for profit and without concern for the migrants' interests. For the roughly 53 million domestic workers across the globe, employment contracts are rare (International Labour Organization 2013: v). Individual country statistics put the numbers of workers who have formal written contracts as low as 8 percent and as high as 30 percent, depending on the country. Even where they do exist, employers frequently violate them. The International Labour Organization (ILO), a branch of the United Nations, estimates that there are 20.9 million victims of *forced* labor worldwide. Included in this statistic are certain domestic migrants, both internal and external, and laborers working under the *kafala* system in the Middle East (see below) (ibid.: 45).

A separate publication of the ILO entitled *Effective Protection for Domestic Workers: A Guide to Designing Labour Laws* (2012) contains a new set of standards adopted in 2011 by the General Conference of the ILO, in the form of the Domestic Workers Convention, along with a set of Recommendations – an historic document the purpose of which is to promote and protect domestic workers' rights through legislation (ibid.: ix). Although legally the pact applies only in the countries that ratify it, many view the agreement as a landmark move toward improving conditions and establishing the international legal and human rights of foreign workers; the hope is that it will put pressure on all countries who employ domestic workers to better monitor and improve their standards of practice (DeParle 2011). The Convention offers guidelines for the establishment of labor laws in all countries who employ domestic workers as well as those from where they originate. The document presents examples from countries where such legislation already exists. Of the many issues addressed, those related to contracts include: a) the need for bilateral and multilateral agreements between sending and receiving countries; b) the adoption of standardized contracts that are signed, enforceable, and recognized by the worker's own government and that of the destination country; and c) *the importance that contracts be translated into a language the migrant worker understands*. The ILO also recommends that monitoring mechanisms be put in place alongside strict regulations and penalties for employers who do not abide by the contract stipulations.

Significantly, the crucial role of translation in helping to ensure workers' rights is alluded to at several points in the document, as the following examples illustrate (ILO 2012, my emphasis):

> A noteworthy feature of the legislation of both the United Republic of Tanzania and South Africa is that in both cases the employer must ensure that the terms are explained to the domestic worker in a manner that she or he understands. Such provisions may be an important corollary to the requirement for a contract in writing, as such a legal requirement is only of practical value *if the worker, who may or may not be literate, fully understands the terms*. Provisions of this kind may also appear in legislative instruments or bilateral agreements concerned with specifically written contracts for migrant workers.
>
> (ibid.: 18)

> Sri Lanka's Bureau of Foreign Employment Act No. 21 of 1985 requires that the contract be forwarded to and certified by the Bureau prior to the departure of the worker. Section 40(1) provides as follows: "The contract of employment between the employer abroad and the person recruited for employment by such employer shall, *before it is signed by such employer or his [or her] agent and such person, be read and explained to such person in a language that he (or she) understands.*"
>
> (ibid.: 22)

> Indonesia and the Republic of Korea concluded a Memorandum of Understanding on 30 July 2004 concerning the sending of Indonesian workers to the Republic of Korea, which provides in paragraph 5 that the "Sending Agency [here a government agency] will explain to the Workers the content of a labour contract (draft) sent by an employer in the Republic of Korea *so that they can fully understand the contract.*"
>
> (ibid.)

The highlighted phrases indicate an important recognition: that in many cases the complex legalese used in a contract necessitates a 'translation' into more everyday language in order to be adequately understood. They also acknowledge the potential range of language variations and literacy skills among the workers signing such contracts. It is unfortunate that these recommendations do not emphasize the equal importance of guaranteeing the quality of sight translations, oral renditions of legalese, or explanations of legal terminology. However, they are an important step toward foregrounding the right of workers to understand fully the terms and conditions of their employment, ideally before they cross the border where they become more vulnerable to corruption and unfair treatment.

The precarious nature of the contractual agreements for overseas contract laborers, whether they involve sweatshops, construction, or domestic work, is directly connected to the restricted rights of these temporary workers once they arrive in the receiving countries. Their enduring non-permanent immigration status – even for those who remain in these countries for decades or a lifetime – is purposely designed to maintain clear and absolute cultural and national distinctions between migrants and citizens. The strict limitations imposed on migrants' integration in the wider society serve two negative and debilitating purposes: to reinforce their immutable otherness and to guarantee a constant source of temporary low-wage labor. Their restricted freedom of movement – social, cultural, and physical – ultimately gives labor migrants little choice in the degree of acculturation or assimilation to which they can aspire. The cultural border crossings and transnational identities associated with globalization are unavailable to them, as are the translation resources that would give them the information necessary to act in their own best interests.

Male contract laborers

Many contract labor recruits who sign up to work in the Gulf States prior to arriving move through recruitment agencies with connections in the Gulf who recruit men (and some women) from remote villages in places like Nepal and the southern Indian state of Kerala for a substantial fee. Here, *dalal*, or labor brokers, often take advantage of the ignorance and naivety of these villagers about the nature of the employment, promising quality work and pay that never materializes. According to the Italian journalist Vittorio Longhi (2013: 13):

> Contracts soon turn out to be swindles, because at the time of the migrants' departure from Kathmandu the middlemen present a new agreement under worse conditions. Anyone already committed, who is often in debt to pay the agency and obtain work, is then forced to accept it. Once the migrant reaches his destination, he discovers that the contract signed in Nepal is not valid in the new country and almost

always the terms subsequently become worse, with lower pay and longer hours. Language complicates matters, because agreements are written predominantly in English and few people really understand what they are reading.[1]

The corruption surrounding these contracts is only one of many forms of exploitation faced by these migrants, however. In many countries or regions, including Singapore and the Gulf States where many male contract laborers from South Asia find work, workers are obliged to live in labor camps set up by their employers or share cheap rental apartments often in derelict or industrial land on the peripheries of the wealthy capitals, from where they are bused to and from construction sites. In interviews with *New York Times* reporters investigating the working and living conditions surrounding the construction of a large new campus for New York University in Abu Dhabi, men described having to work eleven or twelve-hour days, six or seven days a week, in many instances to earn less than what they had been promised before signing on to the work. They all reported having paid recruitment fees of up to a year's wage to get the job. Their living conditions were squalid, with sometimes fifteen men to a small room overcrowded with bunk beds and food supplies.[2]

The system of *kafala*, a form of sponsorship that binds migrants to short-term contracts with a single employer who is financially and legally responsible for the worker, allows employers to retain workers' passports, suspend their pay, and in some countries prohibit them from leaving the country before their contract ends. The ILO has stated that *kafala* "causes distortions in the labor market and may fuel trafficking in human beings" (Longhi 2013: 9). Because workers' migration status under such systems is tied so closely to their employers' will, they hesitate to use complaints procedures against abusive labor practices and violations of their rights, for fear this could put their employment contract and residence status into jeopardy.

In a recent project report entitled *Labour Migrants and Access to Justice in Contemporary Qatar* (Gardner et al 2014), funded by the International Migration Initiative of the Open Society Foundation, the authors recommend as a top priority the guarantee of the availability of basic translation services for both the Labour Court and the Department of Labour Relations in Qatar based on the findings of their three-year research involving in-depth interviews with experts, officials, and community representatives in Qatar. The report notes that:

> The population of foreign labour migrants in Qatar speaks more than twenty different languages. Few speak English, even fewer speak Arabic, and a portion of these migrants [are] illiterate. While the comprehensive provision of translation services is a formidable logistical and bureaucratic challenge, it is a vital juncture in the carriage of

migrant justice. At the current juncture, prioritization should be given to Hindi, Urdu, Nepali, Malayalam, Tamil, and Bengali.[3]

In a previous study of migrant workers in the Gulf, funded by the Qatar National Research Fund, *Constructing Qatar* (Gardner and Watts 2012), a worker's recollection of his arrival at the airport in Doha illustrates the impediments for migrants both to comprehend and feel in control of their fate from the outset. The description of Raju following "at the heels" of the labor camp boss is revealing of the form of servitude that awaits him.

> A man came up and said something in what Raju guessed was Arabic. He just shook his head to say "I don't understand you." With a wave of his hand the man motioned Raju to follow a line. He saw many others with the same bewildered look on their faces standing in line at a counter which said NEW PASSPORTS.
>
> Raju waited in line for a long time. He thought something terrible had happened and that he would be sent back home. Finally, he heard his name called out. He hurried to the counter and saw a man standing there with a bunch of papers in one hand and a cell phone in the other.
>
> "Raju?" Raju nodded. "Passport," he said. Raju handed the man his passport.
>
> "Okay, wait here," the man said in Hindi, a language which Raju barely knew. After thirty minutes, the man, Krishna – who turned out to be the labor camp boss – led Raju to collect his luggage from the pile next to the conveyor belt. Then Krishna quickly walked out of the airport with Raju at his heels.

According to Amnesty International, workers reported that when they tried to use South Asian languages, including Hindi and/or Urdu, in the Qatar Labour Relations Department, officials were not able to help them and they had to leave. They also note that all Labour Relations Department documents are produced in Arabic only and not translated into other languages, meaning that the vast majority of migrant workers do not understand exactly – or at all – what the documents they are given mean. A complaint form submitted by a Nepalese worker showed a "clear and substantial discrepancy between the information the worker believed he had submitted, and the information which had been recorded on the complaint by the official" (Amnesty International 2013: 115). A similar claim is mentioned in the account of another Sri Lankan worker, named Raj, interviewed in *Constructing Qatar*. Due to his support for the Tamil Tigers, he had been living in a refugee camp in India. Fearing his continued safety in the camp, his family secured him an entry visa for Qatar. Raj arrived in Doha without a contract and eventually found a bus company willing to hire him.

The contract seemed fair to him; he was told that he would work eight hours a day and earn QR 1,500 ($412) per month. This didn't seem so bad, and he would be making more money than his friend who was also a driver. He signed a contract written in Arabic. At the time, it didn't occur to Raj that the conditions written in Arabic on the contract were not the same as those verbally promised to him.

A few months later, Raj lay in bed staring at the ceiling. The air conditioning in his prison-sized room had stopped working a few days earlier, and he could barely breathe. His roommates were too afraid to ask their employer to fix it. Recently, they had asked for the lights to be repaired, and their employer made it clear that he would take the cost of maintenance from their salaries. Clearly, things were not going as well as he had hoped. He was only paid QR 1,200 ($330) a month, and to earn that he had to work a ten hour shift – two hours longer and $82 less than the verbal promise.

(Gardner and Watts 2012)

Most labor migrants do not speak the language of their host country either at all or well enough to navigate an alien and often complex legal system (ILO 2013: 52–53), and there is neither opportunity nor encouragement for them to learn given the long hours they work and the fact that they are forced to live isolated from the local population. Despite the questionable ethics of their work and living situations and the long absences from their families and countries of origin, however, these jobs allow these migrants to send home the much-needed remittances to pay for their children's and siblings' education and dowries, and, for some, to save money for the construction of a home to which they hope to return. Viewed in a more negative light, this demonstrates the extent to which these workers have become transnational commodities to be traded between receiving and sending states: cheap labor in exchange for remittances that provide substantial contributions to the national economies of their countries of origin.

Networked organizations such as the Alliance for Migrants' Rights Bangladesh[4] and active workers' unions like the Pakistan Workers Federation and the Hotel Industry Trade Union in Pakistan have spoken out against the deplorable legal and social conditions of overseas contract work. NGOs like Lawyers for Human Rights International based in India campaign for the protection of Indian workers overseas and raise awareness about human rights abuses for South Asians more generally.[5] International organizations like Human Rights Watch[6] also tackle contract labor rights as part of their broader commitment to uphold human dignity and advance the cause of human rights for all. Many male labor migrants, however, work in places typically not covered by local or international labor laws. As a result, in many countries they are denied rights as fundamental as the 'freedom of association,' making them particularly vulnerable to exploitation and abuse.

Labor trafficking

Framing the current state of activity aimed at combating human trafficking is a collection of formal agreements by individual and cooperating countries dating from the year 2000. In that year the United Nations promoted its *Protocol to Prevent, Suppress and Punish Trafficking in Persons Especially Women and Children* and at the same time a *Protocol against the Smuggling of Migrants by Land, Sea and Air*. These protocols, known now as the Palermo Protocols, made a distinction between the smuggling of migrants on the one hand and "trafficking in persons" (TIP) on the other, based on the element of "exploitation," where trafficking is the movement, placement, or maintenance of a person in a situation of exploitation through force, fraud, coercion, or abuse of vulnerability. Smuggling of migrants alternatively involves the provision of a paid service – most commonly transportation – to people who knowingly engage in seeking to gain illegal entry to a foreign country. The primary difference is that a trafficked migrant is deemed to be a victim whose debt to his or her trafficker continues beyond their arrival and who is entitled to protection from governments, while smuggled migrants, being party to an illegal act, and whose economic relationship to their carrier terminates with their arrival, are automatically subject to deportation and the smuggler charged with committing a crime against the state. In the same year, the United States Congress enacted the *Victims of Trafficking and Violence Protection Act*, after which the US State Department published an annual account of international activities aimed at countering trafficking and ranking countries by their commitment to anti-trafficking programs in their own TIP report.

Despite confusions, ambiguities, and overlaps in all of these measures and their applications, and the extreme difficulties in arriving at accurate estimates of numbers of trafficked and smuggled people, they, and others which have flowed from them, have stimulated a growing amount of international concern and involvement among governments, civil society organizations of many kinds, journalists, academics, and others (Gallagher 2015). Furthermore, although forced labor trafficking constitutes some 90 percent of the total, while sex trafficking constitutes just 10 percent, according to the US State Department's follow-up 2014 TIP report, emphasis on the latter placed by many agencies, organizations, governments, and news media internationally for years has tended to obscure the magnitude of and intensity of forced labor until relatively recently. Even prior to this report, the ILO was aware of and drew attention to the scale of labor recruitment abuses where trafficked workers were involved, including debt bondage for repayment of recruitment fees, the growing role of unscrupulous employment agencies, informal labor intermediaries operating outside legal and regulatory frameworks, deceptions about the nature and conditions of work, the retention of workers' passports by employers, illegal wage deductions, and threats of expulsion from a country to workers who wish to leave their employment (Andrees et al 2015).

In 2011, the International Labor Organization for Migration (IOM) published an important report on the cruelties involved in the trafficking of fishermen in Thailand. The report noted that many fishermen were sold to fishing boat owners at a certain price per head (the *kahua*) which had to be paid off by the fishermen themselves before any wages were paid. This could take as long as six to eight months and, in some cases, even years. According to the report:

> Working conditions on fishing boats are extremely arduous. Fishermen are expected to work 18 to 20 hours of backbreaking manual labour per day, seven days per week. Sleeping and eating is possible only when the nets are down and recently caught fish have been sorted. Fishermen live in terribly cramped quarters, face shortages of fresh water and must work even when fatigued or ill, thereby risking injury to themselves or others. Fishermen who do not perform according to the expectations of the boat captain may face severe beatings or other forms of physical maltreatment, denial of medical care and, in the worst cases, maiming or killing.
> (International Labor Organization for Migration 2011: 7)[7]

These trafficked fishermen were largely speakers of Myanmar or Khmer and, in addition to problems of intimidation of informants, investigations into trafficking cases have experienced difficulties in obtaining evidence due to the absence of any government-employed professional translators. Local NGOs rely on migrant volunteers to interpret. However, because these cases came to light predominantly in provinces where local bodies – particularly the police – were not fully on board with the Thai government's policies regarding trafficking, and did not fully understand the role that translators and interpreters fulfill, interpreters reported that they sometimes faced obstacles, harassment, and intimidation in the course of their work. Recommendations in the IOM report included the issuing of official identity cards for translators in their encounters with local officials to legitimate their presence (p.42).

In some parts of the world where labor trafficking occurs, local police forces have developed some basic mechanisms for communicating with trafficked victims. A police force in Sunderland, England, for example, reported having instituted a system using iPods containing pre-programmed messages designed to assist victims in their first contact with officers, due to the difficulty of finding an official interpreter quickly for certain languages. Audio files are recorded in Albanian, Portuguese, Czech, French, Lithuanian, Malay, Mandarin, Romanian, Russian, and Thai. According to the Detective Chief Inspector:

> The iPods are meant to be a basic measure, a first step before we are able to get hold of someone who can speak the same language as the

victim. And if they come from a place where the police are feared or mistrusted, it makes the task of getting vital information from them much more difficult.[8]

Similarly, the UN Global Initiative to Fight Human Trafficking (GIFT) worked together with Austrian Criminal Intelligence and the Austrian NGO LEFOE-IBF, an organization focused on helping trafficked Latin American women, to develop an audio tool called VITA (Victim Assistance Translation) for use with any computer. It contains thirty-five questions and pieces of information translated into forty languages, taking into account special questions for children. The GIFT website describes it as "a unique new tool using audio messages, that allows law enforcement officials to provide a basic level of assistance to victims of human trafficking."[9] In a related vein, the 2015 TIP report of the US Department of State notes that:

> US embassies and consulates worldwide provided a "Know Your Rights" pamphlet that included the national hotline number and confirmed that applicants for temporary work and exchange visitor visas received, read, and understood the pamphlet, an effort that subsequently generated 791 calls to the national hotline. Some embassies and consulates also began to play in consular waiting rooms a new "Know Your Rights" video, available in 13 languages.[10]

Such measures are, of course, a far cry from the adequate provision of a fully functioning investigating team involving competent translators. The obstacles to accurate assessment and judgment are further amplified in a report published by the US-based Urban Institute, *Understanding the Organization, Operation, and Victimization Process of Labor Trafficking in the United States* (2014), which includes commentary on the ineffectual interpreting resources available to victims testifying in court.

> Victim testimony is critical to the successful prosecution of labor trafficking particularly as labor trafficking cases commonly hinge on psychological coercion and fraud, information about which must be provided by victims. The challenge of proving these elements was illustrated in one domestic servitude case we reviewed in which the victim attempted to testify about the coercion she faced but felt the interpreter was not interpreting her words correctly. In the end she did not think her testimony as interpreted clearly articulated her experiences.[11]

The guarantee of communication rights is a crucial element in any effort to ensure human and labor rights for migrants. The increasing recognition on the part of NGOs, law enforcement, and workers' rights organizations of the centrality of translation to their efforts against illegal and abusive practices is therefore significant. Without access to quality translation resources, migrant workers are prevented from giving voice to abusive practices associated with both contractual and forced labor. This contributes to their exploitation and prevents them from receiving the rights and recognition they are entitled to as major contributors to the production and circulation of goods and services in the global economy.

Internal migrants: Female factory workers in China

The intractable authority that language derives from the complex social relations of power created or sustained by the global economy is also evident in the context of internal migration when clashes between rural and urban identities together with regional and ethnic factors define the politics of many migrants' workplaces. In countries like China where regional locality, kin-ethnic identity, and dialect indicate one's status and wealth, the origins of an individual or group of individuals can be used strategically for a migrant's own benefit or, more commonly, for the benefit of the management in the factories in which migrants from diverse regions are often employed.

Over the last three decades China has witnessed a 'Great Migration' with an estimated 200–250 million rural residents moving to cities and towns within the country. In China, rural–urban migration has historically been tightly controlled and regulated by the *hukou* (household registration) system. The system dates back to the Communist Revolution in 1949, when it served a dual function: to curtail rural outflows to the cities and to exclude the rural population from access to state benefits, thereby maintaining a flexible and cheap source of labor (Chan 2012:187). Rural migrant labor continues to have a very specific meaning in China where it refers to industrial and service workers with rural *hukou* status only. Under the terms of this system, rural migrant workers remain officially a part of the rural *hukou* population, even though they may have worked and lived in an urban area for many years. Legally they are and will remain temporary migrants; they are not entitled to welfare benefits and social services, including local schools and public housing, and have little expectation of inclusion or acculturation into the permanent population (ibid.: 189). This "floating population" of migrants in some areas far outnumber the legally permanent residents; statistics from 2011 put them at close to 230 million (ibid.: 190–191).

In the industrial export city of Shenzhen in Guangdong Province, located in China's Pearl River Delta, that was designated a "special economic zone" open to global capital in 1980, 70 percent of the labor force have rural *hukou* status and the great majority of these are young, single, and unmarried females (Ngai 2005: 38–40). Most of these workers,

86 *Translation and labor migrants*

referred to as *dagongmei* (*dagong* means 'hired hands' and *mei* means 'younger sister') (ibid.: 111), are housed in factory dormitories built by mostly foreign-owned companies. Like domestic workers, the work available in these economic zones allows them to escape poor village life and contribute to their family income. For some it allows them to break away from their families' control.

Factory migrant workers in China and elsewhere leave the slower pace of village life for modern assembly lines where they must quickly learn to work in tandem with the speed and timing of the conveyor belt. Writing about the *dagongmei* in the city of Shenzhen with whom she worked on an assembly line in an electronics factory as part of an ethnographic study during the late nineties, Pun Ngai compares the conveyor belt to a chain that "coupled an individual body with a specific position, but at the same time it linked the individuals to form a collective social body devoted to the singular aim of maximizing production" (ibid.: 86). According to Ngai, in front of every seat in the functional test section of the factory a "layout" hung on the shelf that demonstrated each step of the task the worker had to undertake. Step 5 is reproduced in Figure 3.1 (ibid.: 85).

Ngai found that most workers did not know anything about the products they were testing or the meaning of the English words on the products and the layout instructions depicted above. Their line leader would demonstrate the test process only once; after that the workers had to rely on the layout and learn to recognize the English letters alongside the arrows and graphics. Given the repetitive nature of the task (workers are trained in only one process which they do repeatedly for years), once they had it mastered, the worker instinctively pressed the right keys and buttons. When Ngai asked a particularly well-coordinated woman whether she found the layout useful, the worker, who had done the same task for two years, replied (ibid.: 83):

---

5.   At stage 3, press "Q" key; the panel will show back stage 2, then press "V," move

  "➔" to the position of "QUIT COMMS TEST," and then press "O" button on the right side, the panel will resume the following picture:

  TEST ROUTINE OPTIONS

  KEYBOARD TEST
  LCD TEST
  ROM TEST
  ➔COMMS TEST
  QUIT

  Then press "V" and move "➔" to the position of "QUIT." Then press "O" on the right side, and the panel will return to state 1.

Figure 3.1 Assembly lines (Ngai, 2005)

It was useful at the very beginning. You know the line leader will only show you one time how to do it and you never dare to ask a second time. The first time I saw those English letters as 'worms' I was scared to death. I couldn't recognize them, so I copied them down and recited them at night. On the second morning, they were all in my mind and I didn't need to see the layout anymore.

The absence of a translation in this context or of any concern that the women should need to understand the instructions on the layout reveal a number of inter-related issues about the factory and its relationship to its line workers. Most certainly, the company's objective was not that these workers should know about the products they were assembling and testing; their aim was effectively to replace costly machines with workers. As Ngai points out, it was "to produce a body without mind, a mindless body" (ibid.). This was partly due to their knowledge that around 20 percent of the workers leave after only one year, in large part due to the exploitative nature of the work, including long hours, usually twelve-hour days, and low wages, so training had to assume that workers could be quickly and easily replaced. It is also an indication of the value of maintaining a flexible yet disposable labor force for China's growing export-processing industries. Rural *hukou* migrants hired in the export sector generally fall between the ages of 16 and 30, with new workers hired typically before they reach the age of 20.

> With their good eyesight and high manual dexterity and tolerance of dormitory-type environment, combined with the increasing prevalence of education beyond elementary school in the countryside, young rural migrants are more educated than their predecessors and better suited for assembling modern electronics, which often involved small parts and exacting specifications.
>
> (Chan 2012: 198)

The *hukou* system makes it easy for factories to select temporary workers with dexterity and endurance and eventually replace them as their abilities decline or if they begin to make demands regarding wages or working conditions, though without local *hukou* rights, individuals have very little bargaining power.

Another means of maintaining a tightly stratified workforce inside China's 'world's factories' is through the creation and maintenance of local hierarchical forms of linguistic segmentation. In the coastal province of Guangdong where the Shenzhen factory in Ngai's study was located, two prestige varieties of Cantonese, Hong Kong and Guangzhou, took over from the state official language Mandarin as the dominant language of the production and management side within the workplace; evidence of the fact that local market forces in parts of China have overtaken state control (Ngai 2005: 128). Professionals in top engineering and technical positions spoke only in Mandarin and when they met with the Cantonese-speaking managers each group spoke in their preferred language, creating the somewhat odd situation of speaking to one another in different languages, close enough only in that the speakers would recognize occasional words and phrases in each other's languages. On the factory floor, alternating prestige varieties of Cantonese were used among the production managers, line managers, and workers. Workers who spoke only their own rural Cantonese dialects were at a disadvantage both in being more vulnerable to misunderstandings and because competence in the factory-authorized forms of Cantonese was necessary for upward mobility. Rural Cantonese accents or styles were highly stigmatized within the factory; they were considered markers of a rural identity and associated with a lack of sophistication and intelligence. Similar labeling occurred between workers from the Cantonese dialect areas and women considered provincial outsiders, the most marginalized of the workers (ibid.: 122). Despite their proven ability to work long hours, meet their production quotas, and adapt to the repetitive pace of their work on the lines, all the *dagongmei* were frequently reminded by their superiors of an alleged mismatch between their rural selves and the modern industrial world they serviced.

> The Cantonese term *xiangxiamei* (village girl) was often used to depreciate the status of the women from the rural areas. Phrases like "xiangxiamei, you know nothing except farming", "xiangxiamei, what else can you understand? Learn the rules and behave in a civilized way", "a xiangxiamei is always like a xiangxiamei, cushou cujiao [rough hands, rough feet]", and "xiangxiamei can never be taught! [They are] foolish and stupid" were frequently heard in the workplace, especially when a male foreman or line leader came to criticize or scold the workers.
>
> (ibid.: 116–117)

The manipulation of linguistic, regional, and kin-ethnic differences among the rural employees by managers and line leaders in the factories for the purpose of control is similar to the experiences of domestic workers (see below). In both situations, the fact that their different languages or dialects hinder communication among themselves or with others is viewed as something to exploit rather than attempt to mediate through any form of translation, increasing their isolation. In both cases, the *absence* of translation, written or spoken, as a scaffold to help in their training through a period of adjustment, or when more serious concerns arise, speaks volumes about these particular migrants' place in the transnationalized world economy.

China's domestic *hukou* system condemns its workers to exist in a perpetual 'floating' space without access to health, education, or housing benefits, which prevents them from permanent resettlement, despite the government's drive to urbanize the population. For those wishing to raise families, buy property, develop local businesses, and integrate into the local community, obtaining an urban *hukou* in the large and medium-sized cities where factories are located is next to impossible. In order to be eligible to apply for a residence card, an individual first needs to buy a commercial house in the city and pay a large lump-sum charge for using the urban infrastructure and facilities (Tao and Xu 2007: 1308, and see Saunders 2012). The low wages these temporary workers are paid, which make it possible to deliver to the *global* market the 'Made in China' price that allows so many to purchase cheap electronic goods, make such a move prohibitive.

During the global economic recession in 2008, about 23 million migrant workers lost their jobs in China; of these 95 percent were temporary rural migrants without local *hukou* (Chan 2012: 197). At the same time, many manufacturing companies in Shenzhen and other coastal cities relocated production further inland where wages could be set even lower. In 2010, Shenzhen, already considered one of China's first-tier cities, re-emerged to become identified as a "tech nirvana" for hi-tech internet businesses; it is rapidly becoming the 'Silicon Valley' of the world's hardware startups in China.

> "Everything you need is here," says Eric Pan, founder of Seeed Studio, looking out of the dusty windows of his mid-rise office/factory/warehouse. Within walking distance of his building are circuit-board manufacturers, injection-moulding companies, packagers and shippers. He is three hours from factories making every imaginable electronic component, and three days by FedEx from 90% of the world's population.
> (Whitwell 2014)

Most labor migrants, however, find it very difficult to fully partake in the social and economic opportunities that their labor makes possible. The reasons for this are to do with the transnational structures of inclusion and exclusion that these migrants, including internal ones, are trapped by and inadvertently help to sustain.

Female domestic workers: From submission to empowerment

Domestic workers, the vast majority of whom are female, also make the grim choice of staying at home or leaving their families behind in order to provide them with the prospect of a better future, and many find themselves in positions similar to their female counterparts working in factories and their male counterparts in the construction industry. Nicole Constable has compared domestic workers to "commodities in the way they are inspected, bought, traded, owned, generally objectified, and treated like economic investments" (Constable 2007: 51). They work excessive hours without rest, are given few or no days off, and are forbidden to talk on the phone, watch television, or leave their employer's house on their days off. Reports of physical, sexual, and psychological abuse are common.

Although domestic workers with limited competence in English or in the local language express a desire to improve their abilities in these languages, particularly English to better their options and opportunities for work in the future, many employers show little interest in helping them develop their language skills. It is more common for families to use "foreigner talk," i.e. the tendency of native speakers to use simple grammatical constructions, simplified registers, increased volume, and repetition when talking to their non-native-speaker domestic employees. Underlying the use of foreigner talk is an implicit or explicit assumption of migrants' inferiority, presumed from their lack of competence in the language of their employers. Though the use of foreigner talk is often claimed to be for the purpose of facilitating comprehension, its use toward domestic workers by the members of a household, including the children, also demonstrates and reinforces their authority over these women and men (Dashti 2013). The following examples illustrate the use of foreigner talk in several interactions between two members of a Kuwaiti family and their domestic help.

> Daughter to domestic servant (ibid.: 71, 75)
>
> (1) ana jguːlič misaː? Ikwi Qamiːṣ
> I tell (present) you from hour iron shirt
> I told you an hour ago to iron my shirt
>
> (2) malaːbis naÐːf wen?
> clothes clean where?
> Where are the clean clothes?
>
> Son to domestic worker (ibid.: 78)
>
> (3) guːli la jǧassil xamsa sajjara
> tell him wash 5 car (singular)
> tell him (the driver) to wash the five cars
>
> (4) dʒiːbi qamiːṣ aħmɛr min daːri
> bring shirt red from room my
> bring the red shirt from my room

When combined with the use of the imperative form of address, the routine use of foreigner talk in these examples by the son and daughter implies a lack of respect toward the adult migrant they are addressing and an explicit connotation of inferiority. Preventing domestic workers from interacting in the language of the home as learners and potential speakers of that language also allows these families to sustain a view of the women who care for them as perpetually 'other'; at the same time it serves to isolate the women from the wider social environment that surrounds them. One Lebanese woman reported that she intentionally employed three domestic workers from different countries. When asked why, she responded:

> [joking] You want them to form a league, a task force against me? No, reason is they get too comfortable with each other. When they come from different countries they do not get too relaxed, they respect the differences and keep a distance. I don't hear them arguing [it's] better for me.
> (Haraty et al 2007)

When asked why she used only English with them and not Arabic, she replied (ibid.):

> I don't want them to understand everything we say at home. Also, I do not want them to get too friendly with the drivers, the janitor, or the neighbors. I do not feel comfortable. I don't even let them go out on Sundays…I don't want you to think that they are prisoners, no.

The manipulation of the physical and communicative environment closes off selected outlets of communication to their domestic workers. In each case, whether through the form of the employers' communication, their attempts to limit possible interlocutors, or the selection of one language over another, these language-centered choices operate as an astute form of social control whereby these women are invariably muted, silenced, or rendered invisible. This exercise of power over a crucial aspect of their identity places the burden of translating between worlds and languages on the employees, while the employers view it as an unwarranted task. These communicative restrictions allow employers to maintain tighter control over what the adult women in their employ can know or think or feel by limiting their ability to operate in whatever way and with whomever they choose. Situations like these may explain the absence of any significant role for translation in these environments to assist these women in the reading of a contract or in their everyday interactions. Translation creates the conditions for better communicative equality; it allows something written or spoken in one language to become accessible to a greater number of people.

In a study of live-in domestic workers in Lebanon, several women reported on the role that "balcony talks" played for them from where they would speak with other domestic workers in adjacent buildings or with women below on the streets. These interactions compensated for their inability to construct a wider support system due to the severe restrictions imposed on their movements by their employers. Two domestic workers reported using a window and a balcony for literal escape routes from their respective employers (Pande 2012: 392).

> We used to talk, talk, talk over the wall. "How it is for you?" "How it is for you?" But it was not good, no phone, no Sunday off, not even

salary every month. It is not right! So we started talking slowly. We lived not far from the embassy and that day we decided to leave. It was a Friday. We were on the second floor. She climbed out of her window and I from the balcony. We climbed out of the house with bed sheets. We climbed from the second to the first floor. From the first floor we jumped. On the street we met an African man and he helped us to get to the embassy. We left our papers, passport, everything behind. But we were out!

For another, the balcony provided a space and an opportunity to alleviate the physical and psychological trauma caused by her employer's abusive treatment (ibid.: 393):

> Whenever I get very mad at her and want to hit back or shout back at her, I tell myself, get away from the kitchen. I slowly walk away to the balcony. She has also learnt this: When I walk to the balcony, she knows I am angry. She lets me alone for some time at least. Now when I am tired after a day's work, she sometimes says kindly, "Why not take your tea and go out to your balcony?"

Live-in domestic workers are not only physically and psychologically tethered to the home. By restricting their ability to choose how they wish to receive and produce language and with whom, the women are, to different degrees, linguistically tethered as well. By imposing different forms of servitude on domestic workers, employers not only maintain a willful disregard for the fact that these women have social, cultural, and linguistic identities of their own, they erect additional walls between the women and their pasts, presents, and futures, as illustrated in Figure 3.2, showing a piece of street art by UK graffiti artist and political activist Banksy.

Domestic workers are often the primary wage earners in their households, fully competent beings, many of them wives and mothers who are working to send remittances and boxes of goods to support their own families back home. Though some women manage to establish relationships of mutual respect with their employers and some employers recognize the difficult situations that bring these women to seek employment in their homes, imbalances of status are written into the domestic worker position. What may not be so clear however, even to the most benevolent of employers, is the near totalizing control they wield over the workers they employ.

Overseas domestic workers as activists

In the ILO document *Effective Protection for Domestic Workers: A Guide to Designing Labour Laws*, under Recommendation 2012 21(f), the organization (ILO 2012: 122) specifically addresses the need for better and more public outreach services:

Figure 3.2 Mural by Banksy, Chalk Farm, London

to inform domestic workers, in languages understood by them, of their rights, relevant laws and regulations, available complaint mechanisms and legal remedies, concerning both employment and immigration law, and legal protection against crimes such as violence, trafficking in persons and deprivation of liberty, and to provide any other pertinent information they may require.

Numerous domestic workers rights' organizations have sprung up across the globe in recent decades, among others: Migrante International,[12] an alliance of Filipino migrant organizations worldwide that advocates for stronger labor protections and penalties for recruitment agencies and employers that violate Filipino and UAE labor laws; the National Domestic Worker Alliance,[13] a non-profit that works for the respect, recognition, and inclusion in labor protections for domestic workers in the United States; Women in Informal Employment: Globalizing and Organizing (WIEGO),[14] a not-for-profit global action–research policy network that seeks to improve the status of working women in the informal economy; and Kalayaan,[15] a charity that provides advice, advocacy, and support services in the UK for migrant domestic workers. A perusal of these and similar websites indicates that translation is used regularly for outreach to the public, allowing them to operate effectively as multilingual information and advice networks. Both written translations of publications and translations of audiovisual materials in the form of voiceovers and subtitles are available; some of the websites themselves can be easily accessed in relevant languages. There are often links to printed and audiovisual informational materials available in translation on other websites; full or part-time members of staff, paid interns, or networks of volunteers appear to be the main sources for the translations. Some websites invite comments or suggestions for improving the posted translations from members of the public.

Domestic workers themselves have led the fight for greater visibility and better services. Activists organize protests and are present at public rallies for worker rights, signaling to the wider public their awareness that the needs of the global political economy cannot continue to be met at their expense. Domestic workers tend to be better educated than many other types of overseas labor migrants and many have prior experience of collective organizing. According to Constable (1999: 203), for example, the majority of Filipina domestic workers in Hong Kong at the time of her research had attained more than a high school education, and some belonged to middle-class families, and Mitra (2004: 497–498) reports on the long tradition of South Asian women's participation in public protests, trade union activity, and the mass media to get their voices heard in their own countries. Domestic workers' unions and organizations have a strong presence on Facebook and other social media sites where members post photos, announce upcoming meetings or demonstrations, and display links with similar groups.

Freeing up the space

In the same way that the Chinese factories aim to transform the young women who work in them into robotic bodies without independent minds, employers of female domestic workers attempt to control their behavior by controlling their bodies, primarily through their perceived sexuality. Before arriving in a particular country, women are commonly given training or, at the very least, a list of suitable conduct expected of them with dress, hygiene, and obedience stressed over their domestic skills. In most countries with large populations of domestic workers, these women have established places where they spend whatever leisure time they are permitted, usually on weekends, to gather with other domestic workers to attend religious activities, shop, picnic, or in the evening go out dancing or to karaoke bars. These become occasions for the women to reject the prohibitions on things like make-up, nail polish, perfume, and clothes deemed too provocative while on duty. It is also a way for them to disassociate from the subordination experienced within their employer's home. These occasions can also become opportunities for women to dress in traditional clothing that is otherwise prohibited by the families they work for. In many countries, for example, including majority Muslim ones, non-Muslim families do not permit their domestic employees to pray or wear Islamic dress, including the *hijab*, or have food that is *halal* (Ho 2013: 17). This is the case in Hong Kong, where over 91 percent of Indonesian domestic workers, mostly Muslim, work for local Chinese families (O'Connor 2012: 48).

Employers' attempts to repress their sexuality, and the outright prohibition of Islamic practices by non-Muslim employers, present particular challenges for Indonesian Muslim female domestic workers that have elicited varied responses from this community. Some move further toward their faith and cultural traditions – during the period of O'Connor's research (ibid.: 51–52) Sundays at the Osman Ramju Saddick Islamic Center in Hong Kong became a female and Indonesian space – while others adopt more secular attitudes and practices, including involvement in same-sex relationships with other Indonesian domestic workers, something forbidden in the Islamic tradition. O'Connor notes that lesbian relationships were "undeniably" visible in Victoria Park (a well-known meeting point for domestic workers) on Sunday mornings with some women dressed in "'tomboy' roles, dressing in funky baggy clothes with short, cropped spikey hair" (ibid.: 49). One such woman describes her evolution in this way:

> When I arrived in Hong Kong, I saw many [Indonesian] women dressing like males and being with other women. I was far away from home, no one was controlling me, and so I finally felt free to become a boy.
> (Ho 2013: 18)

For many of these women, this transformation is, like their migrant status, a temporary coping strategy to deal with a particular set of circumstances; the identities they adopt in Hong Kong are as much a matter of context as of content. The places where they spend their limited free time, whether mosques, parks, or discos, allow them to experience a sense of freedom and mobility regularly denied them in the context of their work. These weekend enclaves are one of the few 'perks' they embrace for the high cost of being away from their families. Temporarily, at least, they become the sentient beings that they are, and not the least valued members of the societies they enable to prosper.

In the twenty-first century, for factory workers and domestic workers the global economy operates more like a lawless state in which less visible and unmonitored localized forms of authority and control are exercised. For factory workers, the vast distances between the goods they produce and the export markets they are destined for renders them invisible to the world; they are but one link in an extensive global commodity chain. For domestic workers, the private domain in which they work acts as a fortress that protects only their employers from public scrutiny. Though their migration may help to alleviate poverty and improve the material conditions of their families, most encounter barriers that exclude them from residency and citizenship, on the one hand, and opportunities for advancement in the global economy, on the other.

Sex workers, migration, and translation

While the moral and ethical arguments against prostitution remain what they are for each individual, just as, say, arguments against taking human life lead some to conscientiously object to military service, the injunction to avoid promiscuity *beyond* the realm of individual conscience has been socially interpreted, constructed, and de-constructed in a variety of ways. From ancient Mesopotamia through Greece, Rome, India, and medieval European and Asian history, norms and attitudes have dealt with the social fact of sex for payment in a variety of ways. Social and political contexts vary but today, as often in the past, human migration and commercial sex are frequently found in tandem, where a person's body can become a primary source of their sexual capital, transferable across many cultural contexts. Globalization has not only facilitated the translation of commercial sexual practices across national borders, it has also encouraged the development of international consensus in ideological and legal responses to its existence. These have been particularly sharpened by the focus on human trafficking that has intensified in recent years, as tragic and perilous journeys by the vulnerable become painfully familiar.

As a result of these developments – and for reasons often having more to do with domestic governance than human rights – laws and policing practices aimed at containing the commercial sex industry have been applied that conflate sex for payment in all cases with human trafficking, thus allowing far more serious penalties to be applied to offenders including deportation and imprisonment, in addition to the public opprobrium attached to trafficking regardless of whether any cross-border migration took place or, where it did, whether the migration was voluntary or coerced. The potential for manifest injustices this has brought about impelled Amnesty International in August 2015, following painstaking case-study-based research, to publish its "Resolution on Protecting the Human Rights of Sex Workers." A Q & A on their website page states:

> Sex workers are one of the most marginalized groups in the world. In many countries, they are threatened with a whole host of abuses, including rape, beatings, trafficking, extortion, forced eviction and discrimination, including exclusion from health services. More often than not, they get no, or very little, legal protection. In fact, in many cases these violations and abuses are carried out by the police, clients, and abusive third parties.[16]

The Resolution makes a number of important recommendations including the full decriminalization of sex work on the grounds that its criminal status contributes most to its vulnerability to abuses, including trafficking. This Resolution has since been developed into a full policy statement published in May 2016 (Amnesty International 2016).

Many other agencies including the World Health Organization, UNAIDS, the International Labour Organization, the Global Alliance Against Trafficking in Women, the Global Network of Sex Work Projects, the Global Commission on HIV and the Law, Human Rights Watch, the Open Society Foundation, and Anti-Slavery International make the same case. As Catherine Murphy, Policy Advisor at Amnesty International explains:

> We have chosen to advocate for the decriminalization of all aspects of consensual adult sex – sex work that does not involve coercion, exploitation or abuse. This is based on evidence and the real-life experience of sex workers themselves that criminalization makes them less safe. We reached this position by consulting a wide array of individuals and groups, including but not limited to: sex workers, survivor and abolitionist groups, HIV agencies, women's and LGBT rights activists, Indigenous women's groups, anti-trafficking groups and leading academics.[17]

This Resolution comes following years of campaigning by many groups and organizations with first-hand knowledge of the stark differences between commercial sex on the one hand and the trafficking of women and children that indebts and enslaves them on the other. For many of these groups, flying in the face of common sense and the powerful voices of national governments and police forces from many parts of the globe, the struggle has been long. Numbering in the hundreds and often with their origins in health campaigns, these activist groups have become particularly focused around a cluster of issues frequently relating to migration and where the frontiers of language themselves present a further challenge. Among these is the Thailand-based sex worker organization *Moolniti Songserm Okard Pooying*, or *Education Means Protection Of Women Engaged in Recreation (EMPOWER)*. 'Empower' is a good example of how local experiences can be imaginatively portrayed and translated into a meaningful contribution to international political discourse over human rights, health, and migrant labor.

Empower – Thailand

Empower was founded in 1985 in Patpong, Bangkok's red light district, as part of the early awareness through publications and education campaigns of the implications raised by the emergence of HIV/AIDS and safe sex. Through plays and songs performed by sex workers from the Honey Bee theater group portraying their daily lives, health issues, and educational challenges, Empower Foundation grew into an organization providing educational courses for young women in the sex work industry and participated in the founding of the Thai NGO Coalition on AIDS. In the early 1990s it made significant international connections in Europe, Asia, the

Pacific, and the United States and became widely known as a sex worker community-based HIV/AIDS organization, forging connections with other sex workers' organizations internationally. The emphasis on sex worker rights and issues was given further focus by the slogan "Sex Work is Work," drawing attention to the economic significance and labor law context of the range of sex work and workplace safety and conditions. Empower was also sharply aware of the particular needs and circumstances of the migrant women who had crossed from Burma.[18] These women were from different tribes and were mostly speakers of Burmese, Tai Yai, Akkha, and Chinese. At the start of the millennium, Empower Foundation opened a center in Mae Sai, a major crossing at the Thai–Burmese border, to help them.

The articulation of the predicament of sex workers in relation to anti-trafficking laws and the nature of their enforcement took significant form in the initiating of a project conducted by Empower Foundation involving over 200 sex workers as informants and researchers, covering eleven provinces of Thailand and involving interviews with an impressive array of people including police, NGO workers, bar owners, brothel owners, and immigration officers. The report of the findings, entitled *Hit and Run: The Impact of Anti-trafficking Policy and Practice on Sex Workers' Human Rights in Thailand* (Empower Foundation 2012),[19] published in Thai and English, includes a preface written in the collective voice of the Burmese migrant sex workers, the first half of which reads as follows (ibid.: i):

> We travel for days up the mountains, across rivers, through dense forest. We follow the paths that others have taken. Small winding paths of dust or mud depending on the season. I carry my bag of clothes and all the hopes of my family on my back. I carry this with pride; it's a precious bundle not a burden. As for the border, for the most part, it does not exist. There is no line drawn on the forest floor. There is no line in the swirling river. I simply put my foot where thousands of other women have stepped before me. My step is excited, weary, hopeful, fearful and defiant. Behind me lies the world I know. It's the world of my grandmothers and their grandmothers. Ahead is the world of my sisters who have gone before me, to build the dreams that keep our families alive. This step is Burma. This step is Thailand. That is the border. If this was a story of a man setting out on an adventure to find a treasure and slay a dragon to make his family rich and safe, he would be the hero. But I am not a man. I am a woman and so the story changes. I cannot be the family provider. I cannot be setting out on an adventure. I am not brave and daring. I am not resourceful and strong. Instead I am called illegal, disease spreader, prostitute, criminal or trafficking victim.

The report goes on to explain the objective of the organization to promote the human rights of sex workers and provide a space for sex workers to "own, belong, organize and assert our rights to education, health, access to justice and political participation" (ibid.: iii). The report also points out how, under the guise of implementing anti-trafficking law and policy, for the previous ten years sex workers in Thailand have been the subjects of human rights violations: "We have experienced an onslaught of slander vilifying our entire industry; violent police raids on our workplaces, arbitrary detention, forced rehabilitation in government shelters and deportation" (ibid.).[20]

Where migrant sex workers were involved, issues of translation frequently contributed to the violation of these women's rights. Translators employed at police stations, the Bangkok Counter Human Trafficking Unit, and the Ministry of Social Development and Human Security were more often than not untrained and inexperienced. Some anti-trafficking NGOs had volunteers they could call on, though these were not trained translators. Women felt that the volunteer translators often had inadequate language skills and brought their own attitudes and agendas about sex work to the interviews. For example:

> Meanwhile at the karaoke bar at 12:30am, 50 uniformed armed police coordinated by the Bangkok Counter Human Trafficking Unit (CTU), raided the bar, running in the doors to cut off the escape and physically apprehend the eight women working there. There were also NGO staff, government welfare officers, immigration officials and people taking photos. The police searched the bar confiscating the women's bags, telephones, clothes and makeup.
>
> [...]
>
> No one at any stage told the women why they were apprehended, or that they had the right to contact family or support persons, or that they could request independent legal assistance.
>
> Interviews began around 1am. Women apprehended in the bar and at the hotel were all interviewed in the police station by police, NGO and welfare officials until 3am. Despite the fact the women were from non-Thai-speaking backgrounds from Burma, no translator was made available at any point. "We thought we were arrested for not having ID cards and we tried to understand what their questions meant and what we should say."
>
> (ibid.: 75)

In another case, women from Burma with limited Thai language skills had trouble understanding the questions, which were poorly translated by an untrained NGO staff member. According to one of the sex workers present, "The translator was saying all the wrong things and the police wrote them down. I said the translator was wrong but no one seemed to be interested. Pi Nong from Empower told [the NGO staff] as well but nothing changed." The volunteer who was called on to translate later contacted Empower to apologize saying, "I'm really sorry about what happened to those women. I said I couldn't translate but they (the NGO) talked me into it. I thought it wasn't serious, that they would be let go. I'm sorry." (ibid.: 80)

On another occasion in court, both volunteer and court-appointed translators had trouble making things clear and understandable for the women.

> At the first court session it was observed that there were no official translators – instead it appeared that one of the women judged as being just 16 years old and allegedly a trafficked person was translating for the prosecutor and other women on the stand. She stated her age as twenty and the other young woman supposed by the court to be 15 years gave her age as 18 years.
>
> At the second session there was a court appointed translator but the woman on the stand complained repeatedly about the translation until the judge had no choice but to adjourn until a replacement could be found.
>
> (ibid.: 82)

In other cases of police questioning, the report found that women were given a printed statement of their rights to sign. However, because the statements were in Thai and there was no effective translator the women did not understand what they were signing. Migrant women and illiterate women are also sometimes forced to put their thumb print as a signature to legal documents provided by police which they do not understand or to put their thumb print to documents which apparently provide a list of their belongings that have been confiscated by police – which they cannot read or understand due to language and literacy issues. These are all considered violations of their rights under the Thai Constitution, the Thai criminal justice system, and international human rights law (ibid.: 89). Women apprehended in such raids also routinely undergo mandatory medical tests and screenings with no information provided to them as to why they are required, and no opportunity to refuse these procedures as there are no trained translators available (ibid.: xi)

Bad girls news

> People don't seem to take into account or understand that being asked why you are a sex worker is a loaded question. The question asks are you just a bad woman, or are you a good girl made bad? Answer one way and you may be treated with disgust. The other way may get you pity. One answer makes you a criminal, the other makes you a victim... either way you end up in a cage.
>
> (ibid.)

Translation and labor migrants 101

The *Hit and Run* report demonstrates the seriousness and opposition of organizations like Empower – within its broad support for sex worker rights – to all forms of labor trafficking that exist from neighboring countries into Thailand. In the playful saying, "Good girls go to heaven, bad girls go everywhere," the connection between sex work and migration is acknowledged by the Thai sex worker community. The saying also gave its name to one of the predominantly Thai language newspapers, *Bad Girls News* – published by Empower Foundation as part of a wider creative response to the predicament of sex workers. The consistently imaginative utilization of the arts in articulating and conveying the important work of Empower Foundation for over thirty years is everywhere apparent on their website, which is in Thai with available English translations, thereby helping to contribute to the international dialogue on relevant issues.

Among its impressive activities is an installation project of large papier-maché dolls representing the hundreds of women migrants who journey to Thailand to earn money to send back to their families (Figure 3.3). Growing out of a small arts training program, the project, entitled 'Labour Sans Frontieres', supports the creation of the dolls, handmade by these women, and a traveling exhibition meant to represent the right of these women to go "wherever their dreams may take them." Each doll is named 'Kumjing,' a common Thai name. However, these Kumjings, rather than being recognized as

Figure 3.3 'Kumjings.' Courtesy of Empower Foundation

genuine labor migrants, are pejoratively labeled cross-border criminals, illegals, disease spreaders, prostitutes, or trafficking victims.[21]

After the first public display of around one hundred dolls, more than 250 were installed at the 2004 International AIDS Conference held in Bangkok. Since then 'Kumjing' has been to many cities including Singapore, London, Barcelona, Seoul, Kyoto, and Zurich. In each city, 'Kumjing' further extends her "international family," which advocates the protection of all migrants' human rights. The local situation of the migrant workers is also represented in the 'Mida Tapestry' project – a ten-meter piece of cloth with thirteen embroidered panels sewn along its length, depicting how women experience the 'raid and rescue' missions of the anti-trafficking police. Each panel is hand-embroidered by migrant sex workers (Figure 3.4). The panel below reads, below in Thai and above in English, "Fifty armed police just to arrest us little women?!"[22]

Another excellent example of the creative political imagination of Empower Foundation is a short video called *Last Rescue in Siam* done in the style of an old silent film of the Keystone Cops variety, complete with ragtime piano and early jazz soundtrack and narrative placards reproduced in Thai and English flashing up between the scenes.[23] It features first a young female sex worker and her client in a bar. With classic silent-movie comic energy, the man at every opportunity slyly fills the woman's glass

Figure 3.4 'Mida Tapestry.' Courtesy of Empower Foundation

with more alcohol, while she in turn distracts him, tossing the drink away. Like other sections of the video, this visual humor lightly comments on a serious concern of sex workers in bars and clubs – the requirement by management that the women encourage their clients to purchase as many drinks as possible from the house to add to the revenue generated from the sex work. This forced consumption of alcohol night after night has a direct impact on the women's health and can also intoxicate them, undermining their judgment and vigilance, making them vulnerable to unprotected sex and sexually transmitted diseases.

The scene that follows shows a social worker, police officer, and an NGO 'hero' planning a raid on the bar, then roaring off in a large truck crowded with officers, zooming past various serious crime scenes and accidents to storm the bar. A tip-off warns the people in the bar and many escape but the young woman we first met is caught up in a chaotic chase throughout the building and is finally caught – with flash photographers capturing the successful arrest. The woman is made to sit down at a table with a police officer and an interpreter who mistranslates her age, changing nineteen to sixteen. Finally the medical examination completes the formalities despite the woman's crazy pranks, all to no avail as she is locked up. She ultimately escapes down an improvised ladder to rejoin her friends in the bar. At present, because of the illegality of their profession sex workers have no power to negotiate different workplace rules and practices. The video tells a serious but apparently overfamiliar story in a well-produced and humorous way. The fact that faulty translation has a sufficiently prominent role in the film is also a comment on the centrality of translation where migrant sex workers are concerned.

The stark absence of translation as a reliable resource in the multiple encounters described in this chapter significantly disadvantages workers already exploited by more powerful employers and misunderstood by law enforcement and NGOs. There are direct consequences for individuals when they cannot read a document they sign because it has not been translated in a language they understand, either because of their lack of literacy skills or because it is written in a formal legal, medical, or other technical discourse. Likewise, there are implications attached to adults not being provided with the resources to communicate with employers, law enforcement officials, or medical personnel *as adults* in a language in which they are fully or sufficiently competent, particularly about matters of fair treatment, wages, or to report an abuse. The limited availability and poor quality of translation resources in the experiences of male and female labor migrants shows that, despite some progress, quality translation provision is still not fully comprehended as an integral component of human and labor rights. Labor migrants certainly understand this given the abundance of examples of individuals-turned-activists located in different countries and continents working together on projects and toward common goals. The provision of translated materials in multiple languages is understood

104 *Translation and labor migrants*

as essential, helping to make possible communication and collaboration between similar organizations, and contributing to the establishment of global networks. The centrality of translation in these different forms of activism enables men and women to intervene on one another's behalf, even in contexts where protest is difficult or prohibited.

Notes

1 The United Arab Emirates (UAE) Ministry of Labor has initiated new measures regarding job offers and labor contracts that went into effect in January 2016. In addition to Arabic and English, potential employees can request contracts in a language they understand from the following nine languages: Bengali, Chinese, Dari, Hindi, Malayalam, Nepalese, Sinhalese, Tamil, and Urdu. This applies both to workers coming from outside and those residing in the UAE who are seeking a new job or moving from one company to another. See http://gulfnews.com/news/uae/government/job-contracts-to-be-offered-in-11-languages-1.1655089 (Accessed April 2106).
2 www.nytimes.com/2014/05/19/nyregion/workers-at-nyus-abu-dhabi-site-face-harsh-conditions.html?emc=eta1&_r=0 (Accessed May 2016).
3 www.lse.ac.uk/middleEastCentre/publications/Reports/LabourMigrantsQatarEnglish.pdf (Accessed April 2016).
4 http://migration.brac.net (Accessed April 2016).
5 www.migrationpolicy.org/article/labor-migration-united-arab-emirates-challenges-and-responses (Accessed April 2016).
6 www.hrw.org (Accessed April 2016).
7 www.iom.int/jahia/webdav/shared/shared/mainsite/activities/countries/docs/thailand/Trafficking-of-Fishermen-Thailand.pdf (Accessed April 2016).
8 *Sunderland Echo* "Police Use iPods to Help Trafficking Victims," August 8, 2007. www.sunderlandecho.com/news/police-use-ipods-to-help-trafficking-victims-1-1135940 (Accessed April 2016).
9 www.ungift.org/knowledgehub/en/tools/vita.html (Accessed April 2016).
10 www.state.gov/documents/organization/245365.pdf (Accessed April 2016).
11 www.urban.org/research/publication/understanding-organization-operation-and-victimization-process-labor-trafficking-united-states/view/full_report (Accessed May 2016).
12 http://migranteinternational.org/ (Accessed April 2016).
13 www.domesticworkers.org/ (Accessed April 2016).
14 http://wiego.org/sites/wiego.org/files/resources/files/WIEGO-e-news-Jan2012-Jun2012.pdf (Accessed April 2016).
15 www.kalayaan.org.uk (Accessed April 2016).
16 www.amnesty.org/en/qa-policy-to-protect-the-human-rights-of-sex-workers/ (Accessed April 2016).
17 www.amnesty.org/en/latest/news/2015/08/sex-workers-rights-are-human-rights/ (Accessed April 2016).
18 'Burma' is used for Myanmar, as migrant sex workers from Burma do not accept the military regime's legitimacy in changing the country's name, and they still call home 'Burma.'
19 At the time of publication of the report, Empower claimed centers in eleven provinces in Thailand, reaching over 20,000 women, with most managed by sex workers from within the local communities. More than 50,000 sex workers from Thailand and the Mekong countries of Laos, Burma, China, and Cambodia have been members of Empower since its inception.

20 The raids referred to here were conducted by multidisciplinary anti-trafficking teams comprising police, members of the Bangkok Counter Human Trafficking Unit and other government bodies, legal professionals, social workers, and members of the NGOs that were funded by the US State Department, channeled through USAID and The Asia Foundation (USAID 2009: 56–58). Despite acknowledged problems with the anti-trafficking teams, the US State Department funded five further Thai-based anti-trafficking NGOs in financial year 2009–2010. Amounts ranged from 2.5 million baht ($85,000) to 22.5 million baht ($750,000), each for one to two-year programs (Empower Foundation 2012: 73).
21 www.empowerfoundation.org/kumjing_en.html (Accessed April 2016).
22 https://researchprojectkorea.wordpress.com/tag/swff/ (Accessed April 2016).
23 www.youtube.com/watch?v=70rPAxLFFKU (Accessed April 2016).

References

Amnesty International 2013 *The Dark Side of Migration: Spotlight on Qatar's Construction Sector Ahead of The World Cup*. www.amnestyusa.org/sites/default/files/mde220102013eng.pdf (Accessed April 2016).

—— 2016 Policy on State Obligations to Respect, Protect and Fulfil the Human Rights of Sex Workers. Pol 30/4062/2016 (May 26, 2016). www.amnesty.org/en/documents/pol30/4062/2016/en/ (Accessed May 2016).

Anam, Tahmima 2014 "Migrant Worker Nations, Unite!" *New York Times*, April 4. www.nytimes.com/2014/04/05/opinion/anam-migrant-worker-nations-unite.html?emc=eta1 (Accessed April 2016).

Andrees, Beate, Alix Nasri and Peter Swiniarski 2015 *Regulating Labour Recruitment to Prevent Human Trafficking and to Foster Fair Migration: Models, Challenges and Opportunities*. International Labour Organization. www.ilo.org/wcmsp5/groups/public/---ed_norm/---declaration/documents/publication/wcms_377813.pdf (Accessed April 2016).

Bailyn, Bernard 2012 *The Barbarous Years*. New York: Vintage Books.

Booth, Ken 1991 "Security and Emancipation," *Review of International Studies* 17: 313–326.

Chan, Kam Wing 2012 "Migration and Development in China: Trends, Geography and Current Issues," *Migration and Development* 1(2): 185–205.

Constable, Nicole 1999 "At Home but Not at Home: Filipina Narratives of Ambivalent Returns," *Cultural Anthropology* 14(2): 203–228.

—— 2007 Made to Order in Hong Kong: Stories of Migrant Workers. Second edition. Ithaca: Cornell University Press.

Dashti, Abdulmohsen A. 2013 "Interacting with Domestic Workers in Kuwait: Grammatical Features of Foreigner Talk: A Case Study," *International Journal of the Sociology of Language* 224: 63–84.

Davidson, Brad 2000 "The Interpreter as Institutional Gatekeeper: The Social-Linguistic Role of Interpreters in Spanish-English Medical Discourse," *Journal of Sociolinguistics* 4(3): 379–405.

DeParle, Jason 2011 "Domestic Workers Convention May Be Landmark," *New York Times*, October 8. www.nytimes.com/2011/10/09/world/domestic-workers-convention-may-be-landmark.html?pagewanted=all (Accessed May 2016).

Empower Foundation 2012 *Hit and Run: The Impact of Anti-trafficking Policy and Practice on Sex Workers' Human Rights in Thailand.* www.empowerfoundation.org/sexy_file/Hit%20and%20Run%20%20RATSW%20Eng%20online.pdf (Accessed April 2016).

Gallagher, Anne T. 2015 "Exploitation in Migration: Unacceptable but Inevitable," *Journal of International Affairs* 68(2): 55–74.

Gardner, Andrew and Autumn Watts (eds) 2012 *Constructing Qatar: Migrant Narratives from the Margins of the Global System.* Smashwords edition [e-book]. http://soundideas.pugetsound.edu/cgi/viewcontent.cgi?article=1735&context=faculty_pubs (Accessed October 2016).

Gardner, Andrew, Silvia Pessoa and Laura Harkness 2014 *Labour Migrants and Access to Contemporary Justice in Contemporary Qatar.* London: Middle East Centre, London School of Economics and Political Science.

Goldstein, Tara 2001 "Researching Women's Language Practices in the Multilingual Workplace," in Aneta Pavlenko, Adrian Blackledge, Ingrid Piller, and Marya Teutsch Dwyer (eds) *Multilingualism, Second Language Learning and Gender.* New York and Berlin: Mouton de Gruyter, 77–101.

Gorney, Cynthia 2014 "Far from Home," *National Geographic* (January): 70–95.

Haraty, Nabelah, Ahmad Oueni and Rima Bahous 2007 "Speaking to Domestics in Lebanon: Power Issue or Misguided Communication?," *Journal of Intercultural Communication* 14. www.immi.se/intercultural/ (Accessed April 2016).

Ho, Wai-Yip 2013 *Islam and China's Hong Kong: Ethnic Identity, Muslim Networks and the New Silk Road.* London: Routledge.

Hoerder, Dirk (ed) 1985 *Labor Migration in the Atlantic Economies: The European and North American Working Classes during the Period of Industrialization.* Westport, CT: Greenwood.

—— 2011 "Overlapping Spaces: Transregional and Transcultural," in Leon Fink (ed) Workers Across the Americas. Oxford: Oxford University Press, 3–38.

Inghilleri, Moira 2003 "Habitus, Field and Discourse: Interpreting as a Socially-situated Activity," *Target* 15(2): 243–268.

—— 2007 "National Sovereignty vs. Universal Rights: Interpreting Justice in a Global Context," Social Semiotics 17(2): 195–212. Reprinted, with editorial apparatus, in Mona Baker (ed) 2009 Critical Readings in Translation Studies. London and New York: Routledge, 229–244.

—— 2012 Interpreting Justice: Language, Ethics and Politics. New York and London: Routledge.

International Labour Organization 2012 *Effective Protection for Domestic Workers: A Guide to Designing Labour Laws.* Geneva: International Labour Office.

—— 2013 Domestic Workers Across the World: Global and Regional Statistics and the Extent of Legal Protection. Geneva: International Labour Office.

Koser, Khalid 2007 "Refugees, Transnationalism and the State," *Journal of Ethnic and Migration Studies* 33(2): 233–254.

Longhi, Vittorio 2013 *The Immigrant War.* Trans. Janet Eastwood. London: The Polity Press.

Mitra, Ananda 2004 "Voices of the Marginalized on the Internet: Examples from a Website for Women of South Asia," *Journal of Communication* 54(3): 492–510.

Ngai, Pun 2005 *Made in China: Women Factory Workers in a Global Workplace*. Durham, NC: Duke University Press.

O'Connor, Paul 2012 *Islam in Hong Kong: Muslims and Everyday Life in China's World City*. Hong Kong: Hong Kong University Press.

Pande, Amrita 2012 "'Weekend-Families' of Migrant Domestic Workers in Lebanon," in Maria Kontos and Glenda Tibe Bonifacio (eds) *Migrant Domestic Workers and Family Life*. London: Palgrave Macmillan, 300–316.

Rubdy, Rani and Sandra Lee McKay 2013 "'Foreign Workers' in Singapore: Conflicting Discourses, Language Politics and the Negotiation of Immigrant Identities," *International Journal of the Sociology of Language* 222: 157–185.

Saunders, Doug 2012 *Arrival City: How the Largest Migration in History is Reshaping our World*. New York: Vintage Books.

Sirkeci, Ibrahim 2007 "Human Insecurity and Streams of Conflict for a Reconceptualization of International Migration," *Population Review* 46(2): 32–50.

Tao, Ran and Zhigang Xu 2007 "Urbanization, Rural Land System and Social Security for Migrants," *The Journal of Development Studies* 43(7): 1301–1320.

USAID 2009 "Thailand," in *Antitrafficking in Persons Programs in Asia: A Synthesis*. USAID, 56–58.

Whitwell, Tom 2014 "Inside Shenzhen: China's Silicon Valley," *The Guardian*, June 13. www.theguardian.com/cities/2014/jun/13/inside-shenzen-china-silicon-valley-tech-nirvana-pearl-river (Accessed May 2016).

4 Translating the landscape

In his book, *The Presentation of Self in Everyday Life* (1959), Erving Goffman considered the way in which individuals present themselves to others in order to project forms of identity. He made a distinction between signs *given*, the things people do consciously to make a specific impression of themselves in certain contexts, and signs *given off*, the impressions given to others – the meanings others interpret – that an individual may or may not consciously intend (1959: 2). He proposed that certain aspects of social life could be apprehended through the microanalysis of the numerous everyday routine encounters in which members of a society interact with one another – simultaneously as *individuals* performing particular roles and as *social categories* based on their gender, race, or ethnic origins, for example. He saw face-to-face and other types of close encounters – both fleeting and recurring – as performing a key social function. They demonstrated a certain regularity, but also a vulnerability, in the mutually constructed social relationships conducted or attempted among members of a society. In doing so, Goffman drew attention to the significance of what he termed "the interaction order" which, he suggested, served as a "membrane" or set of "transformational rules" for the conduct of society (Goffman 1983: 11).

Goffman left the matter of the relationship between these 'rules' and more intransigent structural issues an open question, and made little reference to the function of the interaction order in societies undergoing major population transformations due to migration, shifting demographics, or globalization. Nevertheless, these larger social phenomena contribute significantly to the interpretive shaping of the *given*. For migrants attempting to have some agency over their reception, the creation of counter-discourses becomes a complex challenge as they map themselves onto different terrains, carving out their place in pre-existing spaces, possessing and altering them in meaningful ways.

The next two chapters consider the semiotics of migrants' visibility, historically and in present-day communities, beyond their mere presence as selective statistics in the media or in official documents. The present chapter examines, in particular, the configurations of photographs and political cartoons of migrants, religious and other cultural markers, together with the often forgotten manifestations of the presence of migrants in the constructed and 'natural' landscapes they helped to create. These signs play a critical role in the reconstruction of the interaction order and in the public imaginary regarding migration and multiculturalism. They are important indicators of which aspects of migrant selves or migrant groups are represented, foregrounded, or forgotten, by whom, and the factors influencing these.

Marks on the land

In the United States, in the valley of the Ohio River and its tributaries, over 10,000 earthen heaps lie at the heart of a cultural complex that began to establish itself some two to three thousand years ago, marking the landscape with conical burial mounds up to ninety feet tall and geometrical enclosures with earthen walls five to thirty feet high creating broad octagons, squares, and circles, some encompassing up to 200 acres. There are large 'image-mounds' in the form of reptiles, birds, and beasts, as well as massive flat-topped pyramids, some terraced, created by an heroic investment of labor by early Native American Adena and Hopewellian peoples. To the south lie the more recent earthworks of the Mississippian culture (800 to 1600 AD) stretching down into Florida and across toward the Mexican border, where more flat-topped pyramids are in abundance. Where preserved, these monuments of past engineering, calculation, artistry, and sweat were once obscured by trees, bushes, and undergrowth, and not until the late eighteenth century did Americans begin to take serious note of their presence. But while the earliest scholarly observers took it for granted that the Native American Indians had constructed them, soon layer after layer of myth was created by the more speculative migrant settlers who were increasingly flooding into Ohio. They suggested that it must not have been the Indians but some superior race who stayed long enough to build these wonders before heading south to create even greater civilizations elsewhere (Woodward and McDonald 1986). In the 1830s, William Cullen Bryant famously captured this myth in the second stanza of his poem *The Prairies*.

> As o'er the verdant waste I guide my steed,
> Among the high rank grass that sweeps his sides
> The hollow beating of his footsteps seems
> A sacrilegious sound. I think of those
> Upon whose rest he tramples. Are they here –
> The dead of other days? – and did the dust
> Of these fair solitudes once stir with life
> And burn with passion? Let the mighty mounds
> That overlook the rivers, or that rise
> In the dim forest crowded with old oaks,
> Answer. A race, that long has passed away,
> Built them; – a disciplined and populous race

> Heaped, with long toil, the earth, while yet the Greek
> Was hewing the Pentelicus to forms
> Of symmetry, and rearing on its rock
> The glittering Parthenon. These ample fields
> Nourished their harvest, here their herds were fed,
> When haply by their stalls the bison lowed,
> And bowed his maned shoulder to the yoke.
> All day this desert murmured with their toils,
> Till twilight blushed, and lovers walked, and wooed
> In a forgotten language, and old tunes,
> From instruments of unremembered form,
> Gave the soft winds a voice. The red man came –
> The roaming hunter tribes, warlike and fierce,
> And the mound-builders vanished from the earth.
> The solitude of centuries untold
> Has settled where they dwelt. [...][1]

Many versions of the myth thrived throughout the nineteenth century despite a strong scholarly tradition that argued rigorously to the contrary. By the 1860s, Bryant's imaginary mound-building "lovers" who "walked and wooed in a forgotten language" had turned into a highly successful romantic novel by Daniel Pierce Thompson titled *Centeola: Or The Maid of the Mounds* about a young and beautiful mound-builder woman and her lover. (Their entire civilization was destroyed and they were the only survivors.) Robert Southey, the English poet and author of the story of Goldilocks and the Three Bears, wrote a long poem, *Madoc*, about a group of Welshmen in the twelfth century who sailed to the New World and built cities of which the mounds were all that remained. Other speculations on how such sophisticated earthworks could become abandoned by their makers included pseudo-scientific works such as Josiah Priest's *American Antiquities and Discoveries in the West*, which apparently sold 22,000 copies within 30 months (Silverberg 1968: 65), though Priest remained unsure of which glorious world civilization might have created the mounds. Earlier versions included the wanderings of the lost tribe of Israel; others suggested Danish Vikings who were said to have later moved on to become the Toltecs in Mexico. What was clear, as Robert Silverberg argues, is that most writers and scholars rejected the belief that native Indians had built the mounds.

> The United States was then busy fighting an undeclared war against the Indians, who blocked their path to expansion; the Indians were being pushed out of their territory, imprisoned, forced to migrate, or simply massacred; and as this century-long campaign of genocide proceeded it may have been comforting to the conquerors to imagine that there once had been another race that these Indians had pushed out in the same way. Consciences might ache a bit over the uprooting of the Indians

but not if it could be shown that the Indians, far from being long-established settlers in the land, were themselves mere intruders who had brutally shattered the glorious old Mound Builder civilization.

(ibid.: 48)

Once the Homestead Act was signed by President Lincoln in 1862, previously native Indian land was granted for agricultural use, enabling thousands of White settlers and migrants to acquire land, build homes, and farm it for a minimum of five years. By the time research conducted by the Bureau of American Ethnology between 1882 and 1894 established without a doubt that the "widespread pre-historic earthworks had indeed been built by American Indians and by different cultural groups at that" (Woodward and McDonald 1986: 28), the kind of ethical legitimation alluded to by Silverberg had served the Homesteaders well enough.

'Navvies,' 'Paddies,' and 'Celestials': Migrant specters of the canals and the rails

If the innumerable mounds of North America turned out not to be the creation of some exotic highly civilized 'lost' tribe but the work of the descendants of those first migrants who had spread out of Eurasia millenia before, more recent marks on the land are undoubtedly of much more recent origin. Migration has always had an impact on human geography, serving an important function as the 'eye of history,' and of the many major public works projects that made the first (1760–1840) and second (1840–1870) Industrial Revolutions possible, two that remain highly visible are the canals and railroads built across Britain and the United States. What is not so well recognized is that their construction – an arduous and sometimes deadly undertaking – was accomplished by tens of thousands of migrants, the largest numbers of whom were Irish (in Britain and the United States) and Chinese (in the latter). These two groups of mostly unskilled, itinerant, and casual workers constituted a sizeable part of the migrant labor force in two of the largest burgeoning economies of the nineteenth century.

Irish navvies in Britain

The late eighteenth and early nineteenth century is considered the golden age of canal building in Britain. Prior to the railroads, canals created the infrastructure that linked towns and cities, making the first Industrial Revolution possible. Irish seasonal migrants, due to poverty and lack of employment opportunities in Ireland throughout the year, joined the scores of British men who were known as 'navigators' or 'navvies.' Together they did the slow laborious work of carving out the waterways from rock and soil, blasting tunnels through solid rock using picks, shovels, and gunpowder.

Despite their major contribution to the British economy, navvies were for the most part seen as a source of cheap expendable labor whose lost lives and limbs were viewed largely with indifference (Cowley 2001: 68–69). The loss of limbs was common enough that navvies with artificial arms or legs were referred to as "Walker's Fragments" after Thomas Walker, one of the main contractors on the Manchester Ship Canal who was known for his generosity toward any worker who was maimed on a site under his supervision (ibid.: 66).

Although the navvies came from many regions across Britain and elsewhere, it was the Irish navvies who:

> lodged in the public image because of their numbers and their 'separateness'. They spoke another language, had a particular cultural identity, different religious practices (80 per cent were Roman Catholic) and, most importantly, were not bound by family or community to England. If they wanted to behave badly, there wasn't much to stop them. Any settled community would be put out by the sudden appearance of young, unattached men living in makeshift camps, working all day and, so it was said, drinking all night.
> (McIvor 2015: 162, 164)

[…]

There are references in newspapers as well as in verse to men in corduroy breeches and leather tunics with brightly coloured headgear, as well as with a shovel or wheelbarrow.

A theatre audience knew that as soon as such a figure appeared on the stage, he would speak with a ridiculous, laboured West of Ireland accent and drink or fight everything in sight.
(ibid.: 164)

McIvor's account avoids mention of the fact that the centuries of hostility, some would say hatred, between the Irish and the English reached a peak in the nineteenth century, brought on by two significant events, the signing of the Act of Union in 1801 and the Great Famine of 1845–1848.[2] The behavior attributed to the Irish navvies – who, though large in number compared to other migrants, made up just under one-third of the labor force of 16,000 men working on the Manchester Ship Canal – was likely connected to deep-rooted prejudices and latent xenophobia directed toward the Irish by the English in this period. There was a marked tendency for English and Irish workers to monopolize different streets or settlements and much of the company housing seemed to support a policy of segregation between the two groups (Cowley 2001: 65–67). There is certainly evidence that the English navvies were as disposed to drink and violence, yet the "settled communities" of England with whom and for whom the navvies labored regarded the Irish alone with a mixture of fear and contempt (ibid.: 44–48).

If the broadsheet songs of the nineteenth century lambasted the Irish navvy, lyricists in the twentieth century – for example, Dominic Behan's "McAlpine's Fusiliers," Ian Campbell's "Here Come the Navvies," The Pogues' "Navigator," XTC's "Tower of London," and Genesis' "Driving the Last Spike" – re-wrote earlier representations of the navvy, eschewing negative stereotypes in favor of evocative images of stinging sweat, spikes being pounded in rails, families left behind in tears, navvies washing down blood and mud with beer, and showing no fear despite the many navvies who had died as they helped Britain thrive.

Irish 'Paddies' in the United States

The Irish fared no better in the United States, another major destination for them in the nineteenth century both before and after the Great Famine, with respect to the treatment they received by the anti-Catholic Protestant majority. One and a half million arrived before the Famine, another one and a half million during the Famine between 1846 and 1855, and three million more from 1855 to 1930 (Lee 2006: 16). The historian J.J. Lee and others have suggested that Irish migrants in the nineteenth century lived one way or another "in the Famine's shadow." Successive generations of migrants would have either lost parents, grandparents, or siblings to the Famine or heard tales of its horrors from others or in the US press (ibid.: 18–19).

In a three-volume work, *America, Its Realities and Resources* (1846), Francis Wyse, a prosperous Irish landowner, wrote a comprehensive guide for prospective British and Irish emigrants to the United States in which he covered with considerable detail the state of mid-nineteenth-century social and political life there. Based on an extended visit to the United States, the book is more treatise than travelogue; Wyse covers some of the major questions affecting the country at the time, including slavery, the state of the union, and immigration. With regard to the latter, he offers the following advice to Irish immigrants to avoid the "vexed and angry feelings that are every day springing up against him in this country" (Wyse 1846: 57).[3]

> He will find it necessary to remodel himself with more becoming care, to the practice, and national peculiarities of the people he is amongst, than to which he has generally been accustomed; to abandon, or at least to modify, many of his peculiar notions, and to identify himself more in spirit, as in his conduct, with the habits, and national feeling, than the generality of those of his countrymen who have preceded him, have deemed it of importance to attend to.
>
> (ibid.)

Wyse's suggestion that Irish immigrants should work harder to assimilate to the dominant culture contained criticism of the Irish fight for independence and the repeal of the Act of Union which he opposed.

They carry with them, in too many instances, to the New World, the prejudices and dislikes, engendered by earlier associations in the Old. The sectarian animosity; the unsettled and peculiar notions, which the absence of all liberal and enlightened instruction, together with the sickly influence of a morbid political excitement, to which they are ever subject in their own country, cannot fail to produce. While acting under their varied influences, they become obnoxious to the native citizen [...] frequently carrying [their] notions of liberty, in the exercise of [their] newly acquired right [to vote] to the verge of licentiousness.

(ibid.: 59–60)

For the contemporary reader, Wyse's writings provide both a synchronic and a diachronic account of the strategic role that transnationalism and assimilation played for the Irish, particularly the less well-off, in negotiating a place for themselves. Notwithstanding his own political and commercial interests, Wyse's careful observations about the signs his fellow Irish nationals both gave and gave off provide valuable insight into the competing narratives that vied for control in the representations of their history and their character.

Despite this censure of his compatriots, Wyse also expressed concern over what he saw as certain established political parties using the Irish immigrants as a political weapon: sympathizing with their treatment, inciting them to act, and then remaining silent when their character, religion, and fitness for self-governance were called into question. He was also critical of the tendency of the nativist working classes to blame "the great annual influx of a foreign population" for their economic woes, given his observation that "to the emigrant's exertions, their labor and industry, is the nation in great part indebted for its extended national improvements, its public works that bear daily and irrefragable evidence of their usefulness, with very many other advantages derivable from their sojourn in the country" (ibid.: 62).

Canal construction was one of the principal ways the Irish contributed to the development of the commercial infrastructure required to support the Industrial Revolution in the United States; though many were highly skilled professional canallers due to previous experience in Britain, they were all referred to as "ditchdiggers," perceived as "not merely ignorant and poor – which might be their misfortune rather than their fault – but [they are] drunken, dirty, indolent, and riotous" (Dearinger 2016: 62). Kirby Miller reports how British visitors to the United States in the 1820s and 1830s remarked "with astonishment" about the resemblances between the congested shanty towns of the Irish excavating the canals in the United States and their peasant villages in Ireland, both characterized by "those sterling Irish comforts, a cow, a pig and a 'praty garden' " (Miller 1985: 274).

The Irish provided much of the labor for the construction of the Wabash and Erie Canal, North America's longest canal, that extended 468 miles from Lake Erie to southern Indiana (Dearinger 2016: 17–18). They were also major assets in the creation of cities like Lowell, Massachusetts, doing the backbreaking labor of digging canals and laying foundations along the Merrimack River to power the textile mills that contributed to that city's rise as a cloth-making capital during the 1820s and 1830s (Blewett, M. 1976: 168). When the Lowell Canal System was completed in 1848, it was the largest in the world. The photo in Figure 4.1 shows some of these Irish laborers at work – every Saturday night the canals were drained so that on Sunday the workers could repair canal walls and remove debris. The photo in Figure 4.2 shows the same spot in 2016 – with the water present, only the tops of the arches are visible.

Canal construction was associated with diseases like Asiatic cholera brought on by the working and living conditions of canallers and their families (Dearinger 2016: 24). As Peter Blewett reports, Irish canallers in Lowell were not provided any housing by the increasingly prosperous mill owners, obliging them to fend for themselves in "Lowell's first slum," the segregated shanty towns known as "Paddy Camp Lands," "New Dublin," or "The Acre" where the majority resided until the early twentieth century (Blewett, P. 1976: 190–191).

> The wooden tenement houses, built close together, showed no design for life: sun and air reached only a few of the rooms. Generations of

Figure 4.1 Moody Street feeder, Irish canal workers, circa 1896. Lowell, Massachusetts. Courtesy of The University of Massachusetts Lowell, Center for Lowell History

Figure 4.2 Moody Street feeder, Lowell, Massachusetts, 2016. Photograph by Roger Hewitt

tubercular people spat on the floors and left a killing bequest for those who followed them into the buildings. There was no attention to sanitation and well into the twentieth century many of the buildings had no sewerage except for the 'vaults' which seldom were cleaned and often overflowed. In the tiny yards, in the alleys, in the streets, junk and garbage collected. A typical slum, the Acre was infested with disease, misery and death.

(ibid.: 208).

Despite the enduring physical evidence of their hard work across the United States, native-born American Protestants continually criticized Irish immigrants for their poverty and manners, their supposed laziness and lack of discipline, their public drinking style, their Catholic religion, and their capacity for criminality and collective violence. Between 1845 and 1921 the continuous arrival of Irish immigrants from Ireland ensured a steady infusion of individuals from home, compensating for their dispersal and rapid assimilation within the United States. Inter-generational loyalty between the Irish- and American-born throughout this period was another important factor in the community's continued strong identification with home and its support for the independence movement (Doyle 2006: 214). As William H. A. Williams notes, "The Irish immigrants in America came to realize that they shared a uniquely (tragic) experience, and in the face of Yankee hostility, a common destiny" (Williams 1996: 1). The stereotypes of the Irish became so ingrained among individuals with nativist beliefs about this group that the lines between Protestants' theatrical or political cartoon parodies of the Irish and the reality of Irish culture became blurred.

> An Irishman taking a drink, getting into a fight, or just generally having a high old time, was not like other men who might drink, fight, or celebrate. He was acting an elaboratedly scripted role. He was filling a grimly comic prophecy. He was playing the stereotype of himself.
>
> (ibid.: xx)

The Irish cultural historian Gearoid O'Tuathaigh has noted that "faction fighting" was part of the culture of the Irish peasantry during the eighteenth and nineteenth centuries, "a peculiarly Irish form of entertainment in which groups of men would club each other with cudgels, sometimes to settle a feud between families or villages but more often simply as a sort of bravado exhibition of strength" (O'Tuathaigh, qtd. in Williams 1996: 53). A typical fight of this kind is captured in the Irish novelist William Carleton's short story, "The Battle of the Factions" (1830). The narrator describes, somewhat tongue in cheek, the unique character of the "faction fight":

> Paddy's at home here; all song, dance, good-humour, and affection [...] his eye is lit with real glee – he tosses his hat in the air, in the height of mirth – and leaps, like a mounteback, two yards from the ground. Then, with what a gracious dexterity he brandishes his cudgel! what a joyous spirit is heard in his shout at the face of a friend from another faction! His very 'whoo!' is contagious, and would make a man, that had settled on running away, return and join the sport with an appetite truly Irish. He is, in fact, while under the influence of this heavenly *afflatus*, in love with every one, man, woman, and child. If he meet his sweetheart, he will give her a kiss and a hug, and that with double kindness, because he is on his way to thrash her father or brother. It is the *acumen* of his enjoyment; and woe be to him who will adventure to go between him and his amusements. To be sure, skulls and bones are broken, and lives lost; but they are lost in pleasant fighting – they are the consequences of the sport, the beauty of which consists in breaking as many heads and necks as you can; and certainly when a man enters into the spirit of any exercise, there is nothing like elevating himself to the point of excellence.

While faction fighting was an undeniably violent form of conflict resolution, it was but one part of what the Irish writer Alf MacLochlainn describes as "an intense and distinctive vernacular culture, a culture expressed in music, song and dance, social amusements, shared superstitions, marriage and funeral customs, housing styles, seasonal observances, organization of craft work, all these things we now call folk-life" (MacLochlainn, qtd. in Williams 1996: 52). The type of faction fighting Carleton describes can be seen as representative of the "rural parochialism and familism" that characterizes folk-life.[4]

By the early nineteenth century fights increasingly occurred in commercial farming districts between small farmers and laborers. Addressing the Irish immigrants' propensity toward collective violence, Kevin Kenny writes that, coming from a predominantly rural country divided by territorial boundaries and county loyalties, Irish men (and some women) had traditionally resolved land-related and other types of disputes through both covert activity and violence. He suggests, "the faction fight and the secret society, rather than negotiation and arbitration were the classic forms of protest" (Kenny 2006: 373). Kenny makes the important point that during the nineteenth century Irish immigrants in the United States fought each other not due to some innate temperament, as the stereotypes suggested, but in a context where they were involved in "a desperate struggle for access to employment with each side attempting to drive the other off the job" (ibid.).

Williams has suggested that what made the Anglo-Saxon majority so uncomfortable and even fearful in their encounters with the Irish was not solely due to the latter's distinct cultural practices but to the fact that the two groups were more *alike* than different in language and appearance. The use of English was common among the Irish immigrant population due in part to pressure from the Irish clergy who embraced the ideal of Americanization (Lee 2006: 27) and despite the fact that one-quarter to one-third of post-Famine Irish immigrants spoke English and fluent Gaelic (Miller 1985: 350). It is also significant that the Irish were the first 'ethnic' immigrant group to arrive in extremely large numbers and to gain high visibility across the cities and towns along the East Coast of the United States where most settled in the mid-nineteenth century.

> While frowned upon, fighting and drinking were hardly rare in American society. What set the Irish immigrant apart was the unfamiliar folk culture that provided the context for Irish behavior. By the end of the century, America would receive representatives from scores of southern and eastern European peasant societies, who came into our industrial cities trailing the traditions and customs of their pre-modern cultures. The Irish peasants, however were the first numerous representatives from such societies to arrive in America. Without the wall of language to hide behind, the peculiarities and archaisms of the Irish folk tradition were very evident for Yankee bemusement and concern.
>
> (Williams 1996: 53)

The majority of immigrants had been rural peasants, subsistence farmers accustomed to living in densely populated clachans or villages made up of hundreds or thousands of people living in clusters of small thatched cottages situated on or near jointly leased lands.[5] During the nineteenth century, even before the Famine, for most of those who emigrated, their scant holdings in Ireland were increasingly unable to sustain them or their families. There the poorest among them were "dressed in cast-off rags, through which naked arms and legs protruded, and lived in one-room, mud-floored cabins without chimneys or windows" in which "beds were considered luxuries, and many poor families slept huddled together on straw laid on the bare floor." Many had taken to "eating only one meal per day or every other day, and consuming their remaining potatoes 'with a bone' in them – that is half raw – to slow their digestion" (Miller 1985: 53).

For the Irish immigrants of the nineteenth century, like many newly arrived immigrants, the cultural and physical impressions they *gave* of themselves were constituted in their country of origin and by the conditions there that compelled them to leave. The signs or impressions they *gave off*, on the other hand, were created and circulated through the representations of members of the majority Protestant culture who observed the Irish through a colonialist/nativist lens, whether depicting them as dull-witted but comic and harmless 'Micks' to menacing simianized 'Paddies,' i.e. somewhere between primitive man and monstrous apes (Kenny 2006: 364). Signs given *off* also instigated competition between the Irish and two other groups who were situated at the bottom rungs of the social and economic ladder for much of the nineteenth century: the free Blacks and Chinese immigrants with whom they shared a place in history for their work in constructing the transcontinental railroad.

Chinese 'Celestials' and the building of the railroads in the United States

At around the same time the second wave of Irish entered the port of New York, a much smaller number of Chinese immigrants made a similar journey following China's defeat by the British in the first Opium War in 1842.[6] New York merchants and traders who had benefited from the China trade approved of the more 'gentlemanly' Chinese merchants among the new arrivals; at the same time however they maintained ambivalence toward them due to the perceived resistance of the Chinese to Western notions of progress and modernization.

> Once admired for its splendors and wisdom, China became increasingly measured by how friendly it was to Western economic and cultural expansion. Chinese workers entering the port of New York at this time not only walked into a spatial hierarchy but were also deemed targets of racial backwardness and ridicule, the perfect foil for progressive,

Anglo-Saxon, and Protestant patrician society becoming more and more assured of its self-declared special destiny.

(Tchen 1996: 146)

The relatively small number of Chinese immigrants, especially the merchant class, was greeted with less hostility than their Irish counterparts, though they settled in the same Lower East Side immigrant neighborhoods of New York where the Irish lived. There they formed temporary and permanent alliances with the thousands of other immigrants to whom they sold their goods and with whom, particularly though not exclusively the Irish, they married.[7]

While Chinese immigrants on the East Coast numbered only in the hundreds through the mid-nineteenth century, many thousands headed for the West Coast of the United States, lured by the promise of striking gold, after the economic and political turmoil in China that followed the first Opium War. These migrants were fleeing conditions not unlike those suffered by the Irish: social unrest, poverty, and increasing famine caused by the growing British economic penetration of their country as well as the Taiping Rebellion against the ruling Qing dynasty, which by 1864 had claimed the lives of between 20 and 30 million people (Dearinger 2016: 153). The vast majority who left were men from the interior of Guangdong Province in the Pearl River Delta assisted by Chinese benevolent associations in San Francisco who coordinated their passage from Hong Kong to San Francisco. Typically they were contracted to merchants or companies in the United States who advanced them "the rate of a ticket plus interest which the laborers contracted to repay" (ibid.: 154). Many of these associations would eventually help to direct Chinese workers to the Central Pacific Railroad, which was in competition with the Union Pacific Railroad to lay the most rail lines across the Great Plains.

Like canal work, railroad construction was a grueling and dangerous occupation. Reports of Chinese workers killed by snow slides, freezing to death, and disease, especially smallpox, were not uncommon. A brief report entitled "Bones in Transit" in the *Sacramento Union* in 1870 describes the transportation of "accumulated bones" of perhaps "1,200 Chinamen," nearly all "the remains of the company who were engaged in building the road." The report also mentions the religious custom of the "Celestial Empire" that "wherever possible, the bones of its subjects shall be interred upon its own soil," a tradition the benevolent societies appeared to honor as best they could (ibid.: 166).

Yet despite the enormous contribution of the Chinese railroad workers to US industrial progress throughout the nineteenth century, they were situated at the bottom of the social and economic hierarchy and, much like their Irish counterparts, subjected to denigration in words, images, and in the conditions of their labor.

> Invariably cast as "John Chinaman", epithets targeted male immigrants as a faceless homogeneous mass. Anti-Chinese commentators depicted

Chinese immigrant laborers as "coolies" or forced contract laborers, no better off than slaves. The Chinese were considered weak, feminine, and submissive, yet also uncivilized and loathsome. Politicians such as Ohio representative William Mungen condemned them as a "poor, miserable, dwarfish race of inferior beings," who were "docile ... effeminate, pedantic, and ... cowardly."[8]

(ibid.: 155)

The Chinese American writer Frank Chin has made it his particular mission to reclaim a central role for Chinese Americans in the history of American Western expansion, particularly the part played by the Chinese immigrants who made a major contribution to the construction of the transcontinental railroad. In a series of plays and short stories produced from the 1970s onwards, he sets out to unmask attempts made in eighteenth and nineteenth-century narratives of the American West to exclude the Chinese from that history and to represent the "Chinese truth about China." Chin describes himself as a fifth-generation Chinaman who, after graduating from university in 1966, worked for a year on the Southern Pacific railroad where several of his forebears, including his great-grandfather, also worked and where Chin became the first Chinese American brakeman in the company's history.[9]

Visibility re-envisioned

In an effort to reclaim the pioneer spirit of the Chinese immigrants who built the railroads, prospected for gold, and created successful businesses, Chin's twentieth-century Chinese American characters challenge enduring stereotypes of themselves and their ancestors as passive peons, effeminate and compliant.

In Chin's novel *Donald Duk* (1991), for example, the eponymous eleven-year-old protagonist tangles with these specters of history growing up in San Francisco's Chinatown where his father is a locally celebrated chef in their family-owned restaurant. Donald, who is named after his uncle, an internationally renowned opera singer, attends a private school the narrator describes as "a place where the Chinese are comfortable hating Chinese." As the novel begins, it is Chinese New Year, for Donald the "worst time of year," when all the teachers "are making a big deal about Chinese stuff" in his classes. As he listens to his teacher, Mr. Meanright, read from a book written by his former history professor from Berkeley about the "timid, introverted Chinese" who were "made passive and nonassertive by centuries of Confucian thought and Zen mysticism" making them "helpless against the relentless victimization by aggressive, highly competitive Americans," Donald just "wants to barf pink and green stuff all over the teacher's book." When his friend Arnold asks him what the teacher is talking about, Donald whispers, "Same thing as everybody—Chinese are artsy, cutesy and chickendick" (Chin 1991: 2–3). Although Donald understands that something is not quite right about this characterization, he internalizes the distortions nonetheless, to the point where he consistently rejects Chinese culture: what he wants is to dance like Fred Astaire.

A visit from his Uncle Donald, however, precipitates a shift in Donald's perceptions. His uncle reveals that their real last name is not Duk but Lee,[10] like Lee Huey, one of the 108 outlaws in the Chinese classic, 浒传 (shui-hu-zhuan), Water Margin, a collection of folktales about the real-life rebel Soong Jiang who led a peasant uprising in the early twelfth century.[11] He tells Donald that his great-great-grandfather Lee worked on the Central Pacific Railroad, and shows him a photograph in a book of a young boy his own age among the workers. From this point on in the novel, Donald begins to experience lucid dreaming about the Chinese railroad workers.[12]

He inserts himself among these men whose masculinity is asserted in Chin's descriptions of the type of labor they performed, their strike over pay, and their resolve to carve or ink their names in the last crosstie of the transcontinental railroad as a record of their achievements. The actions of the railroad men are interspersed with appearances from some of the 108 outlaws as well as the Chinese war hero, Kwan Kung (or Gwan Gung), a prominent general from the first century who continues to be worshiped as a deity in the Taoist tradition.

In the novel, Chin constructs Donald's recurrent dream narrative around an actual event that took place involving the Union Pacific Railroad (built mostly by Irish immigrants) and the Central Pacific Railroad (constructed primarily by Chinese immigrants). The occasion is described in the historical record as a competition, instigated by James Strowbridge, chief engineer and labor boss, and Charles Crocker, Superintendent of Construction for the Central Pacific Railroad, over whose workers could lay the most tracks in a single day to achieve the world record. The focus of the event was the driving of the "Golden Spike" where the lines of these two railroads intersected at Promontory Point, Utah, the spot designated by Congress "at which rails shall meet and form one continuous line" from east to west.[13] The ceremony, which took place on May 10, 1869, has since come to occupy near-mythic status in railroad history. The joining of the rails was to serve as a symbol of "a nation of diverse sections" coming together to become "one nation, indivisible" (Arrington 1969: 4), taking place as it did just a few years after the end of the Civil War. It was also intended to reinforce the Western frontier as a place of economic opportunity.

In the history of Chinese railroad workers, however, the event has taken on a rather different meaning due to the notable absence of any Chinese workers in the most famous photo taken of the event, Andrew J. Russell's "East and West Shaking Hands at Laying of Last Rail," (Figure 4.3) and the omission of their names in reports in the press.

Figure 4.3 "East and West Shaking Hands at Laying of Last Rail." Golden Spike ceremony, Promontory Summit, Utah Territory, May 10, 1869. Photograph by A.J. Russell. Collection of the Oakland Museum of California

In Donald's dream, the war hero Kwan Kung appears as the fictional foreman of the Chinese crew who participated in the competition. Chin introduces an important indisputable fact about the event: the bias of the journalists who mentioned eight of the Irish workers by name, while omitting any Chinese names. In one dream scene, as Strobridge surveys the workers laying six miles of track in a half a day from a distance, a reporter watching the same scene through a telescope remarks:

> "Six miles! The Celestials seem to have set themselves an extraordinary pace. How do you make them do it, Mr. Strobridge?"
>
> "To be perfectly truthful, sir, they have too much pride to work for me. I do not make them do a thing. Tis not in my power," Strobridge says.
>
> "It is then a tribute to your superior organization of the coolie labor, Mr. Strobridge. Six miles! Brilliant organization of 400 small, weak ...
>
> "Whoa, sir. Not weak."

"Nonetheless, a heathen race versus 400 hot-tempered individualistic Christian Irish who love nothing but a yard of beer and a brawl. It is clear to me superior generalship of inferior troops will triumph over inferior generalship of superior troops."

Kwan steps into the scope of Strobridge's transit. Strobridge follows him. Kwan carries the length of smoldering rope in his hand. He comes to the fuse of the large rocket. "Kwaan," Strobridge mutters in anticipation.

The reporter with the telescope asks, "By the way, what are the names of the Irishmen unloading the rail?"

Kwan lights the fuse, the rocket goes off leaving a trail of sparks and explodes. Work starts.

(Chin 1991: 110–111)

The reporter's seeming disregard for Kwan's fearlessness while making sure to note the names of the "eight burly Irishmen armed with heavy track tongs" (while making derisive comments about both the Chinese and the Irish) are later recalled by Donald who complains to his father about the injustice of it all. He tells his father, "We made history. Twelve hundred Chinese. And they don't even put the name of our foreman in the books about the railroad" [...] "It's not fair," to which his father responds, "Fair? What's fair? History is war, not sport!" (ibid.: 122–123). Echoing Chin, Donald's father tells his son that Chinese Americans have to write their own history to counter the misconceptions about Chinese history and culture that have persisted in histories of the West. If history is war, Chin suggests in his blog, the Chinese need to fight back:

CHIN: I see the stereotype as an invitation to either prove it or disprove it. And if you study it, I've been lucky enough to find that the stereotype is mostly disproved. For instance, we were not slaves building the railroad. There has been a campaign to pity the poor workers on the railroad. The only thing that we should be pitied for was that when we struck we didn't ask for more pay at that time. But we did go on strike. We did strike for back pay, we did strike for food allowance, we did strike for Chinese foremen. None of that is in the railroad history. We say that we worked on the railroad, yet at the Golden Spike ceremony, that famous photograph of the two engines meeting cowcatcher to cowcatcher, and the men leaning across with bottles of champagne toasting each other, there was not one Chinese in that photo. And yet we are mentioned in the caption that Chinese were there, or that we had finished building the railroad just that day, but no Chinese in the photo. And what really pissed me off was, that not one Chinese had noticed.

EHII: Not one Chinese historian or scholar, you are saying?

CHIN: Right and we don't write about the railroad. We seem to be ashamed of the railroad. And I was always taught to be proud of the railroad because we built it, that the Irish were always leaving the railroad to get drunk and they refused to work with nitroglycerin, which was just invented [laughs] and the Chinese said, 'Oh, any explosive, we're not afraid of.' And the Chinese weren't afraid, and they'd go out and they mastered it, but the Irish? No. There were accomplishments to be proud of, we won the track-laying contest, etcetera. But no one had really gone and looked. The Chinese seemed just to accept what Whites said about us and not look for themselves.[14]

Chin's comments point to three separate issues: the misplaced sympathy for Chinese railroad workers in the public consciousness, the lack of awareness among Chinese intellectuals of the specific nature of the contribution of Chinese Americans to the building of the railroads, and the interpretation of the photo as emblematic of the racialized underpinnings of the history of Western expansion. He suggests that the most effective way to challenge these distortions concerning these nineteenth-century migrants' contribution to that history is to re-articulate the unreliable signs given *off*, and in both *Donald Duk* and the excerpt above, Chin constructively fills in these signs with references to legendary figures in Chinese history and to historical facts. His references to the photo and to their victimization are less well aimed however. Like many others, Chin is inclined to interpret the absence of Chinese workers in the photo negatively, making the absence itself a crucial feature of the sign, along with the extra-textual fact that Chinese scholars did not see fit to remark on it. There is an implication of intentionality or at least neglect on the part of the photographer and/or in the particular function the photograph has served within the dominant, or 'White,' culture. The first reading of intention is materially contradicted, however, by the existence of a number of related images by Russell (Figure 4.4) and other photographers, artists, and illustrators in which Chinese workers do appear in the record of that particular day.[15]

There is also other strong evidence that, though absent from this particular photo, the Chinese workers and their foreman were celebrated at a separate more private occasion later the same day.[16]

The second reading of the photo as a dismissal of the workers' significance to the railroad and a sign of broader public anti-Chinese sentiment is more complicated. While the photo could well have contributed to existing sentiment, there are a number of other likely readings given the historical context. Two alternative readings are particularly plausible.

The Golden Spike ceremony was primarily intended to demonstrate to the commercial sector and the US government, who had partly subsidized its construction, that the country was open for business. The Pacific Railroad took four years to build with an estimated cost of $500 million to the Union Pacific and Central Pacific Railroads (Arrington 1969:13). The

126 *Translating the landscape*

Figure 4.4 "Chinese Laying Last Rail / U.P.R.R." Promontory Summit, Utah Territory, May 10, 1869, A.J. Russell's Stereoview #539 H69.459.2426. Collection of the Oakland Museum of California

main credit for its completion went to the American-born railroad associates, industrialists, financiers, and politicians, supporting Chin's fictional reporter's assertion that "superior generalship of inferior troops will triumph over inferior generalship of superior troops." As Leland Stanford, Governor of California from 1862–1863, noted in the first words of his speech at the ceremony:

> Gentlemen: The Pacific Railroad Companies accept with pride and satisfaction these golden and silver tokens of your appreciation of the importance of our enterprise to the material interest of the section which you represent on this occasion – the material interest of our whole country East and West, North and South. These gifts shall receive a fitting place in the superstructure of our road. Before laying the tie and driving the spikes, in the completion of the Pacific Railway, allow me to express the hope that the great importance which you are pleased to attach to our undertaking, may be in all respects fully realized.[17]

Russell's photo can be read as sending a sign about the knowledge, power, and influence of these representatives of American capitalist enterprise to reconfigure the West according to their image and likeness, as indicated in a cartoon that appeared a few weeks after the Golden Spike ceremony

Figure 4.5 "Does Not SUCH a Meeting Make Amends?" Wood engraving, May 29, 1869. Courtesy of the Library of Congress, Prints and Photographs Division, LC-USZC2-747

(Figure 4.5). The public viewed the presence of all the migrant workers in their towns, as well as the free Blacks and Mormons, as at best a necessary evil in the fulfillment of America's Manifest Destiny. Though some non-Chinese laborers do appear in Russell's shot, no details are given or can be discerned regarding their specific skills, their names, cultures, or countries of origin. In this regard, they are as invisible as the Chinese. The photo can thus also be read as a sign of the threat that immigrants posed to a growing class of Americans (themselves immigrants from the two centuries prior) who were worried and feared that these outside-others challenged the norms of behavior established within what was essentially a Protestant pluralist hierarchic order. The railroads, like the canals, were constructed during a time when nativist sentiment was high, though it was certainly the case that the Irish fared better out west than they did on the East Coast where social status continued to mean more than wealth. This helped modulate the intense nativist bigotry directed at them in the east. However, it is also the case that all the railroad workers were perceived as cultural others by the White Protestant majority. This is evident in the denigrating statements that were frequently uttered about these groups, the invidious comparisons invoked about their characters calculated to create ill will between them, and in the negative, often parodic, representations of more positive relationships that developed between them, including inter-marriage.

Chin himself gives voice in his blog commentary to what was in fact a manufactured exaggerated rivalry between the Chinese and the Irish railroad workers (Dearinger 2016: 188–191). His negative characterizations of the Irish draw attention away from the effort expended by both groups to accomplish the unforgiving task of laying ten miles of track in a single day, described by David Haward Bain as follows:

> One by one, platform cars dumped their iron, two miles of material in each trainload, and teams of Irishmen fairly ran the five-hundred-pound rails and hardware forward; straighteners led the Chinese gangs, shoving the rails into place and keeping them to gauge while spikers walked down the ties, each man driving one particular spike and not stopping for another, moving on to the next rail; levelers and fillers followed, raising ties where needed, shoveling dirt beneath, tamping, and moving on – "no man stops" Charley Crocker directed, "nor allows another man to pass" – and no man, Irish or Chinese, did more than one task, each a cog in that large dusty, sweating machine advancing up the incline toward the summit.
>
> (Bain 1999: 639, see also 658)

None of these workers had as much to gain by the joining of the rails as the men who drove them to complete the task. In fact, for the vast majority, the ceremony meant the end of this relatively lucrative employment. To focus the Irish–Chinese struggle on aspects of their character or their courage ends up reproducing the nativist attacks both groups suffered which fueled the competition between them as they fought to change their status from poor and oppressed outsiders that many had occupied in their country of origin.

The Irish were undoubtedly guilty of demonizing the Chinese to improve their own status at the time, encouraged by the fact that support for the Chinese was often used as a means of demonstrating hostility toward the Irish (Tchen 1996: 132–134). Positive relationships between the Irish and Chinese were not uncommon in the mid-nineteenth century, however, including marriage. Yet even these were frequently satirized in political cartoons, popular songs on the minstrel circuit, and in vaudeville acts, most famously, T.S. Denison's "Patsy O'Wang: An Irish Farce with a Chinese Mix-Up" (1900) about the son, known as "Chin Sun," of a Chinese mother and an Irish father who by the end of the play "transforms into 'Patsy O'Wang' by drinking from a bottle of brandy" (Lee 1999: 78–79).

In the play, Chin Sun is hired, much to the chagrin of the two Irish domestics, Mike and Nora, as a cook in the home of Dr. Fluke who runs a "modern sanitarium." When Chin Sun inadvertently drinks some brandy, "the spirit of Hibernia" [the Latin name for Ireland] is released and he suddenly becomes his Irish self – much to the disappointment of Dr. Fluke ("I hired you for a Chinaman. A bargain is a bargain."), who attempts to turn him back by "feeding him great quantities of tea, measuring progress by how obedient he perceives Patsy to be" while "Patsy siphons off the tea and declares that he has always been and is determined to remain "Irish forever" (ibid.: 79).

The play operates on the popular stereotypes of the Chinese and Irish working-class communities and highlights the onus on both groups in the late nineteenth century to prove their capacity to serve as respectable and loyal citizens suitable for American democracy, while underscoring the growing advantage of the Irish in the racialized politics and immigration policies in full force during that period, culminating in the Chinese Exclusion Act. As Robert G. Lee describes (ibid.: 80):

> In the schizophrenic mixed-race Chin Sun/Patsy O'Wang, the "wild" Irish and the "docile" Chinese together represent the duality of working-class nature as simultaneously fearsome and childlike, in need of both training and discipline. Irish wildness is controlled and reformed by the presence of the Chinese. Once his true Irish nature is unleashed by liquor, Patsy becomes potentially dangerous. Nevertheless, the plot must end with Patsy choosing his Irish whiteness, however tainted it may be by ethnic stereotype, because it alone offers a path into America. However divided by class, accent, and religion the Irish might be, whiteness confers upon them the freedom to create a unified ethnic identity as Irish Americans and use it as a vehicle for political power and economic mobility.[18]

In the second half of the nineteenth century, fear operated on a number of levels in the United States with respect to who should qualify as a citizen. The cartoon image shown in Figure 4.6 entitled, "The Great Fear of the Period, That Uncle Sam May Be Swallowed by Foreigners: The Problem Solved" ca. 1860–1869, captures the complex positioning of the Irish and Chinese in relation to the dominant culture, here represented by 'Uncle Sam.'[19]

In the first and second frames, the cartoonist plays on the nativist fear that the Irish and Chinese threaten to consume the dominant culture and replace it with their own, destroying the country in the process. As Uncle Sam is devoured by the caricatured images of the two men, they grow bigger, and presumably more powerful. The third frame suggests a number of possible meanings. One is that the two ethnic groups cannot coexist, that one must ultimately take down the other, and the likely winner will be the Chinese man, now wearing the Irishman's hat. This interpretation would play on the Irish immigrants' fear that increasing numbers of Chinese immigrants were a threat to their economic survival and social position, thus encouraging their support for laws designed to exclude the Chinese.

130 *Translating the landscape*

Figure 4.6 "The Great Fear of the Period, That Uncle Sam May Be Swallowed Up By Foreigners: The Problem Solved," White and Bauer [1860–1869]. Courtesy of the Library of Congress, Prints and Photographs Division, LC-DIG-pga-03047

Another reading is that, like the fictional Chin Sun, the Chinese must possess some distinctive element of 'Irishness,' an equivalent 'Whiteness' perhaps, in order to survive and thrive. The background to the stereotyped racial images though is the barely discernible Western landscape traversed by the railroads.

Translating the migrant self into the landscape

Visual signs can be a powerful means through which migrants locate themselves within a new place. Geographical similarities, in particular, provide tangible evidence of correspondences between the things left behind and the new space of inquiry. Such moments of recognition can stir up nostalgia for home, but they can also indicate the potential for feeling 'at home' in the new space, and the promise of a connection to be fulfilled with others still unknown.

The anthropologist Johannes Fabian has explored this idea of recognition as remembrance (Fabian 2001: 162–163) in the context of the travelogues of European colonizers and explorers in relation to the African countries they visited. In these he scrutinizes their failure – or refusal – to fully recognize the people they encountered as being in any way like themselves, and on the rare times they did, their unwillingness to acknowledge complete parity, so as not to disturb their belief in European superiority.

> [T]he Belgian Camille Coquilhat expressed *recognition* in his observation about drinking parties he saw on the banks of the Congo: "These drinking conventions sometimes take on gargantuan proportions and in that case, instead of ending like a scene in a picture by Teniers [the Flemish genre painter], they often finish with squabbles that degenerate into bloody fights" (1888, 267). Notice that this statement conforms to a pattern we noted earlier: Recognition may be stated ("comme une scène d'un tableau de Teniers") only to be taken back in the same breath. Were the Flemish drinking scenes Teniers had in mind always as peaceful as they were made to appear in genre painting?[20]
>
> (ibid., emphasis in original)

He notes that European explorers were "more likely to suppress recognition with regard to persons, practices or institutions than the natural landscape"(ibid.: 165) and cites several entries in the travelogues as examples. The explorer and lieutenant in the Belgian army Jérôme Becker describes the look of nature overtaking an abandoned village as like the growth that "covers the remnants of castles in Alsace or the Rhineland ..." while members of the German East Africa Expedition, Richard Böhm and Paul Reichard, wrote of some trees along a river "that, with the grotesque forms of their towering trees, reminded one of Dore's illustrations of Dante's *Inferno*." These seemingly neutral descriptions, however, hid an overwhelming Eurocentrism attached to their writings, even about nature. In another letter home, for example, Böhm observed of Usagara (now Tanzania) that it "gives the impression of southern Switzerland. Sometimes the African props make a truly striking impression in scenery that so much resembles European landscapes; the troupes of... black warriors, bands of monkeys, parrots, and hornbills don't really fit this frame" (ibid.: 167).

While non-conquering migrants may also tend to view what appears familiar at a glance through their own 'centric' lens, especially initially, most do so with a different aim than that of these European explorers and colonizers. The intention of the majority of migrants is not to appropriate or contest newly found spaces or their inhabitants, but to use them as starting points to carve out a place for themselves in the lengthy process of mutual recognition.

From Sri Lanka to Australia

In her novel, *A Change of Skies* (1991), novelist and professor of literature Yasmine Gooneratne who immigrated to Australia from Sri Lanka with her husband and two children in 1972 explores many of the challenges faced by Sri Lankan migrants arriving in Australia soon after the Whites Only immigration policy had been effectively dismantled in the late 1960s. With a good dose of humor and irony she tells the story of the newly married Baba and her husband Bharat, a visiting professor of linguistics in New South Wales. Gooneratne recounts their journey from temporary visitors to permanent residents, paying particular attention to their divergent strategies for making the strange familiar over the course of several decades. One way Baba achieves this is through moments of self-recognition she experiences in the natural landscape of Australia where she encounters visual signs in the physical environment that trigger memories of Sri Lanka and her past (Figures 4.7 and 4.8) and help her to feel more physically and spiritually connected to Australia. She recalls some of these moments in a letter to her mother:

> But New South Wales, and Sydney, are full of sights familiar to me. For instance, wherever I looked, on our first day here, I saw plants and trees I have known all my life. There is a frangipani tree growing beside the garage that comes into full bloom each December, with white and gold flowers, exactly like the trees in our verandah in Jaffna, and they have the same scent, too. And there are beds of blue hydrangeas on either side of the front door and a white jasmine creeper on the fence.
>
> [...]
>
> While on the subject of the many things here that remind me of past times, I must tell you that there exists an Australian version of the Ice Cave at Amarnath! The only differences are that the lingam in what they call the Cathedral Cave in the Blue Mountains has formed itself of limestone and not ice, can be seen at any season of the year, and is much smaller than the one we saw on our pilgrimage to India. But there's no doubt about it, it is a lingam! I can't tell you how happy it made me to see it there among the stalactites and stalagmites – I felt Australia wasn't so alien any more, that the Gods must have walked here just as they have walked in India and Sri Lanka.
>
> I just can't understand why the British explorers who discovered the Jenolan Caves didn't grasp the spiritual significance of what they found inside them. As I told Bharat, Cathedral Cave would be attracting millions of pilgrims today, people would be coming here from all over the world, just to see the miracle.[21]
>
> (Gooneratne 1991: 171–173)

Figure 4.7 Shiva lingam. Photo courtesy of Shastri Akella

Figure 4.8 Ice lingam, Amarnath Cave. Photo courtesy of Shastri Akella

Baba's comment regarding the lost opportunity of the British explorers' "discovery" of the caves to exploit their potential for attracting pilgrims is an interesting addition to her letter. As well as commenting on the British explorers' lack of spiritual and/or entrepreneurial instincts, it also exposes Baba's own obliviousness to the fact that well before the British, for thousands of years, the Jenolan Caves were an important part of the spiritual culture of the Gundungurra and Wiradjuri indigenous peoples recognized for the healing power of the waters, and were referred to by other names, including Binoomea, Binomil, or Bin-oo-mur. A number of additional factors also contribute to Baba's oversight to do with her own historical ties to British colonialism.

Baba's mention of these visual signs in her letters home is perfectly in keeping with her character. From the moment of their arrival in Australia, and unlike her husband, Baba endeavors to construct a transnational identity in which her memories are put in the service of linking her past to her present in positive ways. Memories are not used by Baba primarily for nostalgic purposes. The fact that the colors and the scent of flowers near her new home recall her family home in Jaffna eases her into her new space, while the shapes of the stalactites and stalagmites connect her with her enduring faith. Accomplishing the latter involves the translation of three visual signs – the ice lingam in India, which is a translation of other Shiva lingams seen in temples or erected as shrines in Sri Lanka, and, finally, the limestone formations in New South Wales – attributing to them an indisputable equivalence: "But there's no doubt about it, it is a lingam!"

For both Baba and Bharat, however, the construction of a transnational identity involves more than constructing equivalences, it also requires them to erect distinctions between themselves and the Australians on the one hand, and in relation to certain other migrant groups on the other, just as earlier Irish migrants did in the United States. Soon after their arrival, in response to a radio rant by a sociology professor at Bharat's university against Asian immigrants who refuse to assimilate, with specific reference to the Vietnamese, "who pollute the air with the fumes of roasting meat," Bharat insists that they change their names to Barry and Jean (from Navaranjini) Mundy (from Mangala-Davishna). At first Baba is opposed to the change, in part because she is reluctant to lose this part of her identity – the name Navaranjini, she remarks, "has a really auspicious meaning in Sanskrit" (Gooneratne 1991: 124) – but also because she does not recognize the professor's use of the term 'Asian' in his statement to include Sri Lankans.

> "Why should you care what Blackstone says"? I asked. "Your eyes aren't slits and your head doesn't slope. It's obvious he doesn't mean you". My husband just looked depressed. "Want to bet"?
>
> (ibid.: 122)

For Baba, the correct term for persons from East Asia was not Asian but 'Far Eastern' as they were referred to back home in Sri Lanka. She tells her husband, "But we're not 'Asians' here. When Australians say 'Asians', they don't mean *real* Asians, like us. They're talking about…" She is about to use the term "Ching-Chongs," the derogatory term used to refer to Far Eastern people in Sri Lanka and India, before Bharat stops her and reminds her that this is a "racist way of speaking that we learned from the British in our colonial days" (ibid.: 119).

In penning this segment of the novel, Gooneratne both acknowledges the part played by negative racialized perceptions of Asians in Australia at the time in their decision to become 'Barry' and 'Jean,' and admits to racist attitudes that originate in Sri Lanka. By the end of the novel, despite or because of the fact that Bharat's idea to change their names is triggered by a racist rant and his worries about his standing at the university, 'Barry' embraces his otherness by becoming an English teacher to young immigrants. He also edits and publishes *Lifeline*, a biography based on his grandfather's manuscripts of an earlier journey to Australia and back (the notes of which appear in Gooneratne's novel in alternating chapters) and works on a *Guide for Asian Migrants*. 'Jean' goes on to write a bestselling cookbook she calls *Something Rich and Strange* whose great success, she reports in the *Queensland Courier*, finally gives her "true self-fulfillment" in Australia.

> "I realised then that I had found what I was looking for," Jean confided to us as she measured six cups of frothing Queensland beer into the pan in which she was mixing up a batch of delicious cinnamon-flavoured breakfast breads. "A wholesome synthesis of East and West, that's what *Something Rich and Strange* is all about."
>
> (ibid.: 293)

From the Levant to 'Little Syria' to the 'real' America

A wholesome synthesis of East and West is also what the Syrian writer and itinerant preacher the Reverend Abraham Mitrie Rihbany sought when he migrated to the United States in 1891. Rihbany was born in 1869 to Greek Orthodox parents in the town of El-Shweir in Mount Lebanon, then under Ottoman rule. He was schooled up to the age of nine when, following his family tradition, he became an apprentice stonemason. At seventeen his family consented to his attendance at the American Missionary High School of Suk-al-Gharb in Beirut where he studied classical Arabic and eventually converted to Protestantism. Protestantism, he recalled, gave him close engagement with the Bible, something that was reserved for priests in the Orthodox Church. He wrote of his conversion, "Sentimentally, I was still a Greek Orthodox; intellectually I had leaned perceptibly toward Protestantism" (Rihbany 1914a: 243). At twenty-two Rihbany emigrated to the United States where he hoped to establish himself as a Protestant minister. He arrived at Ellis Island in 1891 and for the first eighteen months lived in the Syrian colony in New York.[22]

In his autobiographical writings about the Syrian colony in the essay "In New York With Nine Cents," Rihbany describes its mercantile atmosphere (ibid.: 239):

> The Syrian colony in New York consisted in those days of a few store and restaurant keepers, a multitude of peddlers of 'jewelry and notions' and a few silk merchants who, although they peddled their wares, bore the more dignified designation of "silk-sellers." For lack of better pursuits, college men often took up silk-selling as a means of livelihood.

He recalls being questioned upon his arrival by Syrians like these who lived and worked in the colony:

> "Do you have money so that you can at least buy an interest in a store, or deal in silk?"
>
> "No, I have no money at all."
>
> "Do you have letters of recommendation from missionaries in Syria to persons in this country?"
>
> "No."
>
> "Can you speak the English language?"
>
> "Not so that I can be understood."
>
> "How old are you?"
>
> "Twenty-two."
>
> "Twenty-two! Too old to master the English language. The only thing you could do, and which thousands of Syrians are doing, would be to peddle 'jewelry and notions.'"

To which he remembers thinking:

> Call it pride, vanity, or whatever you please, whenever I thought of peddling 'jewelry and notions,' death lost its meaning for me. Come what might, I would not carry the 'keshah' (a colloquial Arabic name for the peddlers pack).
>
> (ibid.: 239–240)

It was during this same period that Rihbany came to know Khawaja Najib Arbeely, a Syrian inspector of immigrants, who had, as it happens, facilitated his entry at Ellis Island despite the fact that he did not meet the financial requirements. When Arbeely started *Kowab Amrika* (Star of America), the first Arabic newspaper to be published in the United States, he asked Rihbany to serve as literary editor due to his knowledge of classical Arabic, a post he held for a year until politics in Syria caused the newspaper to fold. The two met regularly with "the few college men in the Syrian colony" and eventually formed the "Syrian Scientific and Ethical Society" with Arbeely as president and Rihbany as vice-president. According to Rihbany, they would discuss:

> history, philosophy, the good and evil of immigration, the greatness of the United States of America, the superiority of the Syrian to the Irish population of Washington Street, – these and many other subjects called forth the impassioned eloquence of the orators among us, who spoke with perfect confidence and freedom, and often regardless of the facts.
>
> (ibid.: 244)

In a report on New York's 'Little Syria' published in 1899 in *The New York Times*, the journalist Cromwell Childe describes in the piece, typical for its time, a neighborhood "made up of Orientals of many stations in life," including the poor who made up the majority and the families of the "small merchants, the very prosperous peddlers."[23] Childe makes some effort in his article to emphasize the "American" customs the Syrians had embraced in contrast to other migrant groups living in the lower Manhattan "Ghettos" in and around Washington Street. He writes about this not so much to herald their embrace of these customs but to counter the image of the Syrian colony as a typical immigrant enclave made up of dirty foreigners and "to disabuse the minds of those who have read that it possesses extraordinary romance" based in stereotyped images of "red-fezzed heads and languorous eyes."[24] Though not without traces of orientalism, he writes, for example:

> In a manner, the Ghetto, or one of New York's "Italies," is more romantic, for at least some hints of national costumes. Syria, down in Washington Street, shows nothing beyond an occasional headdress of black on the part of the women.
>
> In the Ghetto, the "molders of public thought" are frequently unwashed and greasy. Syria's editors, on the other hand, are delicately nurtured gentlemen, of the highest mercantile order.
>
> There are plenty of low grade groceries and restaurants for the colony's 3,000 Syrians are poor. But, many of those Orientals are well off, comparatively. Kaydouh, save for his olive skin and his cast of features, scarcely seems a Syrian at all. His English is pure and has little foreign accent. [...] Americanized completely already he may yet become a political leader to the quarter, and swing the Syrian vote.
>
> In these restaurants at night, then transmuted into cafes, a red Syrian wine is drunk and the "hubble bubbles" appear. These lose none of

their attractions because the man smoking them is in American clothes instead of a national costume.

Rihbany, like other Syrians of his day, was eventually convinced not only that the ethnic communities of New York did not constitute the '*real* America' but that to get closer to the Yankee sensibilities of White Protestant America that he had come to the United States to embrace, he would have to leave his own community behind.

> The loose composition of a population of many and mutually exclusive nationalities, the grotesque manners, and the multitude of saloons and other haunts of vice and crime in the "lower regions" of American cities, where the foreign colonies are generally located, soon tend to awaken in the mind of that foreigner, who finds himself yearning for a better order of things, the significant question, Where is America?
>
> I often asked myself, in those days, where and how do the *real* Americans live? Who are the people who foster and maintain that American civilization of which I hear so much, but which I have not yet known? I have seen a multitude of Irish, Italian, Poles, Russians and Chinese, and other human elements which make up the community in which I am living, but where are the Americans? It seemed to me that in a cosmopolitan city like New York it was well-nigh impossible for a poor foreigner like me to come into helpful contact with its real American families.
>
> (Rihbany 1914a: 248–249, emphasis in original)

Rihbany's construction of a transnational self that was White, Syrian, Arab, Protestant, and American that had begun in Mount Lebanon and Beirut was further realized in the Syrian colony itself where he continued the work of trying to ameliorate or otherwise address the gap between a number of divided selves. These were not just the dilemmas of what was ascribed or made possible or not to him within his newly chosen society. They were issues that grew out of a longer history of discontinuities and his efforts to resolve them.

Still a very young man, Rihbany's second migration from New York to the American heartland in search of a place to preach to "its real American families" initially rendered him destitute, as he writes in "Out From My Kindred": "In my travels westward, the expressions, 'These are very hard times.', 'The summer is a dull season for the churches.', 'Not many people care for lectures this time of year.', tortured my hearing everywhere" (Rihbany 1914b: 366). Nonetheless, he persisted in his efforts to locate Protestant churches wherever he went, seeking to establish his rightful place within them: "Upon coming into a town, the sight of church spires rising above the houses and the trees as witnesses to man's desire for God, always gave me inward delight" (ibid.: 371). In the meantime, his Bibles, one Arabic, the other English, were reminders of the past, the present, and the synthesis he sought between the two: "…as a sojourner in this Western world, whenever I pick up my Bible it reads like a letter from home" (Rihbany 1916: 309).

> I owe a great deal to the live language of the English Bible. On occasions, I would open my Arabic Bible at church and follow the scripture lesson as read by the minister, and thus learn what was meant. On other occasions, I would open my English Bible and learn how the words were pronounced. Thus the English has come to me saturated and mellowed with feeling. The phrases of the English Bible are elemental human sentiments made tangible.
> (Rihbany 2014b: 371)

Rihbany forged an unambiguously orientalist discursive apparatus, grounded in his own contradictions, with which to translate himself culturally between these two worlds. As Sirène Harb suggests, this discourse "provides Rihbany with the tools to rework his inscription in time and space" (2008: 133). Although he had viewed his departure from 'Little Syria' as a radical break with his parent stock, "a complete departure, inwardly and outwardly" (Rihbany 1914a: 248), his preaching was consistently framed in the Orient–Occident binary (or rather, his specific constructions of these categories) that he deemed recognizable to his target audience. Rihbany was not alone in this, as Evelyn Shakir and others have noted of early twentieth-century Arab writers and intellectuals:

> In the early decades of this century, they themselves seemed locked into the Orientalist discourse with which their readers were familiar, at least insofar as they too, spoke of Orient and Occident (terms implying immutable opposition) and followed conventional practice in attributing traits of temperament to one or the other. Thus Rihbany speaks rather glibly of Western enterprise and of Eastern effusiveness and mysticism.
> (Shakir 1988: 43)

Rihbany has been sharply criticized for using his profession as a preacher to propagate stereotyped images of the East to the conservative mainstream in the United States at the time, encouraging the perpetuation of certain beliefs and attitudes about people they viewed as inferior. He was, in this sense, according to Waïl Hassan, a perfect example of "what Said described as the modern Orient participating in its own Orientalizing" (Hassan 2011: 98). He has also been identified with Arab Americans in the first half of the twentieth century who "struggled for inclusion as 'white' Americans," suggesting the possibility of a more "pragmatic, historically situated rationale" underlying his decisions (Majaj 2000: 328). Harb views the autobiographical narrative of his evolution from his Syrian childhood to American manhood as echoing "the ideological construction of temporality of the colonial project" (Harb 2008: 138) and its reliance on an evolutionary perception of time.

It seems doubtful that Rihbany would not have noted the tensions and even contradictions between the negative racialized perceptions of Syrians in the United States, his own racist dismissal of the other migrants he encountered in Washington Street, and his desire to reside among the Protestant elite with whom he identified. He was in this sense similar to both the Irish (with whom he and his fellow Syrians contrasted themselves) and the educated Sri Lankans in Australia (particularly after the White policy ban was lifted), each of whom made a concerted attempt to distance themselves from those groups they perceived as undesirable in order to improve their own social standing.

Rihbany, like other nineteenth-century Arabic-speaking immigrants from the Levant, though seen as 'Oriental' was classified as 'White' and, significantly, not 'Chinese.' Given his complex brew of ascribed and assumed identities, whether Rihbany ever achieved the 'wholesome' synthesis between East and West that he and the fictional Baba/Jean sought is unclear from his writings. One of his earliest attempts to do so is captured in the following passage in which he describes his very first appearance preaching before an American audience.

> The nouns and the verbs often stood at cross purposes in my remarks, and the adjectives and adverbs interchanged positions, regardless of consequences. My impromptu literal translation of Arabic into English greatly puzzled the minds of my hearers, and, at times, it was difficult for me to know fully what I wanted to say. Notwithstanding all that, however, I managed in closing to shift from Syria to America and eulogize George Washington.
>
> (Rihbany 1914a: 369)

Though three years later Rihbany would realize his wish to be a regular minister of an American congregation, his recollection of such moments demonstrates the difficult task for him, as for other migrants, of culturally and linguistically translating (and being translated by) a new place.

Invisible/visible specters

The act of situating the self into a new space, regardless of the degree of assimilation permitted or desired, inevitably involves some degree of surrender to stereotypical representations, at least initially and in places undergoing intense demographic change. In the history of migration, the real and metaphorical landscape on which this process takes place represents for the first generation of migrants the 'not yet begun,' and for the generations that follow, the 'the not yet over.' In the field of cultural geography, landscape has been identified as "the discursive terrain across which the struggle between the different, often hostile, codes of meaning construction has been engaged" (Daniels and Cosgrove 1993: 59). These authors are referring here to their attempts to interpret the worlds they survey, but migrants are involved in a similar struggle to interpret the people and places with which they interact. Landscapes not only offer evidence of the enduring signs of an earlier presence of migrants whose origins have gone unrecognized or underacknowledged in the public consciousness – an archaeological record of visibility and invisibility in the translation of cultures – they are forever shaped by this presence as well.

In this sense, landscapes are also powerful spectral spaces. As such, they are particularly vulnerable to multiple mappings of meaning and susceptible to what the sociologist Avery F. Gordon has theorized as "haunting," her proposed method for understanding "how that which appears to be not there is often a seething presence, acting on and often meddling with taken-for-granted realities ... dense sites where history and subjectivity make social life" (Gordon 1997: 8). The absence of the Chinese workers in the photograph at Promontory Point is a good example. Despite other possible readings of the photograph, the one foregrounding the "seething presence" of the missing Chinese workers produced an opening in which distinctly Chinese truths about the railroads could be told. It demanded a proper acknowledgment, by their descendants and the country as a whole, of these men's place in history, delivering the type of justice to this "generation of ghosts" to which Derrida refers in *Specters of Marx*:

> If I am getting ready to speak at length about ghosts, inheritance, and generations, generations of ghosts, which is to say about certain *others* who are not present, not presently living, either to us, in us, or outside us, it is in the name of *justice*.
>
> (Derrida 1994: 15)

Landscapes can also be a powerful means through which living migrants demonstrate agency with regard to a place, uncompromised by anyone else's gaze. Gooneratne's character Baba built her heritage into the spiritual cave-scape of Australia's Blue Mountains while Rihbany resolutely willed his identity into the Protestant church spires of America. Similarly, the Chinese workers on the Central Pacific Railroad can be said to have exemplified in their "pedantic," "feminized" expectation of and insistence on the essence of Chinese food, dress, and intoxicant, the way the *given* can be collectively achieved despite and beyond the competitive nature of migratory life, and, in the modern context, the politics of recognition, as the following passage illustrates:

> The new workers were organized into gangs of twelve or twenty men including a foreman and a cook. The foreman kept records, collected

the gang's pay (it had risen by midsummer to $27 per month and would soon climb to $30), deducted for food and for any outstanding amount owed to the labor contractor, and dropped the remainder of the gold coins—perhaps $20—into the hands of his charges. The cook obtained food, usually dried, from Chinese merchants in Sacramento and San Francisco, and it was decidedly unlike anything the whites had ever seen before. The cookfires sent up fragrant clouds of peanut oil and garlic, of simmering white rice or clear noodles, of stir-fried cuttlefish, abalone, shrimp, and oysters, of mushrooms, bamboo shoots, bok choy, mung beans, snow peas, and kelp, and, most often on Sundays, of pork or chicken slaughtered on the spot. Seeing this alien cornucopia, the Irishmen shuddered—and turned smugly to their unvarying menus of boiled beef, boiled potatoes, boiled beans, boiled coffee, and bread and butter. And the following day the mountainside was waiting for all.

Toiling in the sun, everyone turned frequently to the water boys, but there again stood the cultural difference; the Chinese drank lukewarm tea, boiled at dawn in great pots and poured into glass jugs for distribution to the gangs, then dispensed from powder kegs throughout the day: the whites merely drank dippers of unboiled water, more often than not bringing on the dysentery which plagued their ranks and caused absenteeism to soar.

(Bain 1999: 221–222)

There is clearly more than simple disgust at the unfamiliar Chinese food here in the Irishmen's shudder and smug relish for their own food. Chinese elaborations beyond beans and boiled beef may have seemed at one glance to be merely a neutral sign *given* but could be taken defensively as a sign *given off* by the Irish workers, unsettled at many a turn by racist discourses aimed at them. Where signs given and given off are simultaneously in play, it can be difficult to extricate one from the other.

The anthropologist Tim Ingold suggests that landscape be viewed not as objects, detached from the humans who shape them and are shaped by them, but as "the homeland of our thoughts," borrowing a phrase from Merleau-Ponty.

> The landscape, in short, is not a totality that you or anyone else can look *at*, it is rather the world *in* which we stand in taking up a point of view on our surroundings. And it is within the context of this attentive involvement in the landscape that the human imagination gets to work in fashioning ideas about it.
>
> (Ingold 1997: 171, emphasis in original)

Although accounts of the Irish and Chinese migrants in the American West and on the railroads tend to foreground the conflicts between them, their historic encounter, their labor, and the landscape they shared connect them through history, creating what Ingold calls a taskscape: "landscape constituted as an enduring record – and testimony to – the lives and works of past generations who have dwelt within it, and in so doing have left something of themselves there" (ibid.: 152).

The process of resituating and renegotiating cultural signs cannot be reduced to ethnic struggles floating free of history or economics, nor of the landscapes that from time to time come to embody them both. The work involved for migrants, like all people, in translating space into place, of developing a sense of belonging, is ongoing. For migrants, it begins with the hard-fought battles of the first generation and continues in other more subtle ways in the generations that follow. Gaps between intention and interpretation in the presentation of the self in everyday life can emerge even where greater shared understanding may be expected. The interaction order thus effectively operates like a membrane; it is both pliable and structuring, allowing some things to pass through while stopping others.

Notes

1 www.poemhunter.com/poem/the-prairies/(Accessed April 2016).
2 The Act of Union agreed between England and Ireland held out certain promises to improve economic conditions for Ireland and to initiate the process of Catholic emancipation that would guarantee Catholics the right to hold seats in the British Parliament. According to Woodham-Smith (1962: 15–16), "The Union was bitterly opposed; contemporaries described it not as a marriage but as a 'brutal rape,' and Ireland was compared to an heiress whose chambermaid and trustees have been bribed, while she herself is dragged, protesting to the altar." In the end, the Act proved disastrous for the Irish: It effectively increased Ireland's political and economic dependence on England. The Great Famine forced millions of Irish to emigrate to the United States, the UK, Australia and elsewhere to avoid the fate of at least a million others who died from starvation and disease (ibid.: 20).
3 Wyse is referring to incidents like the violence that occurred in 1844 in Philadelphia which was triggered by a request from a representative of the Catholic archdiocese of that city's school board to allow the optional use of the Douai version of the Bible where requested. The America Protestant Association and the local nativist party held a meeting in an Irish district of the city to oppose such a measure and riots ensued. Among other destruction, sixty Catholic houses and two churches were burned by nativists and Orangemen over six days, leaving twelve nativists dead (Doyle 2006: 200). The Douai Bible translation was produced by English Catholics in the sixteenth century in response to perceived biases in the existing Protestant versions. It was done so that "men should have a faithful and Catholic translation rather than they should use corrupt versions to their peril if not to their destruction" (Pope 1910: 108). That modern Protestants should have objected to the use of a Bible in a vernacular chosen by Catholics represents an interesting historical irony. Just as Wycliffe and Tyndale had done centuries before, the original Douai Bible also used the Vulgate Latin as its source text and was motivated by a similar political intent.
4 Irish stick fighting, or the art of *bataireacht* or *boiscín*, is part of a historical tradition dating back millennia of martial arts around the globe involving

sticks, clubs, canes, swords, etc. For a brief account of this history and its development in Ireland, see https://hemamisfits.com/2015/02/03/what-is-irish-stick-fighting/ (Accessed April 2016).
5 Ireland in the early nineteenth century remained "a colonial appendage to the world's most advanced industrial economy" in which the great majority of farmers were tenants at will or tenants on short lease laboring under a "grossly inequitable system of landownership" (Miller 1985: 32).
6 The first of two Opium Wars fought between China and Great Britain was prompted by the Qing Dynasty's attempt to ban the trade of opium from China. The conflict ended with China's defeat by the British and the subsequent signing of the Treaty of Nanjing, a treaty considered the first of many unequal treaties between China and Western powers. China agreed to pay the British government all of the debts accrued by Chinese merchants during the conflict, to cede the territory of Hong Kong in perpetuity, and to permit British merchants to trade at five named ports with whomever they pleased, i.e. not, as had been the case, exclusively with Chinese merchants at the main port of Canton (Guangzhou). http://afe.easia.columbia.edu/ps/china/nanjing.pdf (Accessed April 2016).
7 These Chinese male immigrants were generally single, of marrying age, and few in number compared to the Irish. There were hardly any Chinese women among them. Irish women of marrying age in New York at one time, on the other hand, far outnumbered Irish men (Tchen 1996: 128–129).
8 It was also during this period that the pejorative term 'Celestials' came to be used, a term that had been used for thousands of years by China that reflected its view of itself as the Middle Kingdom or Celestial Empire, "positioned between heaven above and all the rest of the world below" and whose emperor was understood to be the 'Son of Heaven' who ruled by divine inspiration (Dolan 2012: 29). One of these rulers, Emperor Kangxi, had prophetically warned in 1717 of the dangers of a "collision with the various barbarians of the west, who come hither from beyond the seas" (ibid.: 37). Ironically, it would be the Chinese who would be deemed uncivilized barbarians less than a century later.
9 See the Frank Chin papers in the University of California Santa Barbara Library, Department of Special Collections, http://pdf.oac.cdlib.org/pdf/ucsb/spcoll/chin_frank.pdf. (Accessed April 2016).
10 His uncle is most likely referring to the practice used by Chinese migrants to get around the exclusion laws. Chinese American citizens would sometimes claim others, family members, friends, or fellow villagers, as their biological sons in order to allow them to enter the United States. Known as 'paper sons' even where no blood ties were shared, the 'paper kinship' established a bond and sense of mutual obligation between the bestower and the recipient of the family name (Lee 2003: 195).
11 Chin introduces *Water Margin* into the novel to highlight the parallels between this legendary band of Chinese outlaws, Robin Hood and his Merry Men, and the iconic heroes and anti-heroes of the American West: cowboys and gun fighters. The source of the Chinese classic is somewhat uncertain, though Shi Nai'an and Luo Guanzhong are generally accepted as its authors. The stories were first translated into English in 1933 by Pearl S. Buck as *All Men Are Brothers* and in 1937 by J.H. Jackson as *Water Margin*. A more recent and more popular version is Sidney Shapiro's 1980 translation *Outlaws of the Marsh*. In 2010 an updated edition of Jackson's translation was published in which Edwin Lowe edited Jackson's translation to retain more of the flavor of the original.
12 See, for example, *John Chinaman On the Railroad*. Retrieved from http://digitalcollections.nypl.org/items/510d47e0-336c-a3d9-e040-e00a18064a99 (Accessed April 2016).

13 http://cprr.org/Museum/Done!.html#Shaking_Hands (Accessed April 2016).
14 http://chintalks.blogspot.com/search?q=railroad (Accessed April 2016).
15 It has been suggested that there were as few as eight Chinese workers at Promontory Point on that day as most had finished their work and had been moved westward "leaving only a few, perhaps a dozen, to do the grading, lay the ties and drive the few spikes of the west rail, lay the east rail for the ceremony, and replace the laurel tie." The same estimate was likely true for the Union Pacific (Irish) workmen, most of whom had already been sent to undertake the eastern points of the line improvement (Bowman 1957). http://cprr.org/Museum/Bowman_Last_Spike_CHS.html (Accessed April 2016).
16 The following was reported in an issue of the *San Francisco Newsletter, California Advertiser* (May 15, 1869, IX: XV), dedicated to the Golden Spike ceremony in the *Transcontinental Railroad Postscript* under the heading HONORS TO JOHN CHINAMAN: "Mr. Strowbridge, when work was all over, invited the Chinamen who had been brought over from Victory for the purpose, to dine in his boarding car. When they entered all the guests and officers present cheered the chosen representatives of the race which have greatly helped to build the road – a tribute they well deserved, and which evidently gave them much pleasure" (ibid.: 4). Just above this section it is reported that "The Chinese really laid the last tie and drove the last spike." http://cprr.org/Museum/Newspapers/SF_Newsletter_1869.html (Accessed April 2016).
17 *Salt Lake Daily Telegraph* "The Pacific R.R. Finished," May 11, 1869.
18 In Brian Castro's *Birds of Passage*, the protagonist Seamus O'Young is an orphan with blue eyes and Chinese features born in nineteenth-century Australia during the Gold Rush of a Chinese 'digger' and an Irish prostitute and raised by an Australian couple. As a grown man in search of his biological identity he remarks, "I believe my real name is Sham Oh Yung, but I am unable to find any records of my past. I am a truly stateless person. When I go to Chinatown I feel at one with the people, but then the strange tones of their language only serve to isolate me" (Castro 1983: 8–9).
19 This nativist image appeared at around the same time that 140,00 Irish-born men were fighting in the US Civil War, the majority on the side of the Democratic pro-slavery south (Spann 1996: 193–209). Of the 58 known Chinese men fighting in the War, only one of whom was US-born, most served for the Union, though at least five are recorded as having fought on the side of the Confederacy (see "Chinese in the Civil War: Ten Who Served," Ruthanne Lum McCunn, 1995. www.mccunn.com/Civil-War.pdf). See also www.voanews.com/content/surprise-asians-fought-in-the-us-civil-war-120282254/163158.html (Accessed April 2016). The oppositional stance many Irish immigrants took regarding abolition, however much the motive was fear of economic competition, indicates a similar paradoxical position with regard to the Black population that many had toward the Chinese. David Roediger has suggested that the mutually expedient relationship that Irish American Catholics entered into with the Democratic Party appealed to Irish Catholics in large part because the party's view of American nationality stressed the relevance of "race," which placed the Irish "safely within an Anglo-Celtic racial majority," resolving the matter of their qualifications for citizenship. He writes, "Under other circumstances, Irish-American Catholics might not have accepted so keenly the 'association of nationality with blood – but not with ethnicity', which racially conflated them with the otherwise hated English" (Roediger 1991: 144).
20 In his book, *Out of Our Minds: Reason and Madness in the Explorations of Central Africa* (2000), Fabian also notes, "there is overwhelming indirect evidence that European travelers seldom met their hosts in a state of what we would expect of scientific explorers: clear minded and self-controlled. More

often than not they too were 'out of their minds' with extreme fatigue, fear, delusions of grandeur, and feelings ranging from anger to contempt. Much of the time they were in the thralls of 'fever' and other tropical diseases, under the influence of opiates ... high doses of quinine, arsenic and other ingredients from the expedition's medicine chest" (Fabian 2000: 3).

21 Since ancient times Hindus have made a yearly pilgrimage to the sacred Amarnath Cave near Baltal, Kashmir, India. According to Hindu legend, this is the cave where the Hindu deity Shiva explained the secret of life and eternity to Maa Parvati, his divine consort. The cave is covered with snow most times of the year except for the summer months when it is possible to view three ice stalagmites, the largest of which is worshiped by Hindus as a symbol of Shiva. The Shiva lingam (the Sanskrit word for 'sign' or 'distinguishing symbol') is the representation of Shiva used for worship in temples, which traditionally takes the form of a cylindrical pillar. The ice Shiva lingam resembles this form as a result of water dripping from the roof of the cave that accumulates and starts to freeze. According to Hindu belief, Shiva lingams can be made from permanent or transitory materials, reflecting the belief that Shiva is beyond the qualities of form and formlessness.

22 According to the writer Louis Werner, "Accurate numbers of the Arabs living on Washington Street are not available, partly because they were registered as 'Syrians' upon arrival but in later census counts were identified as 'Turks'." One estimate was of 300 families in 1890. In 1904, a newspaper estimated a total of 1,300 people. The total number of Arab immigrants admitted to the United States between 1899 and 1907 was 41,404, and 15,000 more arrived in the following three years, though few of the later arrivals ended up in what was known as 'Little Syria'. www.saudiaramcoworld.com/issue/201206/little.syria.ny.htm (Accessed April 2016) (See also Naff 1985: 107–112).

23 This enduring occupation has been explored by Alixa Naff in *Becoming American: The Early Arab Immigrant Experience* (1985). She estimates that an itinerant peddler in 1910 working 200 days a year and earning an average of $5.00 a day would have a yearly income of $1000.00 as compared to earning $233.00 in agricultural work, $651.00 in manufacturing, $657.00 in coal mining and $630.00 in retail sales (Naff 1985: 197–198).

24 Childe, Cromwell, "New York's Syrian Quarter," *The New York Times*, August 20, 1899.

References

Arrington, Leonard J. 1969 "The Transcontinental Railroad and the Development of the West," *Utah Historical Quarterly* 37(1): 3–15.

Bain, David Haward 1999 *Empire Express: Building the Transcontinental Railroad*. New York: Penguin Group.

Blewett, Mary H. 1976 "The Mills and the Multitudes: A Political History," in Arthur L. Eno (ed) *Cotton Was King: A History of Lowell, Massachusetts*. Somersworth, NH: New Hampshire Publishing Co, 161–189.

Blewett, Peter F. 1976 "The New People: An Introduction to the Ethnic History of Lowell," in Arthur L. Eno (ed) *Cotton Was King: A History of Lowell, Massachusetts*. Somersworth, NH: New Hampshire Publishing Co, 190–217.

Bowman, J.N. 1957 "Driving the Last Spike At Promontory," 1869, *California Historical Society Quarterly*, Vol. XXXVI (2): 96–106.

Carleton, William 1830 "The Battle of the Factions," in *Traits and Stories of the Irish Peasantry*. London: George Routledge & Co. www.irishhistorylinks.net/Historical_Documents/Carleton_Factions.html (Accessed April 2016).
Castro, Brian 1983 *Birds of Passage*. St. Leonards, NSW, Australia: Allen & Unwin.
Chin, Frank 1991 *Donald Duk*. Saint Paul, MN: Coffee House Press.
Cowley, Ultan 2001 *The Men Who Built Britain: A History of the Irish Navvy*. Dublin: Wolfhound Press Ltd.
Daniels, Stephen and Denis Cosgrove 1993 "Spectacle and Text: Landscape Metaphors in Cultural Geography," in James Duncan and David Ley (eds) *place/ culture/ representation*. London: Routledge, 57–77.
Dearinger, Ryan 2016 *The Filth of Progress*. Berkeley: University of California Press.
Derrida, Jacques 1994 *Specters of Marx*. Trans. Peggy Kamuf. New York and London: Routledge.
Dolan, Eric Jay 2012 *When America First Met China*. New York: Liveright Publishing Corporation.
Doyle, David Noel 2006 "The Remaking of Irish America, 1845–1880," in J. J. Lee and Marion R. Casey (eds) *Making the Irish Americans*. New York: New York University Press, 213–252.
Fabian, Johannes 2000 *Out of Our Minds: Reason and Madness in the Explorations of Central Africa*. Berkeley: University of California Press.
—— 2001 *Anthropology with an Attitude*. Stanford: Stanford University Press.
Goffman, Erving 1959 *The Presentation of Self in Everyday Life*. New York: Anchor Books.
—— 1983 "The Interaction Order: American Sociological Association, 1982 Presidential Address," American Sociological Review 48(1): 1–17.
Gooneratne, Yasmine 1991 *A Change of Skies*. Victoria: Penguin Books.
Gordon, Avery F. 1997 *Ghostly Matters: Haunting and the Sociological Imagination*. Minneapolis: University of Minnesota Press.
Harb, Sirène 2008 "Orientalism and the Construction of American Identity in Abraham Mitrie Rihbany's 'A Far Journey,'" *MELUS* 33(3): 131–145.
Hassan, Waïl. S. 2011 *Immigrant Narratives*. Oxford: Oxford University Press.
Hodges, Graham 1996 "'Desirable Companions and Lovers': Irish and African-Americans in the Sixth Ward, 1830–1870," in Ronald H. Bayor and Timothy J. Meagher (eds) *The New York Irish*. Baltimore: Johns Hopkins University Press, 107–124.
Ingold, Tim 1997 "The Temporality of the Landscape," *World Archaeology* 25(2): 152–174.
Kenny, Kevin 2006 "Race, Violence, and Anti-Irish Sentiment in the Nineteenth Century," in J.J. Lee and Marion R. Casey (eds) *Making the Irish Americans*. New York: New York University Press, 364–378.
Lee, Erica 2003 *At America's Gates: Chinese Immigration During the Exclusion Era, 1882-1943*. Chapel Hill: University of North Carolina Press.
Lee, J.J. 2006 "Introduction: Interpreting Irish America," in J.J. Lee and Marion R. Casey (eds) *Making the Irish Americans*. New York: New York University Press, 1–61.
Lee, Robert G. 1999 *Orientals: Asian Americans in Popular Culture*. Philadelphia: Temple University Press.
McIvor, Liz 2015 *Canals: The Making of a Nation*. London: BBC Books.

Majaj, Lisa Suhair 2000 "Arab-Americans and the Meaning of Race," in Amritjit Singh and Peter Schmidt (eds) *Postcolonial Theory and the United States: Race, Ethnicity and American Literature*. Jackson: University of Mississippi Press, 320–337.

Miller, Kirby A. 1985 *Emigrants and Exiles: Ireland and the Irish Exodus to North America*. Oxford: Oxford University Press.

Naff, Alixa 1985 *Becoming American: The Early Arab Immigrant Experience*. Carbondale and Edwardsville: Southern Illinois University Press.

Pope, Hugh 1910 "The Origin of the Douay," *The Dublin Review* 147: 97–118.

Rihbany, Abraham Mitrie 1914a "In New York with Nine Cents," *The Atlantic Monthly*, Making of America Project 113: 236–249.

—— 1914b "Out From My Kindred," The Atlantic Monthly, Making of America Project 113: 364–375.

—— 1916. "The Syrian Christ," The Atlantic Monthly, Making of America Project 117: 309–319.

Roediger, David 1991 *The Wages of Whiteness*. New York: Verso Books.

Shakir, Evelyn 1988 "Mother's Milk: Women in Arab-American Autobiography," *MELUS* 15(4): 39–50.

Silverberg, Robert 1968. *The Mound Builders*. Athens, OH: Ohio University Press.

Spann, Edward K. 1996 "Union Green: The Irish Community and the Civil War," in Ronald H. Bayor and Timothy J. Meagher (eds) *The New York Irish*. Baltimore: Johns Hopkins University Press, 193–209.

Tchen, John Kuo Wei 1996 "Quimbo Appo's Fear of Fenians: Chinese-Irish-Anglo Relations in New York City," in Ronald H. Bayor and Timothy J. Meagher (eds) *The New York Irish*. Baltimore: Johns Hopkins University Press, 125–152.

Williams, Williams H.A. 1996 *'Twas Only An Irishman's Dream*. Urbana and Chicago: University of Illinois Press.

Woodham-Smith, Cecil 1962 *The Great Hunger*. New York: Harper and Row.

Woodward, Susan and Jerry N. McDonald 1986. *Indian Mounds of the Middle Ohio Valley*. Newark, OH: The McDonald and Woodward Publishing Company.

Wyse, Francis 1846 *America, its Realities and Resources, Vol. 1*. London: T.C. Newby.

5 Signs of transnationalism from above and below

The previous chapter explored the social and semiotic function of landscapes for migrants involved in mapping a sense of connection and belonging in relation to place. This chapter shifts the focus more specifically to visible signs in public places that indicate or anticipate the presence of individuals from more than one language community. Whether viewed from a distance or in close proximity, these signs create an impression. They elicit some type of immediate response. In certain contexts, the public appearance of multilingual signs unavoidably interrupts prior assumptions of homogeneity, opening them to diverse interpretations or recontextualizations. Public signs have a social and interactional function; they 'signify' beyond the particular groups they reference. And like all signifiers there can be gaps between their intention and their interpretation. In some cases, particularly where there is insufficient understanding of what or whom they represent, their indexical or symbolic functions can easily be obscured.

Languages in translation on view in public settings function as a welcome relief for some; for others they are an unwelcome blemish on a presumed monolingual space. Signs that display (un)recognizable scripts simultaneously carry a message of exclusivity and inclusivity depending on the viewer and the context. The appearance of a translated signpost, billboard, notice on a place of worship or storefront, etc. in a particular language can shift the 'outsider' status from one group to another, reinforce the target group's 'otherness' within a community, and mark that place with reference to its newest inhabitants. In multicultural cities, untranslated signs or signs in multiple languages are as likely to provoke indifference in urban residents or passersby as to stir pride in their diversity, given the multiplicity of visual and aural stimuli they take in on a regular basis.[1]

Translated signs found on official buildings, public transportation, instructions for use, warnings, public address announcements, voicemails, and so on, appear primarily as inter-lingual messages that more or less replicate the same information for a general public. These are the types of translation presented in written form (no smoking/no fumar) or where an option is given to hear information in another language on the telephone as in the phrase commonly heard in the US, "*para continuar en español* [*oprima, marque,* or *diga*] *el dos.*" Many other translated signs are inter-semiotic in kind, sometimes involving written text with an accompanying visual referent, for example, "La Iglesia En El Camino" in front of a building indicating its status as a church. For a native Spanish speaker, this would not be read as a translation, it is a monolingual sign; it is the non-Spanish speaking person for whom some additional information would be required to make sense of it, involving some sort of translation, including the building itself. With inter-semiotic signs like those in Figure 5.1 that appear outside the British Museum in London, a mecca for tourists from across the globe, the assumption is that either the pictorial images or the English texts, "Do not sit on the steps" and "Emergency escape," or both, will be understood. Failing this, of course, the other option available to visitors is simply to 'interpret' the actions of others.

There are certain instances when the need for translation comes to a halt, as when visual signs in another language are incorporated into the local or national lexicon. English, given its current standing as a lingua franca, is most often associated with this phenomenon, but it occurs with other languages as well. For example, many New York City residents will commonly refer to their neighborhood corner grocery store as a bodega where no such sign is posted and where the owner is neither Spanish-speaking nor from a

Figure 5.1 Inter-semiotic signs at the British Museum, London. Photograph: author's own

Spanish-speaking community. Paradoxically, to understand its use as a name for a corner store would require more effort by some so-called native Spanish speakers, especially first-time visitors to New York, than for non-Spanish speaking inhabitants of that city. For many Spanish speakers, for example, the word *bodega* is more commonly understood to refer to a wine cellar or, if encountered on a sign in front of an establishment open in the evening, either a shop selling wine and champagne or a wine bar. A secondary meaning would be the hold of a ship or an airplane where items are stored.

In New York City, the term *bodega* suggests a specific type of place to buy certain things; it requires no translation for most urban residents, only local knowledge. Figures 5.2 and 5.3 are examples of such establishments. Although the signs read, respectively, (in yellow and red) "Villa Fundacion DELI GROCERY CORP.", and (in green and yellow) "Burj Khaleefa Deli" (an apparent ironic reference to the luxury skyscraper in Dubai, now the tallest building in the world), only one of these shop signs, "Villa Fundacion," indicates a Spanish-speaking proprietor probably with links to the town of La Fundación, Dominican Republic, yet both are likely to be called *bodegas* by most residents of New York City.

Jake Dobkin, a New York native, took to his blog[2] to explain the meaning of *bodega* to a reader who asks: "What is the difference between a

Figure 5.2 Villa Fundacion, New York. Photograph by Milica Bogetic and Stephanie Kaplan

152   Signs of transnationalism

Figure 5.3 Burj Khaleefa Deli, New York. Photograph by Milica Bogetic and Stephanie Kaplan

bodega, a deli, and a corner grocer? Are they all different terms for the same thing?"

> Dear Curious:
>
> Some natives might tell you that these are all expressions for what other Americans call "convenience stores," but this is wrong. The words we New Yorkers use to describe our metropolis are freighted with subtle meaning and reflect our city's long and ethnically diverse history. Allow me to explain!
>
> Bodega is the Spanish word for "warehouse." When Spanish-speaking people began arriving in New York in large numbers during the first half of the twentieth century, they brought this word with them to describe small stores selling a variety of items including packaged food, beverages, cigarettes, newspapers, and candy. When prohibition was

repealed, these stores also began stocking beer; some also sold fresh and prepared food like sandwiches, produce, milk, flowers, and eggs.

As the Spanish-speaking population of New York continued to expand, the word bodega began to be used outside Hispanic communities, where it was used interchangeably with other terms, including ones that referred to a store by what it sold ("candy store," "newsstand," "optimo," etc.)

But critically, when a New Yorker hears the word "bodega" he also pictures a specific style of store design. This includes red and yellow awnings ("cold cuts and cold beer"), a variety of window ads, and a small sign advertising the presence of an ATM in back. The stores are usually small and often (but not always) on a corner. Inside we are not surprised to find a resident cat, slightly dusty groceries, and a few neighborhood guys bullshitting about current events. The proprietor is often behind the register, but is no longer always Puerto Rican. In bodegas with Muslim owners, beer is usually not sold, and instead you find a wider selection of non-alcoholic beverages.

Deli is short for "delicatessen", which is a German word (borrowed from France), meaning "delicacies." Originally used to refer to the food itself, it began to be used to describe the stores selling the food. It arrived in New York with the German immigrants after the Civil War, and reached its fullest expression when used by Yiddish-speaking Jews to describe restaurants selling corned-beef and pastrami sandwiches, among other items. These are now referred to by New Yorkers as "Jewish Delicatessens" or "Kosher Delis." Katz's and The 2nd Avenue Deli are prime examples.

As Yiddish and German speaking New Yorkers filtered out of the Lower East Side and into other neighborhoods, the word "deli" also began to be used to describe any place that sold sandwiches or similar grab-and-go foods. If a store consists mainly of a long counter behind which people are making sandwiches, with a beverage case off to the side and possibly a few tables, it will often be called a deli, but if a bodega has a small sandwich counter, and mainly sells groceries, it will usually still be called a bodega. If the deli mainly sells food from a single ethnic tradition, New Yorkers will often refer to it by that designation (the "Mexican place," "The Chinese place") even if you can also get sandwiches there.

This account illustrates the organic means by which lexical signs attached to a particular language and culture can be reconfigured and reintroduced into a different space over time to become part of a new local lexicon and culture. Words like these that enter a lexicon enrich an existing set of possible signs by adding variation, eclipsing those already established, or adding new ones. The new meanings that emerge are uncoupled from a previously established sign/meaning through repeated encounters with new groups of individuals in new contexts, making its translation no longer necessary, as it becomes reimagined and absorbed into their daily life in similar enough ways. These are not merely loan words, which signify borrowing, nor does it imply, in the case of bodega, that a Spanish concept has become 'assimilated' into the English lexicon in the pejorative sense of this term. What is most significant is not the words themselves, but the micro-processes by which they come to possess new referents by their use by a specific community of users. In both smaller and larger global spaces – official policies notwithstanding – contact among diverse linguistic and cultural practices and the communities with which they are associated tends to occur over time and to varying degrees as firm boundary lines are gradually perceived as open border crossings for any number of reasons. Though in cases of heightened animosity or physical conflict this can become a volatile space, many if not most multicultural spaces involve frequent enough exchange and encounters among their inhabitants to ensure that a certain mutual assimilation of interests is attempted and achieved.

Two decades of sociolinguistic research on the semiotics of public multilingual signage has advanced the notion of the "linguistic landscape" first introduced by Landry and Bourhis (1997) as a site in which to explore questions concerning language variety, ethnic identity, and mobility, particularly in cities characterized by their 'superdiversity,' with a particular interest in assessing the relative power and status of a particular linguistic community in a given, usually urban, setting. The notion has spawned a rich and varied investigative field of research in which a number of sociolinguistic phenomena are addressed, resulting in an impressive body of literature.[3] Though the specific focus of each study varies, most share the view that visible multilingual signs in public places reveal something about the organization of social relationships among members of a society and also serve as significant markers of ethnic and linguistic identity.

Though much of the research on linguistic landscapes has focused on major urban centers, multilingual taskscapes are of course a feature of remote and rural areas as well. Moreover, they are not limited to communities with a migrant presence, but are also common wherever a minority–majority language dynamic has been established as a consequence of history, migration, and/or conflict – the continent of Africa for example. In both types of communities, the translation of particular signs can indicate the degree to which the use of more than one language is perceived as a priority or even a right, as well as the expected or assumed levels of competency regarding the languages in use within that community. The languages that are selected for translation, and the overall quality of the materials or the translations themselves, can underscore the real or perceived relative power or significance of one language or one group over another. Alternatively, the refusal to translate a sign can, though not always, signal a preference for greater insularity, a way of intentionally marking the borders of a community.

Signs of transnationalism 155

The research on linguistic landscapes takes these signs as examples of multilingual writing or multilingualism, which differentiates it somewhat from the approach taken here where multilingual signage, as well as the same signs in different languages, are examined and discussed as instances of translation in all its forms. Viewing such signs primarily as examples of multilingualism tends to accentuate the *juxtaposition* of different languages and cultures, presenting them as separate and, in some cases, not so equal material artifacts situated in the landscape. Understanding them as examples of translation, in contrast, gives greater prominence to their *relational* aspects and to the interpretive processes involved in reading these signs, highlighting their intrinsic *dialogism*. By translation, I am not referring to the task of interpreting their cultural or linguistic meanings, though this is a part of the process. I refer to the more complex task of comprehending the dynamic between the signs given and signs given off through a combination of intellectual and instinctive behavior – a task that activates reflexive responses within a particular environment by assorted individuals or groups, some of whom may even reside outside its presumed boundaries. In other words, there is a presumption of a dialogue between signs and their producers, their multiple viewers, and the settings where individuals come together – sometimes from a distance, sometimes not – to engage in the quotidian activities of social life.

What I have in mind here is elegantly illustrated in the intensive intellectual and aesthetic exchange of over one thousand letters beginning in March 1950 between the poets Charles Olson and Robert Creeley, during which both also moved several times, writing from different landscapes within and outside the United States. Olson moved from Washington to Yucatan, to Black Mountain College in North Carolina, and Creeley from New Hampshire to southern France, to Mallorca, and eventually to New Mexico (Butterick 1980: xiv–xv). The two corresponded for four years, knowing very little about each other until meeting in person in 1954 when Creeley arrived to teach at Black Mountain College.

Olson named Creeley the "Figure of Outward" in dedicating his first volume of *The Maximus Poems* (1960) and referred to Creeley once again in this way in this note to himself toward the end of his life (ibid.: ix).

> the Figure of Outward means way out way out
> *there*: the
> 'World,' I'm sure, otherwise
> why was the pt. then to like write to Creeley
> daily? to make that whole thing
> double, to
> objectify the extension of an
> 'outward'? a[n] opposite to a
> personality which so completely does (did)
> stay at home?

156 *Signs of transnationalism*

In his editor's introduction to the first volume of *Charles Olson & Robert Creeley: The Complete Correspondence*, George Butterick writes (ibid.: xi):

> Each man allowed the other his head, took what came, and found of interest (or at least discussible) each other's preoccupations. Sometimes a dialogue ensued, other times one generously allowed himself to be used as a sounding board for the other's necessities. Together they hammered out a poetics – both the specialized craft of the wordsmith, but also the larger issue of how a man of language must live in the world.

For Olson, in his retrospective reflection on their correspondence, the dialogue was two-faceted, but crucially also one that opened onto the world – prospectively onto new terrain, both aesthetic and material.

In the dialogues that are instigated by more public forms of communication, an opening on to the world is also offered. Minimally, public signs can trigger a fleeting awareness of a community's diversity, creating an opportunity for some type of recognition, if not inclusion, between its members to occur. Maximally, they precipitate an enhanced mindfulness of one another, providing a means toward the (re)consideration of prior understandings and the implementation of new ones. These contexts allow us see how different forms of language are focused dialogically on an 'I' and an 'us' who simultaneously constitute one another's "out *there*." They are thus integral to the interaction order, and an important component of its evolution.

The taskscapes of Koreatown, LA

Koreatown is one of Los Angeles' largest districts; its current population numbers about 130,000, the majority of whom are relatively recent migrants who began to settle in the area in the mid-1960s. Though English is the official language of the state, most of the residents of Koreatown regularly use additional languages in everyday discourse. Despite its name, Koreatown is currently home to a multiplicity of ethnic groups, the largest of whom are Latin Americans who make up around 58 percent of its population, and the majority of these are Mexican. Korean Americans make up only about 22 percent, while the rest include relatively small numbers of Asians (including a growing Bangladeshi community who currently make up 9 percent of the total population) and Pacific Islanders, White, African American, and other Black inhabitants.

Koreans were among the first migrants to settle there after 1965 when new US immigration legislation phased out the national origins quota system in favor of family reunification. The majority of these immigrants came not directly from Korea, but via Germany and Brazil. In 1992, Koreatown found itself at the center of violent conflicts that would leave an enduring mark on the respective communities living there. Over half of the businesses in Koreatown were burned and looted during the Los Angeles riots (known as *Sa-I-Gu* in Korean, which translates as April 29) in response to the brutal beating of an African American man, Rodney King, and the subsequent acquittal of the four policemen responsible. This precipitated a Korean American exodus out of the city and into the suburbs, leaving room for Latin American families to move in due to its proximity to public transportation and the sudden availability of low rent apartments (Eui-Young et al 2004: 31). However, Koreatown still represents the largest concentration of Koreans outside of Korea (Sanchez et al 2012: 4).[4]

Despite the relatively small numbers of Korean Americans in relation to Mexicans, Central and South Americans, Koreatown's commercial areas are awash with Korean signs on small businesses, which sometimes appear alongside signs in English and increasingly in Spanish. In some cases, Korean, English, and Spanish appear together on one sign or on signs in close proximity. The majority of Korean American small-business owners in Koreatown are first and second-generation immigrants who arrived in the second half of the twentieth century.[5] Their shop signs – which are exemplified below – tend to reflect their lower socioeconomic status relative to more recent immigrant-owned businesses and the increasing number of enterprises in this district that are heavily financed by overseas Korean transnational capital; to a more recent Korean visitor, they are reminiscent of pre-1990s street signs in Korea. The majority in this block also represent the colors of the Korean flag, red and blue. In the following commentary on these signs, the intended purpose behind any of the decisions taken in the creation of these particular signs is unknown. I nevertheless consider a number of likely possibilities given the context.

Figure 5.4 is a sign for a tire and auto mechanic shop that brings these three languages together on one sign; the information provided is similar though not exactly the same. The name of the establishment **SMOG**, written in white against a light blue background, is untranslated, followed by the Spanish **LLANTAS** [TIRES] and next to that the Korean words 모든 [ALL] 타이어 [TIRES] 취급 [CARRY/DEAL IN]. A close translation would be "we carry all tires," with "types and sizes" being implied. This is followed by the Spanish **NUEVAS Y USADAS** (NEW AND USED). The next phrase repeats this information in English **NEW AND USED TIRE** (with tire in the singular) followed by **COMPLETE AUTO REPAIR,** which is translated only into Korean 함 [GENERAL/COMPREHENSIVE] 정비 [REPAIR/FIX] 센터 [CENTER/PLACE]. A close translation would be "general repair center," with "car" implied. The vertical signs below the sign provide the additional information **CATALYTIC MUFFLER** in English only.

In this example, though SMOG is not translated, given its reference to LA's characteristic haze of polluted air, the term would be familiar to its residents. Although **COMPLETE AUTO REPAIR** is not translated into

158 *Signs of transnationalism*

Figure 5.4 Smog, Koreatown, Los Angeles. Photograph by Roger Hewitt

Spanish, the English cognates make this intelligible for a Spanish speaker. And although the Korean description of tires is less specific than in either the Spanish or English version, the references to "all tires" suggests that both types are likely to be available.

Figure 5.5 is a typical scene observed across Koreatown's major streets: these particular signs go along Western Ave., a main thoroughfare which runs north to south. From right to left the writing on the vertical signs read as follows: (1) Korean in blue on the top half 한미병원 [*Hanmi Medical Clinic*] and in red on the bottom half 수퍼약국 [*Super Pharmacy*] with the words **SUPER MARKET** written in English vertically on the bottom half to the left and the word **PHARMACY** to the right both in blue; (2) Korean in blue 동양 [*East/Orient*] 건재 [*Herbal Medicine*] 한의원 [*Oriental Medical Clinic*] with English at the bottom **ORIENTAL HERBS ACUPUNCTURE** in red; (3) English only "Party Divine" in light blue and black; (4) Korean in blue 라이프 의료기구 [*Life Medical Equipment*] with English at the top **LIFE MEDICAL SUPPLY** in red and Spanish at the bottom **SE HABLA ESPANOL** – no tilde, in red. The four lines of text that appear in Korean over the Spanish words read 건강식품 [*Health Foods*], 건강서적 [*Health Books*], 운동기구 [*Exercise Equipment*], and 미용재료 [*Beauty Supply*], in blue; and finally (5) Spanish-only in red and blue, **MATERIAL DE LIMPIEZA PAPEL QUÍMICOS BOLSAS, ETC.** [*Cleaning Material, Paper, Chemicals, Bags, etc.*] **SE HABLA ESPAÑOL**

Signs of transnationalism 159

Figure 5.5 Streetview, Koreatown, Los Angeles. Photograph by Roger Hewitt

[*Spanish Spoken*] **MAQUINARIA VENTA REPARACIÓN RENTA** [*Machines (for) Sale Repair Rent*] in red and blue. A horizontal sign below in English reads **IDEAL MAINT EQUIP. INC.** in red, and underneath **SALES•REPAIR•RENTAL** in blue and red.

The horizontal sign to the far right has Korean writing on the top 해피 북 서점 and "Happy Book Store" in English on the front of the green awning, both in white. There is an additional sign in Korean only 약전 녹용 • 동방 침구 [*Medicinal Antlers • Eastern Acupuncture*] in red on a light green painted storefront right before "Party Divine." All the other horizontal signs to the left of the bookstore correspond to the Korean in the signs above, repeating all the informational words: **SUPER MARKET** and **PHARMACY** in English in blue and the additional information **HANMI MEDICAL CENTER** in white. The name Hanmi is formed by the combination of two Korean words meaning Korean American.

At first appearance, some of the signs in this block of Western Ave. function differently from the one sign/multilingual approach – two of them, one in English, one in Korean. Why this is the case is unclear, yet it should not be read as an indication that these businesses do not seek to reach out to more than their own communities. The "Party Divine" website's publicity statement, for example, specifically mentions both "quinceaneras," the Latin American tradition of celebrating fifteen-year-old girls' birthdays

160 *Signs of transnationalism*

Figure 5.6 Life Medical Supply, Koreatown, Los Angeles. Photograph by Roger Hewitt

and "dohl," a reference to the tradition of celebrating Korean babies' first birthdays with lavish parties.

> What's a birthday celebration without balloons? Are you celebrating a sweet sixteen, bar/ bat mitzvah or quinceanera? Create the most amazing décor for your milestone with balloons from Party Divine. A necessity for dohl Korean first birthdays, balloons will set the tone of your event.[6]

It is also significant that in Figure 5.6, which is the front view of sign (5) described above, another mention about Spanish being spoken in this establishment appears in larger letters in blue **SE HABLA ESPAÑOL** – with tilde. Taken together with the visible window displays, at least some of the additional information regarding the products available that appears only in written Korean or English becomes accessible to a Spanish speaker.

In contrast, the sign in Figure 5.7 marks its relation to a specific language and culture in a more pronounced way. The restaurant on the corner displays its name in Korean script written in bold black characters. The name 제부도 **JAE BU DO** refers to an island on the west coast of Korea – frequented by Koreans from the capital Seoul which is about two hours away – that is known for its clams and eels. Additional information is given only in Korean as well. To the left of the restaurant's name in red is written

Signs of transnationalism 161

Figure 5.7 Jae Bu Do, Koreatown, Los Angeles. Photograph by Roger Hewitt

숯불 [*Charcoal Fire*], and to the right, in fine characters, "live" is written in Chinese characters[7] 生 along with more detail about the menu: 조개구이 [*Clam Roast*], 바다장어 [*Sea Eels*], and 꼼장어 [*Conger Eels*]. To the far right in bolder characters the word 전문 "specialty" is added. There are, however, at least three pieces of information provided not in Korean: One in English **WE ARE OPEN** and the other two through visual imagery, one of a crab that lights up at night and the other of photos of clams in the front windows. The visual signs that are not in Korean can be read as an indication that the restaurant specializes in seafood and that you needn't be (or read or speak) Korean to feel welcome. The signs in Korean only, as well as the references to places and dishes more likely to be recognized by the Korean American population, can be read as an indicator of the presence of something especially Korean in their Los Angeles community.

The signs above are situated adjacent to one another on Western Ave.; the actual businesses referred to are located just to the left of the signs in Figure 5.8. The sign at the top advertises in bold black lettering the name of a business in Korean only, 사 랑 의 [*Love's*] 한의원 [*Oriental Medical Clinic*]. In the accompanying English text, however, the two main services provided by the clinic are conveyed – **SLIM DIET CLINIC** and **PAIN CARE CLINIC**. Below these, across the bottom of the sign also in English, is a list of the specific treatments available – Acupuncture, Herbal Rx, Body Wrap, Detox, Skin Care, Massage. The photo of the torso of a young

Figure 5.8 Multimodal signs, Koreatown, Los Angeles. Photograph by Roger Hewitt

Figure 5.9 Multimodal signs, Koreatown, Los Angeles. Photograph by Roger Hewitt

woman measuring her waist illustrates the weight loss objective suggested in the words 'slim' and 'diet'. To the right of this, the sign in Figure 5.9 advertises the same clinic in English and Korean only. The words **Slim Diet Clinic** are repeated in a different font with the name of the clinic directly underneath, once again written only in Korean, but with the English word "Acupuncture" added. Like the other signs examined, the decisions about what information to provide and in what language seems to presume some knowledge about the communities targeted. For example, it is most likely taken for granted that the clinic's name itself would indicate to a Korean viewer the services and treatments available. Thus the detail is given in English only. The relevance of the similarities of the English and Spanish words is less clear in this case (only some are cognates) in understanding why there is no Spanish information provided.

Of the three signs in which Spanish does appear, no Korean is included. The large green and yellow sign on the left for the well-known money transfer kiosk business NEXXO is repeated in a smaller version on the right. Neither of these signs translates **ENVIOS DE DINERO** into English [*Money Transfers*], though **PAGO DE CUENTAS** is translated as **BILL PAY** in the larger of the two. A second sign in Spanish, **TRANSPORTES "Mi Gente,"** includes the words **CARGO EXPRESS**, a common general reference found in many companies in the business of courier or delivery services. The third sign in Spanish, **ESCUELA DE TRAFICO** (with the accent in *tráfico* omitted) appears together with the words **ROYAL'S EN ESPAÑOL**, signaling its relationship to the sign directly above for "Royal's Driving School." (This same wording appears in front of the actual business located just yards away.) The most interesting of these three examples is the last one where the additional signage provided in Spanish, **ESCUELA DE TRAFICO,** refers to a very specific service of the driving school: the traffic schools that are available to individuals who have received one or more traffic tickets and want them dismissed to be eligible for a discount on car insurance or to avoid having points added to their driving record.

Taken together, it seems clear that in all of these businesses the sign owners or producers adopt a strategic pragmatic approach to the presentation and translation of the information on the signs based on their sense of what counts as relevant to a particular audience and of how to target certain audiences with specific information. This requires an explicit awareness of the different cultures and languages in use within this community and beyond. It also suggests both prior knowledge and experience on the part of the business owners or managers that are used to assess which languages and forms of language to prioritize (e.g. written or pictorial). The fact that different languages are often used in tandem suggests that all the language users involved – buyers, sellers, and passersby – recognize and accept as the norm that some negotiation about the meaning of the signs may be required to benefit from the products and services being offered and to gain maximal visibility for the product(s) advertised.

At the same time, some signs appear to be designed explicitly to operate more at the symbolic level. In his 2009 study of Korean signage in Oakland, California, an ethnically and linguistically diverse area that is home to the largest Korean community in the San Francisco Bay area, David Malinowski interviewed twelve small business owners about the relationship between the Korean and English languages displayed on their shop signs. Although more than half of the shop owners reported that they had played little or no role in their sign design, either because they had inherited the business and made no changes to the sign or had left most of the decisions to a local sign company, over half of those interviewed claimed that the reason for the appearance of English on a sign was "the self-evident fact that 'This is America.'" (Malinowski 2009: 114). They also gave varied reasons for the Korean that appeared, including the acknowledgement of its symbolic function. In an interview with the owner of a gift shop called Boa Gifts, for example, the author asks why, given that other local Japanese and Thai businesses only wrote their names in English, she had used Korean on her sign including the name Boa, which can be read in Korean 보 (bo) and 아 (a) as "to look." At first the owner's sister interjects, "Didn't you write it, the Korean, for people like, like the old folks around here who can't read English?" to which the owner replies, "Noo... Korean is... you know, even for the people who can speak English really well, if you put Korean up in the sign, they feel a close connection with the shop right away, since there's Korean. [...] When you're in America, and you're passing by and you see Korean right there, you think, 'Oh, there's some Korean.' You already feel some connection with the place" (ibid.).

"Seeing Korean" is understood here to have an important (symbolic) meta-function; the translation work it performs is not primarily informational, as the sister suggests. The sign serves as an important means toward self-recognition in a still unfamiliar space; it is mostly about translating oneself into place. In the same conversation with the author, the shop owner uses an analogy to help him understand what she means. She says, "like if you're in Korea, right, and you pass by someone on the street who's from America, who speaks English well, and their face looks just like someone from America, do you feel some connection, or not? When you're in a foreign country?" (ibid.).

Not everyone shared this shop owner's sentiment, however. The owner of a Korean grocery store interviewed in Malinowski's research had this to say about the significance of the Korean language both inside and outside his store:

> So the owner is Korean and it's a Korean market but, like I said before, like with the idea of being "international," this is in America, where the Korean community is together with the American community, I don't think it's right to talk about it as if it's all about being Korean-this or Korean-that.
>
> (ibid.: 123)

Ultimately, how any viewer will translate a particular sign is not so easy to predict where signs given and signs given off are in play. For example, the shop owner of Boa Gifts reported that she was repeatedly asked by Korean-speaking potential customers if she sold merchandise associated with the internationally successful Korean singer Kwon Bo Ah, known as the queen of Korean pop, whose stage name is BoA (ibid.: 117).

Buenos días – Ahn-nyung-hah-seh-yo – *Good morning*

In LA's Koreatown, many if not most of the local businesses draw their employees and customers from the multi-ethnic local resident population, as well as the surrounding areas. The relationship is such that some Korean business owners, in addition to English, are learning Spanish – and many Latino workers are learning Korean in addition to English. Though English remains the official language of state and local governance[8] and education, it is often the second or third language of choice for immigrants in their daily lives. In 2007, Miriam Jordan reported on the emergent Spanish–Korean language pairing in the *Wall Street Journal*:

> At the Galleria, a large Korean supermarket here, store manager Yoonah Yoon greets Hispanic cashiers and bag boys each morning with a hearty 'buenos dias' – 'good morning' in Spanish. The Latino workers, who make up more than half the store's 162 employees, answer him with the equivalent greeting in Korean: 'Ahn-nyung-hah-seh-yo.'[9]

Many of these Korean American businesses don't necessarily require English language skills to run them, and their owners want to be able to communicate with their Spanish-speaking employees, who in turn pick up Korean on the job. The growing demand for Spanish has prompted Korean churches, community centers, and language schools to offer inexpensive classes for beginner and more advanced speakers. In addition to employing Latin Americans, their economic potential as consumers is also recognized. In addition to including the notice "se habla español," some business owners have created ties with this community by giving stores, bars, and restaurants distinctively Spanish language names, and by gearing them toward the needs of the Latino community. Adopting more of a fusion approach, the highly popular enterprise Kogi Korean BBQ, whose menu was created by the celebrated Korean American chef Roy Choi, innovatively combines Korean and Mexican cuisine to create dishes such as Korean tacos, bulgogi (marinated beef) burritos, and kimchi (fermented chili peppers and vegetables) quesadillas. Born in Seoul but raised in LA and southern California since the age of one, the food Choi creates, he suggests, has "evolved into a socio-cultural thing for me, my vision of L.A. in one bite." Choi is also considered one of the founders of the food truck movement. Using internet technology, especially Twitter, to provide information about its menu and locations, Kogi operates as a fleet of five mobile food trucks that effectively become mobile signs of the population diversity within the city.[10] (In 2016 Kogi debuted its first brick and mortar location in Palms, an area considered one of the most diverse neighborhoods in Los Angeles.)

The upside downside of transnationalism

In an article in *LA Weekly* in 2012, "60 Korean Dishes Every Angeleno Should Know," the well-known LA food critic Jonathan Gold described Koreatown as "functionally a distant district of Seoul – in capital as well as in culture, in both commerce and cuisine," due to the numbers of spas, nightclubs, karaoke bars, and restaurants that attract local and increasingly city-wide Los Angeles residents. One of the sixty dishes singled out for praise is the aforementioned barbecued clams at Jeh Bu Do. Another is the "Grand Prix pizza" from Mr. Pizza Factory, a popular Seoul-based chain that opened there in 1990. Koreatown's, which Gold writes about with his usual enthusiasm, was the first in the United States in 2008.

> Have you ever seen the Grand Prix pizza at The Pizza Factory? Because even in a culinary crossroads such as Los Angeles, the Grand Prix is a remarkable object. This weighty, doughy construction, swirled like a creamy hypnodisc, so completely warps perceptions of what a pizza might be that it threatens to dent the space-time continuum itself.[11]

The mix of Seoul-based chains and smaller local establishments included in the list not only highlights Koreatown's burgeoning reputation for multi-ethnic culinary and cultural cool, it is the type of transnational investment that is designed to underscore the ties between Seoul and Koreatown. The influx of such intra-ethnic capital into the United States has had as much of an impact on the residents of Koreatown as the inter-ethnic ties that developed within their community in the same period. But while much has been made since then of the favorable cultural and economic impact of increased ties between migrants and their countries of origin, along with an assumed ease of mobility, declaring the positive effects of transnationalism on migrants has come at the expense of more careful attention to the real or potential negative consequences, particularly for the socioeconomically poor and less well-off within these communities. In general, the widespread emphasis on the politics of identity over the past several decades has failed to sufficiently acknowledge or address the politics of social class and of class culture, and the question of differential access to the benefits of transnational economics for members of the same ethnic group.

In her multimedia dissertation project on Koreatown, Kristy Kang (2013) reports on how members of the working-class community of Koreatown "struggle with the very real possibility of forced mobility, of displacement due to transnational real estate investment and the subsequent change in housing affordability in their neighborhood" (ibid.: 7). She adds that:

> [f]or middle class and wealthy Koreans, Koreatown is a consumer space, replicating the kinds of spas, coffee houses, clubs, and restaurants that one would find in Seoul. These spaces and the people they attract are largely segregated from the daily practices of other Koreatown residents who are part of the working-class poor.
>
> (ibid.: 24)

Sociologist and professor emeritus Eui-Young Yu, interviewed for Kang's study, expresses his concern about the degree of control that South Korean politics and capital have over the local economy and culture of Koreatown, through policies that, as presently constituted, are neither particularly beneficial nor mindful of the issues that Korean Americans face in relation to other ethnic minority groups within Koreatown and the wider LA community. Eui-Young also points to South Korea's disproportionate influence over the circulation of Korean media (print, television, and radio) in this community and over the local Korean political leadership which, he suggests, is largely controlled by the South Korea Consulate in Los Angeles.[12]

Kyonghwan Park discusses this same trend as an attempt by the Korean government to "reterritorialize[s] its 'deterritorialized' national territory beyond its geographic, physical limits." (2009: 158). He points to the Overseas Koreans Foundation (OKF) (ibid.: 155), which was set up by the South Korean government after the 1997 financial crisis for the purpose of attracting and facilitating the influx of overseas Korean capital into the national economy. An additional component of what he calls the "transnational nation-state apparatus" (ibid.: 146) is the cultural exchanges between and within Korean diasporic communities organized by the Education Department and the Cultural Affairs Department, among others. Although these programs claim to be for the purpose of "help[ing]" overseas Korean communities, second-generation Korean immigrants, and adopted Koreans by providing a variety of opportunities to learn the Korean language and traditions, Park suggests their actual motive is to "discursively produce Korean subjects, create national imaginations, and ethnic solidarity" (ibid.: 155) in order to ensure their interest in and commitment to the economic well-being of the "motherland."

In an earlier paper, Youngmin Lee and Kyonghwan Park (2008) discuss how this intersection of the economic and the cultural has worked in practice against many working-class Korean Americans who live and work in Koreatown. Rather than creating a united *intra-ethnic* transnational utopia of the kind envisioned by the cultural wing of the OKF, the authors note a number of significant changes that have taken place in Koreatown since the 1990s that has made it "more fragmented, internally heterogeneous, and complicated in terms of investment, Korean and Latino transmigrants, and economic growth" (ibid.: 251). One resident cited in the article who received her permanent residency after years of living undocumented gives voice to these changes.

> Immigrants coming before the 80s had a really hard time, but their situation was widely shared within the Korean community where most were poor and similarly working hard in sewing and garment factories, small restaurants, small business shops, etc. But now, new immigrants called the Well-Off, who are really strange to me, are coming into Koreatown... the IMF crisis caused some wealthy Korean people to move here and enjoy the good life as soon as they arrived. The IMF crisis also pushed totally ruined Koreans to here. [Because of being undocumented] the best places they could work, live, and hide in the United States is this K-town. So, some legally fly here with lots of money, while others run away from Korea to illegally cross into the United States. All these Koreans flock together and meet right here in K-town.
>
> (ibid.: 254)

The situation "Mrs. L" describes seems to have done very little in the way of creating "ethnic solidarity" within the community. On the contrary, it has contributed to the current economic pyramid that Lee and Park use to characterize Koreatown's social structure – with transnational and local investors, property owners, developers, local politicians, and large business owners at the top, followed by the smaller retail business owners who due to supply and demand are forced to pay above-market price for their rents (ibid.: 252). On the bottom two tiers, they situate the Koreans and Latinos – some undocumented – who are employed by Korean-owned small businesses. Latinos, who according to the authors form the backbone of the local economy (ibid.: 259), are placed at the very bottom given the physical, hazardous type of work they tend to do.

The workplace in Koreatown, however, has consistently been an important site where inter-ethnic solidarity has developed around the shared issue of workers' rights. The Koreatown Immigrant Workers Alliance or KIWA was formed in 1992 by 1.5 and second-generation Korean Americans and was originally called the Korean Immigrant Workers Advocates. It has grown into a multi-ethnic immigrant worker civil rights organization operated by Korean Americans, with a growing Latin American membership. Though the word *Mac-Jaak*, a negative and derogatory stereotype to refer to Latinos, is still used by some Koreans, according to Mr. Y, a Korean undocumented worker, working together has created more opportunities for the two communities to interact and develop mutual respect.

> I work at a Korean-owned hotel. My partner is a Mac-Jaak. When I first came here, I looked at them contemptuously as did other Koreans

who call them Mac-Jaak, not Latinos. I don't know the exact meaning of the word, but that's what they're called. I know it is used as a contemptuous expression to Latinos as a group. Working with them, however, I feel they work hard. They hold two jobs to support their large families. My partner has been working and living like that for 13 years with the hotel... The hotel bosses cannot help but to employ this guy because they won't be able to find another competent worker who would accept such small payment.

(ibid.: 256)

Since the earliest period of their migration to the United States, Korean Americans, like many migrants before them, have treated their first arrival point, in this case, Koreatown, as a place to settle temporarily as first and second-generation migrants before moving further out of the city, into the suburbs, or to other parts of California. What makes contemporary Korean migration different is that very few of the more well-off migrants ever live in Koreatown. They are often advised in South Korea against obtaining housing there, though they are encouraged to invest in businesses given its location (ibid.: 254). Although it is the case that those who do invest in Koreatown provide jobs for many of the residents, these are mostly unskilled jobs that do not pay the workers enough to advance economically. If they move out of Koreatown it is due to gentrification, unlike the voluntary exodus available to previous generations. This works against the creation of a community in which something is or appears to be "widely shared." When the owner of Boa wondered in her interview – "If you pass by someone on the street in Korea who's from America, who speaks English well, and their face looks just like someone from America, do you feel some connection, or not? When you're in a foreign country?," she clearly expected the response she was given – "Yes, sure." In the streets of Koreatown, transnationalism from above is making the answer to her question far less certain for the Koreans and Korean Americans who live there.

Yuhaksaeng *and* iminja *in Toronto, Canada*

Affluent Koreans do not just invest in properties, there is also a widespread practice of wealthy Koreans taking their children to English-speaking countries (often the mothers and children only) to live, learn English, and invest in their pre-college education. Hyunjung Shin has studied the encounters between some of these Korean visa students (*yuhaksaeng*) and 1.5 and second-generation Korean Canadians (*iminja*) in the city of Toronto (Shin 2012). Specifically, she examined how language and culture are used as "stylistic resources" by the Korean *yuhaksaeng* who are there on pre-college-age study-abroad programs (*jogi yuhak*) to assert a global cosmopolitan 'cool,' with varying results. Shin found that the young students attempt this together with their families in a number of ways, often involving conspicuous consumption, "investing in activities such as shopping, golfing, skiing, horse-back riding; and receiving private tutoring," using Korean internet slang that includes codeswitching into English, distancing themselves from Toronto's Koreatown where the older and poorer immigrants tend to reside, and by generalizing Korean Canadians as "uneducated, culturally unsophisticated, and lacking in taste." The response from the Korean Canadians *iminja*, according to Shin, is to view *jogi yuhak* students as "FOBs" (Fresh Off the Boats) who fail to adapt to local culture and society and speak 'poor' English (ibid.: 189).

Shin interprets the *yuhaksaeng* wish to distinguish themselves by foregrounding the wealthy, modern, and cosmopolitan aspects of Korean language and culture as a defensive response to other negative experiences as transnational migrants. In Canada, she suggests, it is one way of countering the FOB image and forms of racialized discourse such as 'Asian Nerd' imposed on them from the local population, including the established Korean immigrant community. However, she also notes the irony in the fact that their attempts at "indexing globality through cool registers of Korean" (ibid.: 185) do not necessarily meet with much success, particularly among the members of the local population who do not recognize them as the prestigious forms of cultural or linguistic capital that they are. In the following exchange two visiting students, the sisters Su-bin and Yu-ri compare their experience with wealthy Thai *yuhaksaeng* students in New Zealand with first and second-generation Korean Canadians in this regard. The researcher begins the interview asking the girls why they mostly hung out with *yuhaksaeng*.[13]

RESEARCHER: Is it because it's different when you interact with *iminja* friends and *yuhaksaeng* friends?
SU-BIN: Among *iminja* (.) well (.) not everyone, but I feel different from some of them.
RESEARCHER: What's the difference?
SU-BIN: Um (...) just (.) I don't know (.) something is different (*small laugh*). There is something invisible [...] For example, some *iminja* have lived here for a very long time you know, and they don't understand when we say "Oh, I really want to go to Korea." [...] It's like this. When I first went on *yuhak* I felt *iminja* were a bit *dabdab* [old-fashioned] and I didn't like them [...]
RESEARCHER: What do you mean by *dabdab*?
SU-BIN: [...] for example, like language, when we talk, they don't know things like [youth] slang [*eun-eo*] or they are not trendy [*seryeondoiji anheun*]. I feel they are not up to date [...] I don't remember any specific examples, but you know, when we talk about [Korean television] programs or Korean issues, there are kids who ask "what's that?"
YU-RI: [In my school in New Zealand], there were a lot of foreign students. One of the students from Thailand told me that the Thai students

who went there were all REALLY rich [...] Boy, those students from Thailand really wanted to look like Korean kids. If I told them, "hey, you look Korean", they really liked it. And they really went all out to imitate Korean students!

RESEARCHER: You mean stuff like clothing?

YU-RI: That's right, and hairstyle. If Korean students dyed their hair, they all copied them [...] (*smiling*) I benefited a lot from *hallyu*. If I said for example "*iri wa*" (come here), they would understand it! And they kept asking me about stuff like Korean television programs I had never even heard of.[14]

(ibid.: 190–191)

The girls' comments indicate another potential paradox of one of the assumed benefits of transnationalism: a borderless inter-connectivity among communities of the same ethnicity. In the privileged arena of pre-college study-abroad programs, it is the wealthy Thai students who understand the cosmopolitan cool status of *hallyu* and the Korean aesthetics that go with it, and who value the Korean girls as style setters: people that they want to look like. In contrast, their co-ethnic Korean Canadians who are unexposed to or uninterested in accessing the trendy and prestigious cultural capital of their families' country of origin are considered old-fashioned (*dabdab*). The *yuhaksaeng* girls see this as especially true of the "*iminja* [who] have lived here for a very long time," second-generation Korean Canadians whose families left a rather different Korea behind. This is not of course a new phenomenon. Historically it has often been the case that more fractures than connections begin to appear between generations (of the same or different ages) due to differences in status, wealth, opportunity, and as a result of personal and cultural changes that occur over time. The impact of migration on intra-ethnic relations may not be quite as different as is often assumed; the virtual nature of modern connectivity may simply do more to mask the fissures.

Programs like *jogi yuhak*, however, bring intra-cultural gaps and incompatibilities to the attention of members of diasporic communities as they play themselves out in local settings. Although Shin does not share any data from the point of view of the *iminja*, she does report that the *yuhaksaeng* felt ignored by the White students and Korean Canadians whom they complained did not invite them into their social circles. As an example of this, she relates a story Yu-ri told the researchers about wanting to run for president of the Korean club "as she believed it would look good on her college admission applications" but decided to give up the idea because the current president, a Korean Canadian, wanted to remain in that position (ibid.: 190). Although it is difficult to know precisely how this particular situation unfolded, taken at face value, it does seem to be an odd example of an intrinsically exclusionary practice. Given the stated animosity between the two groups, the apparent disparity in their class status, and the mainly opportunistic reasons Yu-ri states for wanting to serve as president of the club, it is possible to interpret the matter as a conflict between a student who had a vested interest in local school politics and one more concerned with global educational currency. This emphasis on different forms of symbolic capital gives rise to an additional paradox, however. For many of the *yuhaksaeng*, the sought-after linguistic capital of English was not necessarily achieved as "both spoke little English at school, did not participate in class discussions, and interacted minimally with school teachers or 'Canadian' peers" (ibid.: 196). This is in part because:

> [...] in their acquisition of English credentials required for acceptance to universities, the girls chose not to take Grade 12 English in their high school but instead took a class at a 'buy-a-credit' school, a private high school known for giving out generous marks in return for payment of a high tuition fee. While this strategy proved to be successful in terms of gaining admission to a university, it again undermined their investment in legitimate English in their Canadian schools. Thus, they were further marginalized as 'illegitimate' speakers of English in the dominant Canadian market.
>
> (ibid.: 196–197)

Shin views this positioning of the *yuhaksaeng* as 'illegitimate' speakers of English as compared with Canadians or Korean Canadians as reproducing social inequality based on racialized linguistic stigmatization in the Canadian market. While this may be the case, it is also significant that the *yuhaksaeng* and their families view the study abroad experience from the perspective of the 'global' rather than the 'local.' Given their positioning in the global market as elite cosmopolitans, the potential for local stigmatization may be less salient than Shin suggests. The actual substance of a more cosmopolitan ethics remains uncertain however. Indeed, co-ethnicity may no longer be a primary space from which they understand and experience the value of certain forms of symbolic capital, including language and culture, and even shared ethnic identity.

All categories of migration and all types of migrants contribute to the redistribution of sensibilities necessary for a cosmopolitan vision that is oriented not only toward those who migrate, but all individuals within diverse societies. The formation of a critical cosmopolitanism – that is, one aimed at reformulating global and local sensibilities to include ideas and perceptions not already privileged in the global order – is central to this project. And language in all its forms contributes significantly to the process of expanding the ever adaptable interaction order.

When George Butterick wrote of Olson and Creeley that their larger task was to help one another work out "how a man of language must live in the world," their dialogue, their endeavor to hammer out a poetics, and the persistence that entailed was a way of thinking about their relationship as writers to the world. It was about how to put themselves on the page in a way that reflected or grew out of that orientation to the world – how to, through poetry, project 'signs given,' to make a specific impress on the page. For these two men in the 1950s, that meant starting anew, building on some previous poets' work, but imagining themselves making something new from first principles or new ways of writing in relation to, for example, constructing rhythm in poetry, deciding what should determine the length of a line – the breath of the poet – or what kind of language can be part of a poem (Olson 1950). Rather than focus on things like beauty or elegance, they reflected on the energy and physicality constructed through words on the page, even including scientific prose. Their orientation to the 'Real' in poetry led them toward the relevance of history and space: the ocean and the plains as well as the space on the page, the field on which poetry and language are constructed.

Olson and Creely's dialogic exploration of language and poetics generated a deeper understanding of signs in space and history. The geography of signs on and of the urban landscapes in places like New York City and Koreatown announce a parallel encounter. These signs create a dialogic space between shifting populations and the social and physical world. Like the railroads and the canals of the nineteenth century, urban linguistic landscapes comprise powerful traces of different groups who are new and present to one another in a space that will connect them through history. In this sense, they too can be understood as "taskscapes" – records of and testimonies to the lives and labor of their inhabitants and places where their historical and cultural significance will endure.

Notes

1 Though the recognized norm in considering translation is inter-lingual translations, this is not the most common form of translation routinely encountered in the public domain. Inter-semiotic translations are present in many different texts and media that people engage with regularly, including subtitled films, film soundtracks, cartoons and graphic novels, advertisements, song translations, and different types of visual art. Intra-lingual translations are also everywhere apparent in different written and spoken texts, the latter demonstrated perfectly in the comedy sketches of President Obama's "anger translator" Luther by the writers Keegan Michael Key and Jordan Peele (e.g. www.youtube.com/watch?v=eX8tL3PMj7o). (Accessed April 2016).
2 http://gothamist.com/2014/05/02/ask_a_native_new_yorker_whats_the_d.php (Accessed May 2016).
3 See for example, Zabrodskaja and Milani (2014), Blommaert (2013), Jaworski and Thurlow (2010), Shohamy et al (2010), Shohamy and Gorter (2009), Stroud and Mpendukana (2009), and Scollen and Scollen (2003).
4 Although Koreatown's boundaries were not actually made official until 2010, 'Koreatown' signs began to be posted on the highway and on the streets surrounding the neighborhood in 1982. The current official boundaries only came about because of a proposal in 2009 to designate a space for another

ethnic community within the boundaries of Koreatown to be named 'Little Bangladesh' in recognition of the growth of this community. Members representing the Korean and Bangladeshi communities worked with the City Council to negotiate the new official boundaries (Kang 2013: 16).
5 Lee and Park (2008) note that that although Korean immigrants in the United States may be willing to identify themselves broadly as Korean or Korean American, many prefer to use sub-categories that differentiate them from other Koreans, for example, Korean Chinese (*Cho-sun-jok*), Korean Latin American, Chinese Korean (*Hwa-gyo*), or as North Korean defectors.
6 www.partydivine.com (Accessed April 2016).
7 There are a number of possible explanations for the use of Chinese characters here. Practically, the idea of "live" or "raw" seafood in Korean would require four as opposed to one character, and thus would take up more space. Traditionally, Chinese characters have been used in Korea to designate certain enterprises as more 'high end,' though since the 1990s this practice has become far less the norm.
8 In recent history, African American politicians have held many of the district, city, and state government offices that represent the four City Council districts in which Koreatown is currently situated. In 2015, however, David Ryu, a 1.5-generation immigrant, became the first Korean American to hold one of these Council seats. The State Assemblyman currently representing Koreatown is Miguel Santiago, a second-generation Latin American.
9 www.wsj.com/articles/SB118075173328922288 (Accessed May 2016).
10 www.nytimes.com/2009/02/25/dining/25taco.html?_r=0 (Accessed April 2016).
11 www.laweekly.com/restaurants/jonathan-golds-60-korean-dishes-every-angeleno-should-know-2383348 (Accessed April 2016).
12 http://seoulofla.com/#rf1-474=&filter=.prof-eui-young-yu (Accessed April 2016).
13 The interviews in this research were conducted in Korean and translated by the author, Hyunjung Shin. I have removed transcription markers and done some minor editing on the interviews in the interest of readability.
14 Yu-ri's statement about *hallyu* is a reference to 'the Korean wave' of popular culture, including television dramas, music, film and the celebrities and fashion associated with them, that is currently popular in China, Taiwan, and Hong Kong (see Lin and Tong 2008 and Lee 2008 for interesting discussions on the differentiated forms of reception, responses, and re-appropriation of the Korean wave across East and Southeast Asian societies).

References

Blommaert, Jan 2013 *Ethnography, Superdiversity and Linguistic Landscape.* Bristol: Multilingual Matters.
Butterick, George F. (ed) 1980 *Charles Olson & Robert Creeley: The Complete Correspondence: Vol. 1.* Santa Barbara: Black Sparrow Press.
Eui-Young, Yu, Peter Choe, Sang Il Han, and Kimberly Yu 2004 "Emerging Diversity: Los Angeles' Koreatown, 1990–2000," *Amerasia Journal* 30(1): 25–52.
Jaworski, Adam and Chrispin Thurlow (eds) 2010 *Semiotic Landscapes: Language, Image, Space.* London: Continuum.
Kang, Kristy H.A. 2013 *The Seoul of Los Angeles: Contested Identities and Transnationalism in Immigrant Space,* PhD dissertation, School of Cinematic Arts, University of Southern California. http://seoulofla.com/ (Accessed May 2016).

Landry, Rodrigue and Richard Y. Bourhis 1997 "Linguistic Landscape and Ethnolinguistic Vitality," *Journal of Language and Social Psychology* 16(1): 23–49.
Lee, Keehyeung 2008 "Mapping Out the Cultural Politics of "the Korean Wave" in Contemporary South Korea," in Chua Beng Huat and Koichi Iwabuchi (eds) *East Asian Pop Culture*. Hong Kong: Hong Kong University Press, 175–189.
Lee, Youngmin and Kyonghwan Park 2008 "Negotiating Hybridity: Transnational Reconstruction of Migrant Subjectivity in Koreatown, Los Angeles," *Journal of Cultural Geography* 25(3): 245–262.
Lin, Angel and Avin Tong 2008 "Re-imagining a Cosmopolitan 'Asian Us': Korean Media Flows and Imaginaries of Asian Modern Femininities," in Chua Beng Huat and Koichi Iwabuchi (eds) *East Asian Pop Culture*. Hong Kong: Hong Kong University Press, 91–125.
Malinowski, David 2009 "Authorship in the Linguistic Landscape: A Multimodal-Performative View," in Elana Shohamy and Durk Gorter (eds) *Linguistic Landscape: Expanding the Scenery*. New York: Routledge, 107–125.
Olson, Charles [1950] 1967 "Projective Verse," in Donald Allen (ed) *The Human Universe and Other Essays*. New York: Grove Press, 51–61.
—— 1960 *The Maximus Poems*. Oakland: University of California Press.
Park, Kyonghwan 2009 "Transnational Nationalism and the Rise of the Transnational State Apparatus," *Journal of the Korean Geographical Society* 44(2): 146–160.
Sanchez, Jared, Mirabal Auer, Veronica Terriquez and Mi Young Kim 2012 *Koreatown: A Contested Community at a Crossroads*. Prepared in collaboration with the Koreatown Immigrant Workers Alliance (KIWA). Los Angeles: Program for Environmental and Regional Equity (PERE). https://dornsife.usc.edu/pere/koreatown (Accessed April 2016).
Scollen, Ron and Suzie Wong Scollen 2003 *Discourses in Place*. London: Routledge.
Shin, Hyunjung 2012 "From FOB to Cool: Transnational Migrant Students in Toronto and the Styling of Global Linguistic Capital," *Journal of Sociolinguistics* 16(2): 184–200.
Shohamy, Elana and Durk Gorter (eds) 2009 *Linguistic Landscape: Expanding the Scenery*. New York: Routledge.
Shohamy, Elana, Eliezer Ben-Rafael, and Monica Barni (eds) 2010 *Linguistic Landscape in the City*. Bristol: Multilingual Matters.
Stroud, Christopher and Sibonile Mpendukana 2009 "Towards a Material Ethnography of Linguistic Landscape: Multilingualism, Mobility and Space in a South African Township," *Journal of Sociolinguistics* 13(3): 363–386.
Zabrodskaja, Anastassia and Tommaso M. Milani (eds) 2014 "Signs in Context: Multilingual and Multimodal Texts in Semiotic Space," Special Issue of *International Journal of the Sociology of Language* 228: 1–6.

6 Constructing and contesting young migrant identities

The growing interest in the transnational character of contemporary migration has emerged from, or been seen as the cause of, an increasing sense of the fragmented nature of social, cultural, and political communities within modern liberal societies. Present patterns of migration are not the sole or even biggest cause of this fragmentation, however. Other factors are introducing new challenges for communities of all sizes, particularly with regard to the creation and maintenance of social cohesion, including the ubiquity of technology and social media, widening income disparities, and internal ideological divisions. In established and emergent liberal democracies, the question of whether new groups of migrants can wish to contribute to the stability of nationhood and citizenship and, at the same time, maintain strong 'transnational' ties and allegiances, is part of a larger public concern about how a sense of a shared collective identity can be established among a diverse and fragmented populace. In Europe this has been intimately connected to the debates over migration to Europe, the extent of European integration, the possibility of a European constitution, internal economic differences, and challenges over the sustainability of the Euro and even the Union itself. It is not surprising that the issue of 'social cohesion' became the most resonant concern of much European policy during the 1990s and into the twenty-first century, and European identity issues informed many of the agendas set by the European Commission's research frameworks.

The conventional understanding in liberal pluralist democracies is that social and moral unity emerges out of the diverse beliefs and understandings of their members. In theory, a coherent and cohesive 'organic' national identity emerges as a consequence of legislation and political compromise, though this can also be a matter of time, chance, special interests, or external force. 'Cohesion' was once thought especially to characterize European countries in contrast to countries where, under colonial economic impact, differing social and cultural groups became artificially juxtaposed, generating internal disjuncture. However, this contrastive notion of European societies as distinctively homogeneous is itself somewhat mythologizing. For example, the sustained cultural and geographical divisions within the United Kingdom – English, Scottish, Welsh, Northern

Irish, Cornish – along with its deep and persistent divisions of social class have never been a settled matter. Spain is similarly divided by both political and cultural fault lines, where linguistic and administrative barriers between the core regions and the historic regions – Basque country, Galicia, Catalonia, and Andalusia – form part of the complex and weakly integrated diversity of Spanish nationality. In France, not only regional differences and unstable borders were seen as longstanding obstacles to national unity, the level of education of the peasantry was a matter of deep concern into the twentieth century. To Léon Gambetta, a former Prime Minister of France, writing in 1871, the peasantry were: "intellectually several centuries behind the enlightened part of the country [there was] an enormous distance between them and us ... between those who speak our language and those many of our compatriots [who], cruel as it is to say, can no more than stammer in it." According to the historian Eugene Weber:

> The prevailing belief [was] that areas and groups of some importance were uncivilized, that is, unintegrated into, unassimilated to French civilization: poor, backward, ignorant, savage, barbarous, wild, living like beasts with their beasts. They had to be taught manners, morals, literacy, a knowledge of French and of France, a sense of the legal and institutional structure beyond their immediate community.
> (Weber 1976: 5)

Italy and Germany's late-nineteenth-century unifications also barely drew a veil over the many cultural, linguistic, and political internal divisions that persist in both of those countries.

Apart from these historically established divisions, much of the current and past European fragmentation can be layered onto long-term processes of *internal* migration across relatively short distances and more recently across the European Union. This remains highly significant today and dates back to the late eighteenth century as the countrysides across Europe began to send significant parts of their populations to the cities to fulfill the promise of the Industrial Revolution and the need for labor. On the back of the British inventions and Belgium's own traditional weaving industry, the industrial towns of the Walloon-speaking southern provinces of Belgium were expanded by workers from the countryside in the 1820s. In the 1830s the Prussian provinces of Westphalia, Rhine, Berlin, and Brandenburg began their industrial expansion, drawing large numbers of people from the eastern agricultural regions. A clear example of this process in nineteenth-century England was the cotton town of Preston in Lancashire. In 1851 half of its population were migrants, 40 percent of whom had come less than ten miles, 30 percent had come more than 30 miles, and 14 percent had been born in Ireland. Through such highly local migrations Lancashire became the most urbanized county in Britain by the middle of the nineteenth century, sustained by the primary markets for textiles in India, Japan, and China, each forced open by British imperial power and maintained until those countries became free of the military and legal constraints imposed by Britain on their textile industries (Hobsbawm 1968: 151, Anderson 1971: 37). This industrial expansion was critically linked to European colonial expansion opening up new markets across the globe, and the migration of people followed the migration of capital just as it does today.

Drawing attention to the variety of economic niches both internal and international labor migrants have created and occupied, Eric R. Wolf described the ethnicization process during much of the nineteenth and twentieth centuries as follows:

> As each cohort entered the industrial process, outsiders were able to categorize it in terms of putative provenance and supposed affinity to particular segments of the labor market. At the same time, members of the cohort itself came to value membership in the group thus defined, as a qualification for establishing economic and political claims. Such ethnicities rarely coincided with the initial self-identification of the industrial recruits, who first thought of themselves as Hanoverians or Bavarians, rather than as Germans, as members of their village or parish (okilica) rather than as Poles, as Tonga or Yao rather than as 'Nyasalanders.
> (Wolf 2010: 381)

In the United States, the later-starting Industrial Revolution moved seamlessly and very successfully across the seismic shift from coal to oil as the primary energy source and the new world order constituted during the twentieth century. The United States and Germany rapidly overtook the UK in the leadership of the Industrial Revolution toward the end of the nineteenth century and the UK fell increasingly behind. In the United States the successive expropriation of Native American lands was accompanied by wave upon wave of migration from Europe, creating the complex ethnic mix that constitutes the United States today. Across the same period in the United States, substantial internal migration also took place, starting with the first published accounts of the discovery of gold in the West, mid-summer 1848, continuing in the 1930s with the mid-western migration of desperate and starving families to California driven by the ravages of dust-storm-creating macro-agricultural practices (Hine and Faragher 2000), together with the 'Great Migration' of Black families from the south to the industrial north, gradually but increasingly stimulated after 1900 by the slowing-down of European emigration (Grossman 1989, Wilkerson 2010).

The patterns of cultural interchange and transformation created in the 'melting pot' of social and economic change reached a critical point during the civil rights era as the long history of racist exclusion and inequality was challenged through protest and anti-discrimination legislation. This process in itself generated a by-product of many other ethnic recognition claims, creating a field of multicultural identity discourse that was not found in Europe but was to some degree also evident in other countries like the United States that were created out of the immigration process – most notably Canada and Australia (see Novak 1972, Lopez 2000, Abu-Laban and Gabriel 2002).

As international mass movements of people create a persistent churn in social relationships, the discourses in liberal pluralist democracies themselves become subject to re-interpretation, as notions of 'social order,' 'cohesion,' and 'unity' are problematized and very different or opposing sensibilities and categories appear or reappear due to some perceived threat to the social order by members or factions within the population. More recent examples include the challenge to long-held beliefs about religion and the state implied in debates in the United States over marriage equality and resurgent challenges to women's reproduction rights (Phillips 2006) or in France about the right of Muslim citizens to wear the veil (Cesari and McLoughlin 2005, Laborde 2008). Across Europe, the perceived danger of reconfigurations to longstanding secular practices or principles have their origin, not in migration per se but as a result of generational, demographic geopolitical and ideological shifts coupled with, in some cases, economic stagnation for certain groups within their populations.

Even beyond the ebb and flow of migration to Europe from conflict zones in the Middle East, when the threat is associated (even indirectly) with a particular migrant group, members of that group – and migration policies themselves – have become targets of greater scrutiny and acts of protest, sometimes violent. The scapegoating of migrants has occurred throughout history, of course. However, the fear of changes brought about by migrant cultures becomes magnified when linked to the misperception that twenty-first-century migrants all now *choose* whether they stay and acculturate or assimilate, return to their country of origin after a while, or maintain different residences, attachments, and allegiances, and sometimes citizenships.

The expanded presence – some would say prevalence – of transnational norms as a consequence of migration has shifted the focus of attention in migration studies toward post-national models of membership and citizenship (Soysal 1994, Papastergiadis 2000), particularly in spaces where the 'world' appears to reside in one city (Vertovec 2007). This represents the supposed shift from nineteenth and twentieth-century migration norms that assumed permanent resettlement and measured degrees of acculturation and assimilation in phenomena such as spatial concentration, patterns of segregation, inter-marriage, and socioeconomic and linguistic change over time. The extent to which transnational activity can be claimed as the normative mode of adaptation of all or even most immigrant groups has been questioned by others (see, for example, Portes 2003, Snel et al 2006, Levitt 2007, Fink 2011) who look instead to the impact of 'axes of differentiation' among immigrant groups, for example, their region or country of origin, gender, age, language, culture, religion, and particular immigration status (e.g. permanent resident, refugee, asylum seeker, indefinite leave to remain, guest worker). Hoerder (2011: 34), reminiscent of Eric Wolf's remarks above, notes that people who decide to migrate:

> carry with them their specific regional socialization. Thus the scope, or scape, of "trans" requires empirical documentation. For example, around 1900 migrating Slovaks came to the United States from three major cultural regions with distinct linguistic patterns; Chinese migrants traveled from four specific regions in two southern provinces and spoke mutually unintelligible dialects. Today's migrating Filipinas leave Manila's metropolitan culture, the island of Luzon, or economically marginal smaller islands. No migrants are generic nationals, even though they carry the passport of a particular state.

To different degrees these factors impact the manner and extent to which individual migrants maintain ties across physical or virtual borders, and the distinct features of their resettlement.

Managing migrant identities

Despite the fact that most people perceive themselves and live their lives as members of multiple social groups through their occupations, political or religious associations, and national or ethnic attachments, ingroup–outgroup classifications remain fairly common, not only in academic discourses, but in everyday references to group identities. This tendency to assume or impose simple identity appellations on individuals or groups who possess an assemblage of differentiated identities can impede progress toward mutual recognition between members of multicultural societies. The view that diverse populations consist of static ingroups or outgroups relative to one another can also lead to the assumption of unbreachable boundaries between groups and encourage an unwillingness on the part of the individuals within these groups to make an effort to achieve a richer understanding of any common social agenda.

Of course, identities are bound to become entrenched under circumstances of heightened antagonism or violent conflict or those involving ongoing direct conflict between particular groups where a physical, economic, or psychological threat is present. Even in societies where relations are less contentious, real or symbolic violence toward certain individuals or groups is never an absent possibility. Multicultural communities nevertheless remain important sites in which identities are created, negotiated, and contested. They reveal the fact that identity is as much socially and discursively constructed as culturally or biologically determined, and deeply embedded in particular social, historical, and political contexts. Multicultural or multilingual encounters create important opportunities to construct 'cosmopolitanism from below' out of which greater mutual recognition and inclusion can be achieved, or at least attempted, among diverse groups where any number of novel forms of identities can emerge.

Qualitative ethnographic research is a rich source for examining the social construction of identity in specific contexts, allowing greater access to the details of the social and biographical trajectories of individuals and communities. In what follows, I re-examine a number of ethnographic studies conducted by researchers in Spain, France, and the United States, two at the end of the twentieth century and the others at the beginning of the twenty-first, focusing on groups of young migrants. My purpose in discussing these studies here is to highlight the 'transnational' or 'cosmopolitan' features of contemporary migration that play out on a personal level in young migrants' lives and to call attention to the different forms of translation in evidence as they manage their identities in particular geographical, institutional, and social settings. What is unique about young people is that the majority attend educational institutions where they meet and mix with other young people from minority and majority populations at a crucial time of their identity construction. In this context, and related social environments, proximity with others is unavoidable and there is a strong likelihood of some form of interaction between individuals from different groups.

Ethnographic studies of 1.5 and second-generation young people coming to terms with the real and potential tensions that develop between one self and another are particularly illuminating in this regard. Each of these studies focuses on a particular set of issues relevant to different social institutions the young people attended and/or the local environments in which they lived. Their emergent self-perceptions are tied to phenomena commonly associated with migration, e.g. language, culture, race, ethnicity, and regional or national identity. What stands out in these studies is how complex and mutable such phenomena are for the young people involved who are situated geographically, historically, socially, culturally, and virtually in one or more than one place at a time.

Essentializing migrants

The first of these ethnographies was conducted by Immaculada García-Sánchez (2013) during 2005–2006 in a small Spanish agricultural town located approximately 125 miles southwest of Madrid. Since the early 1990s this rural area has been a major settlement area for Moroccan immigrants, who make up the majority of the 38 percent immigrant population. Out of the 678 students at the school, 37 percent were children of Moroccan immigrant families. In the class reported on here, seven out of the twenty-four 8 to 11-year-old students were Moroccan immigrant children, and two were Spanish students of Roma descent.

A primary aim of García-Sánchez's fieldwork was to examine the "linguistic and socio-cultural ecology of the lives of Moroccan immigrant children"

182 Young migrant identities

living within this community (ibid.: 483). In the part of this research discussed here, García-Sánchez considers the function of a local school's multiculturalist-oriented curricular agenda and its representation in teacher-led discursive practices within the classroom. She describes the curriculum as follows:

> The main tenets of the new curriculum centered around creating a strong sense of community and a spirit of tolerance and respect for the cultural and linguistic heterogeneity of the students. In addition, the school instituted a set of core civic values – such as dialogue, friendship, and cooperation – intended to regulate the academic and social life of the school; these were enacted through school-wide activities, as well as through classroom practice.
>
> (ibid.: 484)

Principles like these are designed to positively promote the cultural and linguistic diversity among the student population. In the course of her investigation, however, García-Sánchez noted two prevalent linguistic events that took place in the classroom involving appellation and contrastive deixis which were especially pronounced when the focus of the lesson was the cultural and linguistic heterogeneity of the students. Appellation was used by the classroom teacher, not in the limited sense of 'naming' students as 'Moroccan' or 'Roma' or 'Spanish,' but to characterize students' families by focusing on aspects of their ethnic or national culture through such things as the type of food prepared at home, the language spoken, traditional holidays celebrated, etc. Alongside this practice, contrastive deixis was frequently used to reinforce personal ('we Spaniards/our customs' vs. 'you Moroccans/your customs') and spatial ('here' in Spain) distinctions between the migrant children and their families on the one hand, and mainstream Spanish identities on the other. García-Sánchez also noted a practice of tokenization whereby "each child is chosen as a representative of their ethnicity so that they can each give an ethnically-based exemplar of the topic under discussion, in which difference is usually emphasized" (ibid.: 486). Consequently, despite the school's expressed wish to "create a strong sense of community," the teacher ended up (re)producing oversimplified characterizations of the complex social and biographical trajectories of the migrant students and their families, reinforcing their status as outsiders with respect to the Spanish majority, and overlooking the migrant students' own sense of attachment to multiple communities. With respect to the latter, these classroom interactions also reveal the migrant children's efforts to counter the school's multiculturalist narrative by challenging the teacher's presumptions regarding their 'at home' cultural and linguistic practices, their parents' migration histories, and the children's knowledge of and relationship to Spanish culture more broadly.

The following exchange demonstrates the attempts of several students in the class to correct their teacher's erroneous assumptions.[1] The exchange begins just after their teacher has asked some of the Moroccan children in the class how long they have lived in Spain; their answers range from three to six years. The teacher then expresses her assumption that their parents have lived a longer time in Morocco than in Spain, followed by a question about the customs, including their use of language, that the children and their families practice at home.

I.

TEACHER: But your parents have been more years in Morocco than here, haven't they? (Several Moroccan children nod)
TEACHER: And in your homes, what customs do you have? How do you speak in your homes?
WAFIYA: I with my sib- siblings, I speak in Spanish and with my parents, with my parents Moroccan
MIMON: In Moroccan, in a language – in a language, Miss, šilHa
TEACHER: Let's see, Wafiya, you with your siblings in Spanish and with your parents in Moroccan
MIMON: No, not in Moroccan, šilHa
TEACHER: Okay, šilHa
MIMON: Isn't it Wafiya?
TEACHER: Listen, let's see. We are learning lots of things today, okay? Let's see, and why do you speak with your parents in Moroccan?
MIRIAM: Because, no, (with) my father I sometimes speak in Spanish
S3: There are some parents that do not speak Spanish
TEACHER: But let's see, sometimes, but most of the time why do you speak with your father in Moroccan?
MIRIAM: Most of the times in Spanish
TEACHER: Of course. Let's see, Wafiya, why do you speak with your parents most of the time in Moroccan?
(Miriam raises her hand)
TEACHER: Or you, Miriam, why?
MIRIAM: Because they have been in Morocco for a long time
TEACHER: Because they are from, they are Moroccans, right?
(Miriam nods)
TEACHER: Of course, then they'll have to speak Moroccan
MIMON: but they have been here Miss

In this segment, the children and teacher are at odds with each other regarding the social and pedagogic aims of the lesson. The classroom exchange takes the form of Initiation–Response–Feedback, a recognized mode of classroom discourse where the teacher initiates, the student responds, and the teacher provides feedback on the answer given (Sinclair and Coulthard 1975). This mode of discourse has been criticized for being more about a teacher's attempt to steer students toward a correct response – saying what the teacher wants to hear – rather than encouraging a productive exchange of possible responses. In this instance, once the teacher's initial open question, "How do you speak in your homes?" reveals a complex array of language practices, including the use of šilHa, a dialect of the Amazigh (Berbers), among the migrant students and their families that contradict her own assumptions (and pedagogic objectives), the teacher settles on a different question, one that largely discounts the information that has just been offered by the students.

Essentialist labeling of cultural and linguistic identities, of the kind represented in the teacher's question–answer sequence, "Why do you speak to your parents most of the time in Moroccan?" "Because they are from, they are Moroccans, right?" is often found in multiculturalist discourses, sometimes for strategic reasons. Depending on the context and purpose of their use, such characterizations can serve a positive or a negative function. For new and established immigrants alike, however, mis-classifications always mask complex factors at work in the construction and contestation of identity within multicultural societies. At the end of this sequence, one of the students, Mimon, attempts to demonstrate this with respect to his family as he starts to say, "but they have been here Miss." Although the teacher does not take up his challenge at this point, he will return to it later in the exchange.

The segment on language is followed by a similar exchange with respect to the type of food eaten in the Moroccan children's homes. In this part of the exchange, the contrastive deixis identified by García-Sánchez can be seen in the contrast between *here* [in Spain] and *in your home*, and the analogy, *it's like if we were to go to Morocco, right?* [we would *taste* the food], both of which carry the implication that the migrants' permanent home exists outside Spain, that their stay in Spain is somehow temporary. Again, the teacher insists on making clear distinctions between Moroccan food and Spanish food in relation to the students' identity, even when Miriam disagrees with her assertions about the salience of such distinctions in her home.

II.

TEACHER: And in your house, what do you usually eat, Moroccan food or typical Spanish food?
MIRIAM: Sometimes Spanish sometimes Moroccan
TEACHER: Well, let's see, since you are here, since you are here, it's like if we were to go to Morocco, right? You taste something from here, but what's the custom in your home, to eat your typical food, right? Yes or no?
(Miriam shakes her head)
TEACHER: No
W: Sometimes yes, but sometimes from Morocco.
TEACHER: Of course, sometimes from Morocco, right? Your mother sometimes makes typical food from there, right?
(Wafiya nods)
TEACHER: Yes

In the final sequence, Mimon returns to the teacher's earlier generalization that the children's parents have lived more years in Morocco than in Spain to correct her assumptions about the geographical trajectories of his family members. Despite the indisputable fact that Mimon's parents and maternal grandfather had lived most if not all of their lives outside Morocco, in Spain and France, the teacher dismisses their significance, as this narrative does not fit well with her generalized narrative about the Moroccan migrants.

III.

MIMON: Miss, my father has been in France more than anywhere else
TEACHER: Yes
MIMON: More than in Spain and more than in Morocco he has been 21 years, he was born there
TEACHER: Yes, your father in France
TEACHER: And your mother?
MIMON: What? She has been in Spain more
TEACHER: Your mother more in Spain
TEACHER: Well
MIMON: And her father in France
TEACHER: Well, what I wanted to explain to you [is] that we know our things.

The teacher's final comment in this section of the transcript, "Well, what I wanted to explain to you [is] that we know our things," suggests that her primary pedagogic aim was to emphasize the significance of the *differences* among her students, rather than to explore their *diversity*. The subtle yet significant difference in meaning between the two terms is often overlooked in multiculturalist discourses, including certain uses of the concept of hybridity that presume cultures or language users start out as integrated wholes and as fairly intact, non-evolving entities. This notion of culture downplays differences between members of the same culture as well as the possibility that the distinctions between different cultures do not necessarily differ in kind from the distinctions between members of a single culture. The migrant students and their families 'know' that 'our things' are a consequence of accumulated experiences, across time and space, of crossing borders and negotiating boundaries. The irony of the school's multiculturalist agenda is its failure to consider that for many migrant students and their families Spain may already feel like home.

Worlds in words

The second study focuses on migrant and minority identity construction in the language choices of twenty-two young adult daughters, 18 to 24 years of age, of Portuguese migrants raised in France with specific regard to their use of second-person address forms in both Portuguese and French. In her study, Michele Koven (2009) challenges the view that bilinguals diverge from the pragmatic norms of monolingual usage of a less dominant or heritage language because of insufficient exposure to that language. Instead, she argues, such divergences are often a manifestation of speakers' attempts to navigate across multiple language sociocultural and ideological frameworks. In languages where individuals can access multiple second-person address forms, their decision to use one form over another normally indicates their estimation of the degree of deference or intimacy they can demonstrate toward the addressee (Brown and Gilman 1960). Although pronoun usage is negotiable within an interaction, the use of a particular second-person address form can make an initial positive or negative impression and serve as an important indicator of the extent of the addressor's cultural knowledge and belonging. The forms conventionally available for French and Portuguese are somewhat different. In French, 'you' is indicated by *tu* which signals greater intimacy or *vous* which indicates deference, though in contemporary urban France where the subjects were raised, *vous* has become negatively associated as a marker of upper-class, political conservatism. Portuguese also uses *tu* as the more familiar form, and in Portugal *voce* is the more deferential alternative, and is the form commonly used in rural areas of Portugal from where the subjects' families originated. Portuguese also allows several other possibilities to indicate respect: a third-person verb form (missing a subject pronoun), a kinship term + third-person verb, and an alternative use of *voce* with a third-person verb (Koven 2009: 351–352).

In the Portuguese families reported on in Koven's study, the parents addressed their children as *tu* both in French and Portuguese. Where they diverged was whether their children were permitted to reciprocate with *tu* in either language, which was the normative usage among occupants of their social class in contemporary urban France where they and their daughters lived. Despite the fact that their daughters had been born in France or migrated there as young children, attended French schools, and had 'native' fluency in French, as children of migrants their relational ties to Portugal distinguished them from their peers, where alternative cultural and linguistic norms relating to the parent–child relationship existed. The young women in the study spent time in Portugal during the summer, many had monolingual Portuguese boyfriends, and planned to return to Portugal as adults to live and work. Their parents had migrated mostly from the rural north of Portugal, largely for economic reasons, and had maintained strong ties there.

These women's attempts to manage the differences between their urban sensibilities developed in France and their ties to rural Portugal, and particularly the opposing models of the parent–child relationship that existed within these two contexts, were reflected in their use of address forms in both languages. Although most chose French norms when speaking French with their parents, their Portuguese contained both French and Portuguese influence (ibid.: 348). The variation that exists among the women is closely tied to their interpretation of the current social meaning of established uses and their wish to project a particular self through their individual choices. Implicit in their decisions are their contrastive associations of the two cultures and languages they inhabit – urban, modern, and egalitarian France/French as opposed to rural, conservative, and hierarchical Portugal/Portuguese (ibid.: 362) – and the significance for them of rejecting or reproducing these differences in communicating with their parents. In the following examples, taken from interviews conducted by the author (K) with three of the women (W1–3), a number of different factors are evident in their decisions.[2]

Example 1

W1: In French I *tu* them and in Portuguese I *vous* them so
K: And that doesn't feel strange?
W1: No not at all, people think it's strange, because they don't understand, and me too at the beginning I didn't understand, and then little by little you get used to it, it's that I'm from the north and well in the north we are still very conservative but in the family um, my parents, well it's a question of respect, they've always wanted us to say *vous* to them, in the beginning I didn't understand, I said to myself, "frankly I don't really see how it's respectful"…it's not so bad, because it installs a certain um limit not to cross, I don't talk to them like I'd talk to a friend, let's say that, even if I yell at them with the same words that I use to talk to a friend, there's this border of *vous* that makes it, that well even if I yell at them I know they're older than me, I know that they are my parents and I know that I have to respect them. In French I *tu* them because well *vous* sounds very bourgeois, in Portuguese, no it's a question of respect. Where I live [in Portugal] most of the young people say *vous* to their parents and we are starting to see more and more young people who say *tu* but where I live in my area, it's still very rare, and if you want to look ahead, when I have children, they'll say *tu* to me…now when I see, for example, young people of seven or eight years old, when they talk to me in Portuguese, well it happens that there are some who say *vous*, it makes me uncomfortable, I feel it ages me and I don't like that at all.
(ibid.: 360–361)

Example 2

W2: I don't say *tu* to my mother in Portuguese, and in French never … never.
A: You say *vous*
W2: I say *vous* because in Portuguese I remember a story that happened to me, that left an impression on me. By the way, my mother, a little,

I think that she regrets it by the way. I was young and I didn't understand why I said *vous* to my mother because at the time, at school [in France] everybody said *tu* and I tried so I said to my mother, "*tu* this, *tu* that", until the day when she says to me "You don't get to say *tu* to me".

K: How old were you?

W2: Oh I must have been six, seven, but in fact it was in Portuguese, we were speaking in Portuguese, and as I had attempted the *tu* in Portuguese, and that my mother said "No, I don't want you to say *tu*", and then, that marked me a little bit and then in French the equivalent that I found the most that adapted, it was *vous*, if you will, and then now if she asks me to say *tu* to her, that will be, that will be very strange to me, and now in French it's always um well, "*vous* want this, *vous* want that", you see... because there's no equivalent.

(ibid.: 359)

Example 3

W3: It wouldn't occur to me to say *vous*, to *vouvoyer* my parents or my godmother. Whereas I know that there are people who do it, say *vous* to their parents in Portuguese to them. But I find that it's a distancing of the person. My parents, I've always said *tu* to them. It didn't occur to me to say *vous* to them, because I had the impression of taking a distance, you know of distancing myself from them. So I can't stand it, so well it's true that when I see people say *vous* to their parents it seems completely, I dunno, you put up a barrier between children and parents, it's not normal, I don't like that, I have a hard time accepting it. Really I can't get used to it.

(ibid.: 357)

According to Kovan, the majority of the women in her study, fifteen of the twenty-two women interviewed, shared the view expressed in the third example reflective of the more inclusive, non-hierarchical linguistic and cultural norms of the French urban community in which they were raised and of their relationships with their own parents. This is not surprising given that a large part of their socialization took place in France, in French and in school where formative identity construction occurs, which can recast relationships within migrant families. The second example provides an interesting illustration of this in the mother's reaction to the cultural change she perceives when her young daughter begins using *tu* to address her mother in Portuguese. The daughter recounts her mother's negative reaction, "you don't get to say *tu* to me," to her attempts to adopt French cultural and linguistic norms in Portuguese. The daughter responds by reverting to the *vous* form in both languages and excluding *tu* as a reciprocal form of address in either, a practice she maintains in the present. The woman also mentions her mother's later regret about her disapproving reaction though she does not say why; perhaps the mother worries that her daughter's use of *vous* in French or the equivalent in Portuguese sets her apart from her peers, or creates a false impression of a lack of intimacy in their relationship, or makes her sound "too bourgeois" in French. What is interesting is the significance that this moment has retained for both mother and daughter. The mother's initial reaction was quite possibly an indication of her concern that she and her daughter would become unrecognizable to one another within the cultural and linguistic norms of Portugal and Portuguese. What resulted, however, was that the means to express a more intimate parent–child relationship through *mutually recognizable* social and linguistic norms developed over time were 'lost in translation,' and ultimately unavailable in either language. A similar moment in time is alluded to in the first example. When asked whether it feels strange to use *tu* in one language and *vous* in another, the woman recalls, "at the beginning I didn't understand, and then little by little you get used to it." In this case, the woman gets used to her bilingual and bicultural status seemingly by compartmentalizing her identities in ways that allow France and Portugal to exist as two distinct places calling for two distinct sets of cultural and linguistic practices. The fact that her comments could make it appear that she lives in Portugal permanently (which was not the case at the time of the interview) supports this view.

It is interesting that this woman is the only one of the three to discuss her decisions about usage with specific reference to a wider transnational context. In one sense, she represents what many assume to be the normative mode of transnational migration and migrants, characterized by carefully cultivated boundaries between one culture and another, and one place and another. Yet, according to Koven, all these women regularly traversed the same places and the same two cultures, which suggests that migrants can vary considerably in how they construct and negotiate multiple identities in different locations. What is the case for all the women, however, is that whichever linguistic and cultural norms they adopted, all risked experiencing some form of rupture as a result of their choices. The woman who uses only *tu* risks cultural disapproval in Portugal, outside the co-constructed norms of her immediate family; the woman who uses only *vous* inadvertently constructs a linguistic boundary between herself and her mother regarding the expression of intimacy that over time both come to regret; and the woman who constructs a carefully drawn boundary between her French and Portuguese selves, when addressed as *vous* by Portuguese youth experiences a distortion of her (French) self, and will likely experience some break from her (Portuguese) self when addressed by her future children as *tu*. As young children of migrant families, these young women faced a challenge: to maintain and develop their self-recognition and, at the same time, avoid misrecognition by their peers and teachers, while also trying to manage the changes that occurred in their perceptions of the beliefs and values of their families and countries of origin. Taken together, the decisions taken by the women and their families in the face of this challenging task, symbolized in the use of a few words, demonstrate both the type and extent of the transnational ties migrant families negotiate across real borders, and the role that language and translation play in this process.

Restricted spaces of identity

The focus of the next study is Loukia Sarroub's (2005) school-based ethnography of six adolescent Muslim girls in a Yemeni community in Dearborn, Michigan. The research, conducted between 1997 and 1999, focuses on the cultural, religious, and physical boundaries that structured these girls' lives within their families, communities, and in the public high school they attended. The girls' parents came from rural villages mostly in the more religiously conservative North Yemen, and like other Yemenis from these villages who began to migrate to the United States in the mid-1970s, the parents had little to no formal schooling and were illiterate or semi-literate in Arabic and in English (ibid.: 22). All the girls in the study were first-generation Yemenis who wore the *hijab* and referred to themselves as *hijabat*, the plural feminine noun used in their community to denote those who wore the scarf, as did the members of their local community, the Arab Americans in the wider community and the school (ibid.: 12–13).

Yemenis were attracted to the Detroit area for jobs in the shipping and auto industries and because it has one of the highest concentrations of Arabic-speaking people outside of the Middle East. In the Dearborn school district where the Yemeni families lived, 49 percent of students were Arabic speaking and 15 percent of these were of Yemeni origin (ibid.: 23), and in the high school the girls attended, out of approximately 1,420 students, 40–45 percent were Arabic speakers and 41 percent of these were of Yemeni origin. There were eleven Arabic-speaking teachers and staff (ibid.: 24). The majority of Arab Americans in Dearborn, whose families had been in the United States for over a century, were of Lebanese descent. They lived in the more affluent areas, while the Yemenis resided in the working-class community of Southend. The Yemenis viewed themselves as transnational sojourners; they maintained strong ties with their villages, traveling regularly to Yemen, and most planned to return there to live. The Yemenis of the Southend community also tended to interact primarily, and in some cases exclusively, with residents who were from the same village, both because they spoke the same dialect (village dialects were not mutually intelligible) and because they made social (marriage) and political alliances that benefited them back in Yemen. According to the author, the Yemenis remained "geopolitically, linguistically, religiously and culturally isolated from American life" (ibid.: 22).

One of the main aims of Sarroub's study was to examine how the girls managed their responsibility to support multiple sets of expectations. She notes that "[t]heir responsibilities were threefold: to uphold the honor of the family, to become good mothers (most are engaged or married by the ages of 14 or 15 and earlier), and to succeed in school" (ibid.). While seeking to fulfill these potentially disparate agendas, the girls received mixed messages from their family, their community, and their school that often made them feel they were working toward contradictory aims.

> Despite its minor role in Yemen, education was important, perhaps as important as marriage, to the Yemeni community in the Southend. Although the parents of the *hijabat* had not received much formal education, they took seriously their daughters' and sons' education. They sent their children to public school and to Arabic school on the weekends—most of the Yemeni children in the community attended school seven days a week. At the same time however, the Southend community feared the social aspects of public schooling and limited their children's experiences there. Social life in school was monitored and curtailed by family members.
>
> (ibid.: 33)

Within their families and communities the girls were able to respect the cultural and religious expectations with regard to their gendered roles and relationships. However, while in school, a crucial space for identity formation, the Yemeni girls were required to maneuver across religious, cultural, and gender boundaries that made their lives challenging, confounding, and liberating at the same time. As one of them who was married at fifteen to her cousin explained:

> I came into high school and everybody told me you gotta do this, you gotta do this, you gotta do this and this in order to live a happy life in high school. And that was don't look at guys, don't talk to guys, don't laugh loud in the hallways, don't socialize a lot in the hallways. Just keep up the education.
>
> (ibid.: 36)

Although the school accommodated some of the gendered spaces that the girls were accustomed to outside of school by instigating all-girl gym classes and allowing the girls to sit together during classes, the girls were left on their own to manage common spaces like the hallways and the cafeteria. They did this in the halls by lowering their eyes and avoiding body contact with boys, and in the cafeteria by carving out their own space, keeping their distance not only from the boys, but from girls, non-Arab and Arab Americans or Muslims who did not wear the *hijab*, for fear of being associated with behavior that might be construed as inappropriate. The girls were closely monitored by other *hijabat*, the Yemeni American boys, and particularly the more conservative recent young male Yemeni immigrants they called 'boaters', who would report back to their families about any behavior they observed that they considered forbidden.

As it turned out, the most liberating spaces for the girls were inside their classrooms where they interacted more freely with other students, including boys, than anywhere else in school. Without access to the extracurricular activities available to students through afterschool sports or clubs, the classrooms provided one of the few opportunities for the girls to mix with students unlike themselves, and to hear and explore different sets of beliefs and values. Yet the classroom also served as a reminder of what set the girls apart. For although the girls were expected to "keep up the education," academic success was no guarantee that a marriage would not be arranged for them before or soon after they graduated, or that they would not return to Yemen to live. Doing well in school did not ensure that they would be able to continue their education beyond high school, at least not immediately, though it was a more viable option if they were awarded scholarships and if the men in their families supported this decision (ibid.: 112). The main point of their high school success was to contribute positively to the family's status in the community and in Yemen, and to improve their parents' marriage choices, not to create individualized opportunities for their daughters.

The period of adolescence that high school encompasses is commonly understood as a time of ingroup–outgroup formations of one kind or another. In this sense, certain aspects of the Yemeni girls' experience in high school were not unlike those of other students who form friendships with students most like themselves and have minimal contact with others. For the Yemeni girls, the choice to segregate themselves was an important means to protect themselves against the unwelcome consequence of intimidating surveillance, i.e. being taken out of school. Historically, the role of education for first-generation immigrants like these has been to provide a space – as individuals or as a group and away from their parents – to navigate the social, cultural, and ideological differences they encounter between family and school, parents, and peer groups, and between peers. How this is accomplished, how difficult the task is, and what form these juxtapositions take varies considerably from one individual to the next, as the previous study suggests.

What is striking in the case of the young Yemeni girls is how restricted their space of identity construction was in a place normally designed for this purpose. Despite this, there is a lot of evidence that the girls worked through cultural contrasts and reflected on the evolution in their own thinking in much the same way as the Portuguese girls did, with reference to the specific features of their migrant experience. Though the parents and the girls may have appeared "isolated from American life," the families and their traditions were not unaffected by their migration. Take Saba as an example. The book begins with a quote from Saba expressing her frustrated attempts to reconcile her Yemeni and American lives:

Okay, in their eyes, it means you be quiet, you listen, you obey and you go through, you listen to what we say, regardless, because we know what's best for you. Okay, in my eyes, it's not. It's you take what they say into consideration but you also see your own views. You try to – you have to make the decision on your own. You have to go just beyond what they say, what they're demanding and look at it and look at what you want, how you see it, how do you feel about it, what is the best outcome for you. Because you know yourself best... For me, I consider everything in an Islamic point of view. And being Yemeni, that's basically, you listen to what they say. Being Americanized is the fact that you can stand up and say, "No," you know, "This is what I want. And this is the reason why I want this."

(ibid.: 1)

At the end of the book, Sarroub provides a brief update on what happened to the girls in her study after they graduated from high school. Of Saba, "who had been 'known as a leader among the *hijabat*' " (ibid.: 14), in 2001, she writes:

Saba prevailed in her choice of marriage partner. After high school, she married an Arab American who is not of Yemeni descent. She still works for the community center and hopes to become a certified teacher in a public school bilingual program. She now listens to music and goes to movies and restaurants with her husband and thinks that she can still be a good Muslim despite adopting this popular cultural lifestyle. She is still deeply religious.

(ibid.: 137)

Out of the limited space where her two cultures were permitted to meet, Saba emerged with the belief that she, in dialogue with her family, could determine her own way to be a 'good Muslim.' Some of the other girls' situations were similar to Saba's, others followed more traditional paths, some had moved to Yemen, and one, who had been unhappily married while in high school, had run away, been kidnapped by her family, put under FBI protection, and was living with her boyfriend in Southend shunned by her family. How these young women arrived at their post-high-school destinations is a matter of their individuality, their families, and the relation between the two. This relationship is another important dimension of differentiation among immigrant groups that can have a tremendous impact both on the choices available and the consequences for young migrants of the decisions they make. Given the particular forms of control exercised by these particular families and the communities they resided in, this relationship took on a great deal of importance. The girls' fates were intrinsically tied to how their parents occupied the limited space available to *them* outside the bounds of faith and community.

Negotiating inter-ethnic identities

The fourth study examines issues of identity construction and negotiation in a public urban high school in a US Midwestern city, referred to as Lakes City. In her one-year ethnographic study conducted between 2001 and 2002, Bic Ngo (2010) focused on seven Lao students and their struggles with identity issues in relation to parents, teachers, and students and, in particular, their complex relationship with the majority Hmong student population with whom they share a racial (Asian) and national (Laotian) identity, but not an ethnic one. The Hmong were the largest Asian ethnic group in the city and in the school. At the time of the study, out of the total population of the city of 382,618, 6 percent were of Asian ethnicity and of these the Hmong numbered 9,595, followed by the Vietnamese (2,395), the Chinese (2,369), and the Lao (2,212). Of the students in the high school, the majority consisted of 43 percent African or African American, 38 percent Asian American, of which most were Hmong, Lao comprising 8 percent, and 16 percent White American. The majority second language spoken in the school was Hmong, followed by Liberian standard English (ibid.: 123). The students were from both working-class and middle-class families, though 75 percent were eligible for free or reduced school lunches.

The families of the Lao and Hmong students had almost all originally come to the United States as refugees during the late 1970s and 1980s as a consequence of the Vietnam War. The Lao were part of the exodus of villagers who fled to escape heavy American bombing or were forced to relocate for political or economic reasons after the US military defeat, when a civil war established a communist government in power in Laos. The Hmong, many of whom were allied with the US war effort, also left in significant numbers during this time. Both Lao and Hmong lived in Thai refugee camps for years before the United States began to accept significant numbers of Laotians starting around 1979:

> The camps housing the ethnic Lao were gradually emptied, with most refugees coming to the US. France, Canada, and Australia also took thousands of Laotian refugees. The Hmong faced somewhat different circumstances. The Thai government was less friendly toward this ethnic group and sometimes refused them admission as refugees. The Hmong had fought as irregulars – armed, supplied, and paid by the C.I.A. However, they lacked documentation and found it harder to meet US criteria for refugee status.[3]

It is important to note that Laos' many different ethnic groups have inhabited distinct ecological communities for centuries characterized according to three distinct geographical sectors: the lowland, midland, and upland. The lowland Lao migrants constitute the predominant ethnic group. They make up two-thirds of the population and are clustered along the Mekong

River to the east and in the southern panhandle. The lowland Lao have historically occupied the highest ethnic social status in Laos; many are subsistence rice farmers and they are predominantly Buddhist. The Hmong are the largest group among the upland Lao who make up 10 percent of the whole population. They are Tibeto-Burmese speaking peoples who have migrated southward from China over the last two centuries. The Hmong are Animists who believe that there is no separation between the spiritual and material world, and that not only humans, but animals, plants, mountains, wind, and other features of the natural environment, have souls.

The history of social inequality among the different ethnic groups in Laos has meant that the Hmong, like other ethnic minorities residing in the midlands and uplands, have traditionally been underrepresented in the government and received fewer government services. Whatever differences may have existed in Laos, however, both groups were forced to leave the country, with many arriving as refugees in the United States with little or no education and with few of their skills in subsistence farming suited to life there. They mostly found employment as factory workers; many had to rely on their children to help support the family. Since the first few decades following their arrival, however, members of both groups have found ways to improve their standard of living through commercial agricultural activities, entrepreneurial food service businesses, and more recently in 'white-collar' professions as increasing numbers of first and second-generation Hmong and Lao attend university.

Ngo's ethnography does not set out to describe or explore the impact of the economic, cultural, and social differences between the Hmong and the Lao; she alludes only in passing to the history of inter-ethnic tension between the two groups. Her main concern is to explore the impact of problematical classifications regarding race and ethnicity for the Lao students in particular, where they, like other Asian American students including the Hmong, were routinely referred to by non-Asian students as well as many teachers with the term 'Asian' or 'Chinese' or 'Hmong,' all used as though they were the same or similar terms (see also Flores and Huo 2013). The relative absence of any attempt to make distinctions among the Lao, Thai, and other Asian students' ethnic identities, Ngo suggests, exacerbated hostility between the Hmong and the Lao students. The following exchange between a Ngo and a Lao student illustrates her point.

C: A lot of people call Asian people just Chinese or something. I hear it all the time… I've heard it like, they'll say, "That Chinese boy." And I'm sitting here thinking, "He's not Chinese." Cause I can tell the difference almost all the time.
BN: They don't say he's Hmong or they're all Hmong?
C: No. Some of them say it, because then most of them think that everybody here is Hmong. But most of them think it's like Chinese or something (laughs).

(ibid.: 55)

Many of the Lao students felt that their unique cultural and historical identities went unrecognized or were marginalized at the institutional level within the school. The Asian Club, for example, whose faculty advisor and sponsor was a Hmong bilingual teacher, was supposedly initiated with the objective to provide all Asian American students with a sense of belonging to the local school culture and to instill in them pride and awareness of their individual ethnic identities (ibid.: 59). In practice, the club became a site of contestation and conflict between Hmong Americans and Lao Americans, as well as other Asian ethnics, who referred to it as The Hmong Club, as it was seen to privilege the identities of the Hmong students alone. A non-Asian teacher pointed to the club as an example of the institutional exclusion of all Asians other than Hmong; he recalled that the invitations to events such as 'Asian Parent Night' sponsored by the Asian Club were only translated from English into Hmong, for example (ibid.: 62).

This sense of marginalization was also felt by the Lao students at the interpersonal level. The view that the Hmong students were exclusive in their friendships, restricting them to other Hmong students, was common among the Lao in the study, and contributed to their negative attitudes. The following excerpt from Ngo's field notes was recorded after she had asked a group of students whether they thought there was racism in their school:

> Sompong and Kia say no, and point out there's a lot of mixture or diversity at the school. They tell me that different kinds of students hang out together and are friends. They point to our table as an example, where Lao, Hmong and White students sit together. After a little thought, however, Sompong declares that if there's a racist group at the school, it is the Hmong. She quickly touches Kia [a Hmong student] on the arm and apologizes to her and states that she doesn't mean to disrespect any specific person. She continues to explain that many of the Hmong students sit together and hang out exclusively with other Hmong students. Sompong then pauses and gestures at the Hmong students sitting together at the tables around us and our eyes scan the cafeteria with her. Continuing, she turns to me and asserts that many of the Hmong students "hate on me because I'm Laos." Once again, Sompong remembers that Kia and Bao are Hmong and qualifies her remark by adding, "Not all Hmong people are that way."
>
> (ibid.: 63)

But the Lao students who did hang out with Hmong friends also faced criticism from their Lao peers and their parents. As migrant parents of adolescents, their parents shared the same concern for their children's educational success as other parents, with the added fear that their children would lose their language and abandon their cultural and religious beliefs in favor of other, including "American," values. One of these students, Mindy, told Ngo, "I think my friends are getting mad at me 'cause I'm hanging out with too many Hmong people...I think that they think I'm becoming one of them. I think my parents think that too." According to Mindy, her parents asked her, "Why are you trying to be like Hmong people, dyeing your hair and stuff like that?," which indicated to her parents that she was "like becoming a slut, forgetting your own race" (ibid.: 69).

If the friction that existed between the Hmong and the Lao students had some of its origins in the prior structuring of social relations in Laos, their shared experience as migrants added a particular twist. In relation to the city and the school where Ngo's study took place, as a consequence of demographics the Lao found themselves in the minority, a position the Hmong had traditionally occupied in Laos. The fact that the Hmong's majority position granted them disproportional representation within this school may have disrupted the Laotian students' prior assumptions about their relative social status. The Hmong, as a diasporic ethnic minority, are recognized for the lengths they go to protect their culture from the scrutiny and criticism of outsiders (Lee 2001). In many ways, the Hmong's migration to the United States was yet another chapter in the history of this community which had continuously sustained its identity, not through an attachment to a particular nation state, but by constructing itself as a close-knit clan-like group (Hein 2012: 42). One of the Hmong students whose family had migrated from Laos expressed it in this way:

> When they say, "Where are you from?" I say, "I don't really have a country, but I'm from Laos." That's what I tell them. When I tell them that they say, "Oh, you're from Laos, but how come you're Hmong?" Chinese, Lao, Hmong look similar. I just say my grand, grandparents came from China, so that's how we ended up there.
>
> (ibid.: 52)

Although their inter-ethnic conflict created fissures between them, the Hmong and Lao students were inescapably linked through their common experience as migrants and their determination to claim a place in American culture in the face of their parents' fears or disapproval and their own strong affiliations to their Hmong or Lao identities. One Lao girl described by the author as coming from a "Buddhist, low-income, immigrant background" who preferred to dress like "middle-class White American society" (Ngo 2010: 83) ("Gwyneth Paltrow is my ultimate – love the way she dresses" [ibid.: 84] she had said) and who reported that her peers chastised her because she chose "to act and walk and talk and speak" like she was "try[ing] to act Black" (ibid.: 87) tried to explain what it meant for her to be Lao:

> It means that when I sit down to the table the food I primarily eat is Laotian food. The culture that I follow is Laotian. The family that I am in is Laotian. The beliefs that I have are those of many Laotian people.

> The religion is one that is found in the Laotian culture for the most part. So, I may be Americanized, but when I go home and when I look deep inside myself I'm Laotian. That's who I see myself as. I don't see myself as American, you know. Although I am, I am a citizen of this country, yes, but I mean that doesn't change the fact that yes, of course, I am American. But just to me, I feel Laotian. I feel like, that's how I identify myself.
>
> (ibid.: 83–84)

The inter-ethnic conflict that emerged between the Hmong and the Lao students is a reminder that migrants are not only repositioned in relation to the established inhabitants of the countries to which they migrate. Migration also involves constructing relationships with other migrants. When migrants share some prior history, structures of signification that become rearranged in their transfer from one environment to another may not translate well for all. The loss of a social advantage, especially in the face of increased competition over resources and recognition, can make a decision to translate a letter in one language and not another a highly symbolic act.

What's fresh off the boat?

The transnational social spaces that migrant communities inhabit help them to establish enduring economic, political, and sociocultural ties and give them a presence beyond the borders of the communities and nations where they live. The substance of cosmopolitan spaces, however, is less clear. The belief underlying the cosmopolitan ideal – that to reach a better understanding of the self, you must be open to the perceptions of others – is about more than the type of *connectivity* associated with transnationalism, which can be and often is limited to virtual or limited contact. With cosmopolitanism there is an expectation of a more reflective *connection to* the other. This prospect can be especially daunting for 1.5 and second-generation immigrants who, in traversing the *intra-ethnic* borders between two homelands, sometimes encounter an 'us' that feels more like a 'them.'

This particular convergence of identity structures is explored in the final two studies examined in this chapter involving ethnically Korean migrants in the United States. Though the foci of these studies differed somewhat in the original research from my emphasis here, both explore the relationship between self-ascription and other-imposition of identity within the same ethnic group. The researcher paid particular attention to the (self)categorization of ethnicity and how this was performed discursively by young migrants ranging in age from their late teens to early twenties.[4] Broadly speaking, the data suggest significant variation among Korean Americans in how they categorize (and evaluate) their own and their same ethnic peers' identities. Across both contexts the attempts by the young people, who were at different phases of their migrant histories, to claim or embody a particular identity or set of identities could be scrutinized or challenged by others from within the same ethnic group. Although the term 'transnational migrants' is often used to describe young people like these, there was a strong tendency on their part to categorize the identities of peers within their ethnic group in oppositional terms, e.g., certain individuals were labeled or labeled themselves 'more' or 'less' American or Korean.

In their interviews with young 1.5 and second-generation Korean Americans residing in Los Angeles, M. Agnes Kang and Adrienne Lo (2004) found a rich and varied lexicon circulating within the Korean community which the young men and women used to describe themselves and others regarding their ethnicity, including "Americanized," "whitewashed," "Korean Korean," "American Korean," "Koreanized," "Westernized," "Korean-washed," and "fob," though, they note, there was no particular agreement about what these terms signified outside of the specific context of use. "Korean Korean" or "Koreanized," for example, could refer to someone who celebrated holidays and cultural traditions within the family or community, or expected to marry another Korean. The same expressions could be used to refer to friends who were felt to be spending more time with recently arrived Koreans than with Korean Americans who had lived in the United States for several generations.

> In our interviews with second- and 1.5-generation Korean Americans in Los Angeles, we found that some participants would use a term such as "Koreanized" to point to a voluntary, self-ascribed, mutable identity while others would use that same term to talk about an identity which was conceived of as fixed and unchanging. Moreover, in moving towards a conception of identity as primarily changeable, participants also demonstrated an increasing attention to the negotiated nature of identity as achieved *between* participants, through an active attempt at signifying a particular identity on the one hand, and through a recognition of that identity on the other.
>
> (ibid.: 95, emphasis in original)

The idea of a 'self-ascribed' status of identity was especially in the minds of some of those interviewed with respect to their friends who embraced the aesthetic styles of the 'Korean wave' as a resource through which to express their ethnicity in much the same way as the *yuhaksaeng* in Canada discussed in the previous chapter, though without the added marked class distinction. The term "fobby" was appropriated (from FOB or Fresh Off the Boats) by young people to describe their friends who chose to "act *so* Korean" despite having been born or having lived for a considerable time in the United States.

SARAH: I really get annoyed by fobby people actually *(laughing)* Because like wh-why do you have to like I don't know Why do you have to *(quietly)* s-say that you're *so* Korean, you are *so* proud of being Korean that you make a point of showing that you are Korean in front of everybody like ostentatiously like "Oh I have to get bleached hair," "I have to wear this shade of lipstick" or (...)

ADRIENNE: So um so somebody who's fobby do they do they try to be fobby? Like is it like

SARAH: Yeah I know people who try to be fobby on purpose? Because they they like it when people call them fobby, they're really proud of it? (...)

ADRIENNE: So does being fobby have to do with where you were born or when you came or it doesn't have so much to do with that?

SARAH: Um I don't think so because ok my some of my friends um they were born here? but yet they they always go out of their way to make Korean friends or they that's just who they prefer to be with? so they start to dress like them, they start to talk like them (...) they might have a little bit of accent or they might not or but then it's just like their life style um just the way they dress and the TV shows they watch.

(ibid.: 104–105, emphasis in original)

Sarah's comments reveal a good-natured wrestling on her part with the heterogeneous identity structures in place within her peer group. She views the embrace of Korean popular culture as a voluntary and not a fixed aspect of their Korean identity – they "go out of their way" to be fobby. Another participant, Mike, adds the dimension of time to the issue. He views his and his friends' identity as something that changes (and is expected to change) over time as their 'fixed' or inherited Korean identities turn further from the source and more toward the target culture.

There are certain traits that uh more Koreanized people do that Korean Americans they like won't do like listen to Korean music you know a lot – Me and a lot of my friends we used to listen to Korean music but as you got older you really don't like listen to it anymore but you know more more uh Koreanized people will – They still listen to Korean music like all the time um they'll speak Korean like 50% or more.

(ibid.: 99–100)

Kang (2004) examines a similar set of issues in her study of camp counselors at a Korean Cultural Camp in the northern California Bay area in the context of a meeting to discuss their program agenda. In this setting, the cultural resources under scrutiny do not emanate from the popular culture of contemporary Korean but from its cultural heritage. Different viewpoints are expressed among first, 1.5 and second-generation counselors about "the perceived choice between 'heritage' and 'mentorship' as the main motivation for participating in the camp" (ibid.: 219). The tension between the two sides, as Kang notes (ibid.), gets mapped onto ideologies of ethnic identity as the meeting progresses.

The counselors, through their discursive practices, associate certain motivations, like the emphasis on teaching Korean culture, with notions of being 'more Korean' and the emphasis on mentorship with being 'more American'. The subtle ways in which speakers indexically link ideologies regarding the camp to ethnic identity demonstrate that 'being Korean' is anything but stable, homogenous, or fixed.

The camp's first two stated objectives are the "Promotion of a better understanding and awareness of Korean cultural heritage, tradition, and history" and "Sharing our bi-cultural experiences and expectations as Korean Americans with our campers in that order" (ibid.: 220). But opinions differ among the counselors regarding what *their* priorities are and about the implied view of the camp itself that Koreans share a homogeneous identity or cultural heritage. Counselors who see mentorship as their primary motivation refer to their own experiences of "dealing with one's immigrant parents, inter-racial dating, and developing one's sense of ethnic identity while growing up among European Americans" (ibid.: 221). On the heritage side, topics like the use of kinship terms and their cultural significance are stressed, for example, the idea of *oppa/enni* (older brother/older sister), as are traditional folk art forms such as Korean drumming. What emerges from the interview data, however, is that mentorship based in their lived experiences is viewed as *separate* from a sense of a Korean heritage (ibid.: 228). This idea is reinforced in the counselors' use of terms similar to those found in Kang and Lo's study discussed above to categorize themselves and others on the Korean/American spectrum. It should be noted that part of the background to the interviews is the recent fact that, according to Kang, "many 'Korean American' counselors have been let go in favor of some 'Korean' counselors who are able to teach Korean culture courses, such as Korean language, etiquette, and folk music" (ibid.: 221). Many of the latter group are instructors at the Korean Cultural Center (KCC) who, though present, "do not participate actively in the discussion" (ibid.: 228). Though the authors don't mention it, the camp sounds like an example of the kind of cultural exchanges discussed in the previous chapter set up by the South Korean government to extend its reach to the diasporic Korean community.

In the following excerpt, Ellen's reference to "she" is another counselor, Sara, who has just shared her story about how she came to understand her Korean identity after growing up among European American peers.

> And I think, every year that we have like – every year that we have camp, there's always conflict in what the emphasis is gonna be, more Korean, more Korean American, more American, you know? And everyone comes with different ideas, right? And like, right now, I disagree with the oppa enni, and I can hang with that, just, you know, whatever, and I'll do it? but it's like, I think we all have different ideas, you know? And like, as she said, no one's discussed the ideas? but it just comes out

with our opinions? when we argue like this? you know? and it didn't just come out, we didn't like lay out like, exactly what we're here for. And I'm here more on maybe the American side, not American side, but more of like a different – a different angle than some other people come here for, you know? And I think that that doesn't show unless we argue about like this, but we never just flat out said, "I'm here because, this is what happened to me" as she just did right now.

(ibid.: 223–224)

The idea of wanting to work at the camp because of "what happened to me" is acknowledged by another counselor, Jon. In his comments, he struggles to express the view that the type of knowledge the camp offers of Korean cultural heritage, while important, can be learned elsewhere, at the KCC even, but advice and understanding about growing up as a Korean American can only be imparted by someone who has been there. Therefore, specific skills like playing drums or learning a language should not be viewed as more valuable by the camp.

You got to be able to understand what this kid wants. What he needs from you. And if you can't do that, you shouldn't be at the camp. I don't want KCC to take this personally either but, I don't know how to play the drums, but I can play the drums? You know? I don't know anything about uh uh KOREAN CULTURE, those traditions and etiquettes, but I think I know something about kids. I think I know what they need because I've BEEN there. Had those experiences. And I can talk to them. And tha-that's just a- that's just a matter of information. If I went to KCC, I could learn the drums. And then I would have that as a resource. That doesn't mean no one else just because they don't know the drums, or they can't speak Korean, or they don't speak English, shouldn't go to camp. You see what I'm saying?

(ibid.: 227–228)

Although the authors do not make clear the specific migrant trajectories of each of their informants, a similarity seems to emerge in the dynamic between young people who are 1.5 or second-generation Korean Americans and their first-generation counterparts. For many of these young men and women, Korean pride is less about past and present cultural resources and more about the struggles they have faced and the lessons they have learned. In his memoir, *Fresh Off the Boat: A Memoir* (2013), writer, chef, and restaurateur Eddie Huang recounts how he claimed a place for himself as a 1.5-generation immigrant from Taiwan within Black hip hop culture in the United States, in the face of his parent's cultural values and expectations, and society's racial prejudice.

[Tu]Pac made sense to us. We lived in a world that treated us like deviants and we were outcast. There was always some counselor or administrator pulling us out of class to talk. We stayed in detention and we were surrounded by kids who had no idea what we were going through. We listened to hip hop because there wasn't anything else that welcomed us in, made us feel at home. I could see why Milli wanted to pull a pistol on Santa or why B.I.G was ready to die. Our parents, Confucius, the model-minority bullshit, and kung-fu style discipline are what set us off. But Pac held us down.

(Huang 2013: 60)

The views expressed by the young Korean Americans regarding their relationship to the past and present cultural resources of Korea reveal similar efforts to manage the changes in and challenges to their perceptions about their identity. For these young people the challenge is greater than for many previous generations of migrants. They are called on to maintain a connection with their cultural heritage and to consider their place within popular contemporary Korean culture, while still carving out a space for themselves as Americans or Canadians in the multiple options available to them in the North American context.

Constructing cosmopolitanism from below

The combined synchronic 'snapshots' of these children, adolescents, and young adults at a particular time in their development illustrate the diverse ways that migrant and minority populations both direct and inhabit their transnational or cosmopolitan identities. In all of the examples, different forms of translation played a central role in altering cultural meanings and historical relationships from one social and geographical setting to another. For the Moroccan migrant children, they had to re-translate themselves and their families so that their teacher could recognize them as members of the majority Spanish culture. The young Portuguese women struggle to give expression in language to the changing social and interactional norms they encountered as a result of their families' migration to France. The Yemeni girls' experience in a public school environment demonstrates how seemingly impermeable belief structures can be effectively translated within a secular public context. Although their basic identity structures remained strongly influenced by their Yemeni Muslim culture, some of the girls and their parents did find a way to map one set of values onto another, producing modifications to their traditions that grew out of their migrant experience. The young Lao, Hmong, and Korean Americans give expression to the split structures of identity that they were attempting to manage in relation to multiple cultures and contexts.

Taken together, these studies illuminate the rarely stated processes that to varying degrees erode, mitigate, or attempt to outflank the apparent injuries to traditional social and familial patterns of life, changing and qualifying prevailing daily realities, moving them forward. They also reveal a common ground of ambiguity – ambiguity as a place in which to seek to reconcile contending sides, beliefs, traditions, or in which to deliberately obscure differences so that time and new social and cultural realities can come to take away their power to disrupt or impede movement. Even the youngest migrants, as the Moroccan children demonstrate, come to understand that their sense of identity and belonging may not be as clear to others as it is to them. At the most intimate level it is what was dealt with by the young Portuguese women shuffling and improvising, each in their own way, with the grammatical signs of proximity. And here, surprisingly, there is a striking similarity with de Gaulle's mis/understanding with the *pieds noirs* because it is clear that beneath his '*je vous ai compris*' they heard – or chose to hear – the '*tu*' of intimacy, not the '*vous*' of realpolitik. In its calculated ambiguity it stands as a model of the strategies for dealing with the emergent contradictions and mixed loyalties observable across all of the research. The young people, faced with what were sometimes stark differentiations, attempted to find ways of fending off their potentially negative effects. In highly individual ways the young people sought or found some compromise that worked and carried them forward to whatever happened next. Just as Saba "the leader among the *hijabat*" ultimately chose her own husband, listened to music, and could still be a deeply religious Muslim, and the Lao girl could find a place for melding her two realities in the notion of America as a transcendent social reality, so in their different ways all of the young people in the research examined were oriented toward a promised land of sustained ambiguity, or compromise or other means with which to allow in the tiny incremental exchanges that would free them to embrace rather than be lost within the push–pull of the migrant experience.

Adolescence and young adulthood are a time of intense identity construction when young people, drawing from the array of materials available to them, create a bricolage of altered meanings and forms of expression to fit their immediate purposes. First and second-generation young migrants are engaged in the same process of translating the various 'worlds' they perceive around them, with an additional 'world' that is available locally through their extended family or local communities, and, at a distance, through various forms of media correspondence such as emails, online chat sessions, telephone calls, and internet websites. This latter development, an important reason for reconsidering how migration is experienced in the twenty-first century, has enabled individuals to build social networks that extend well beyond the boundaries of their family and local community. For some young people, this is seen positively as allowing greater flexibility with regard to their identity construction, as their knowledge and understanding about their cultural heritage are no longer solely based on accounts from previous generations; for others, together with their families, it has encouraged greater cultural conservatism out of fear that their values, beliefs, and traditions have strayed too far from their origins.

Some form of translation, increasingly in more than one medium, is involved in these expanded spaces of transnational identity exploration, contributing to the maintaining or blurring of cultural boundaries within a wide mix of genres and languages. But this does not mean that migrant families do not also feel firmly rooted in one place; many still view themselves as residents of their new communities much like anyone else, particularly once the second and third generation have reached adolescence. First-generation migrants historically have attached great significance to specific cultural or religious practices that are regularly observed and link them and their children to specific regions or countries of origin. The main difference for contemporary migrants and their families is that far greater numbers, even those without the economic means or the legal possibility of visiting their countries of origin, can maintain a more proximal, though not exactly tangible, sense of belonging to their past as virtual forms of contact make interactions with extended family, friendship, and business networks cheaper, quicker, and more reliable. It still remains to be seen how or if these forms of inter-connectivity can contribute to a 'cosmopolitanism from below' that has as its aim to unite global and local communities in more profound and meaningful ways. What is clear is that translation will continue to be central to this process.

Notes

1 I have divided what was presented as a continuous exchange (ibid.: 496–497) into three parts (I–III) to allow me to comment on one segment at a time of the original transcript. Transcription markers have also been removed and some minor editing performed in the interest of readability. The original Spanish has also been removed here for copyright reasons.
2 The interviews were conducted in French and appear with their English translations in the original article. In the interest of readability, I have removed some transcription markers from the English texts indicating, for example, short pauses, elongated vowels, and minimal speaker backchanneling, and have changed some punctuation.
3 https://seap.einaudi.cornell.edu/refugees (Accessed April 2016).
4 All these interviews were conducted in English. I have removed transcription markers and done some minor editing on the interviews in the interest of readability.

References

Abu-Laban, Yasmeen and Christina Gabriel 2002 *Selling Diversity: Immigration, Multiculturalism, Employment Equity and Globalization*. Ontario: Broadview Press.
Anderson, Michael 1971 *Family Structure in 19th Century Lancashire*. Cambridge: Cambridge University Press.
Brown, Roger and Albert Gilman 1960 "The Pronouns of Power and Solidarity," in Thomas Sebeok (ed) *Style in Language*. Cambridge, MA: MIT Press, 253–276.

Cesari, Jocelyne and Sean McLoughlin (eds) 2005 *European Muslims and the Secular State*. Aldershot: Ashgate Publishing Company.
Fink, Leon (ed) 2011 *Workers Across the Americas*. Oxford: Oxford University Press.
Flores, Natalia M. and Yuen J. Huo 2013 "'We' Are Not All Alike: Consequences of Neglecting National Origin Identities Among Asians and Latinos," *Social Psychology and Personality Science* 4(2): 143–150.
García-Sánchez, Immaculada 2013 "The Everyday Politics of "Cultural Citizenship" among North African Immigrant School Children in Spain," *Language & Communication* 33: 481–499.
Grossman, James 1989 *Land of Hope: Chicago, Black Southerners and the Great Migration*. Chicago: University of Chicago Press.
Hein, Jeremy 2012 "Homeland Narratives and Hmong Americans in Wisconsin," Vincent K. Her and Mary Louise Buley-Meissner (eds) *Hmong and American: From Refugees to Citizens*. St. Paul: Minnesota Historical Press, 47–58.
Hine, Robert V. and John M. Faragher 2000 *The American West*. New Haven: Yale University Press.
Hobsbawm, E.J. 1968 *Industry and Empire: The Pelican Economic History of Britain, Vol. 3: From 1750 to the Present Day*. Harmondsworth: Penguin Books.
Hoerder, Dirk 2011 "Overlapping Spaces: Transregional and Transcultural," in Leon Fink (ed) *Workers Across the Americas*. Oxford: Oxford University Press, 33–38.
Huang, Eddie 2013 *Fresh Off the Boat: A Memoir*. New York: Random House.
Kang, M. Agnes 2004 "Constructing Ethnic Identity through Discourse: Self-Categorization among Korean American Camp Counselors," *Pragmatics* 14(2/3): 217–233.
Kang, M. Agnes and Adrienne Lo 2004 "Two Ways of Articulating Heterogeneity in Korean American Narratives of Ethnic Identity," *Journal of Asian American Studies* 7(2): 93–116.
Koven, Michele 2009 "Managing Relationships and Identities through Forms of Address: What French-Portuguese Bilinguals Call Their Parents in Each Language," *Language & Communication* 29: 343–365.
Laborde, Cécile, 2008 *Critical Republicanism: The Hijab Controversy and Political Philosophy*. Oxford: Oxford University Press.
Lee, Keehyeung 2008 "Mapping Out the Cultural Politics of 'the Korean Wave' in Contemporary South Korea," in Chua Beng Huat and Koichi Iwabuchi (eds) *East Asian Pop Culture*. Hong Kong: Hong Kong University Press, 175–189.
Lee, Stacey E. 2001 "More than 'Model Minorities' or 'Delinquents': A Look at Hmong American High School Students," *Harvard Educational Review* 71(3): 505–528.
Levitt, Peggy 2007 *God Needs No Passport*. New York: The New Press.
Lin, Angel and Avin Tong 2008 "Re-imagining a Cosmopolitan 'Asian Us': Korean Media Flows and Imaginaries of Asian Modern Femininities," in Chua Beng Huat and Koichi Iwabuchi (eds) *East Asian Pop Culture*. Hong Kong: Hong Kong University Press, 91–125.
Lopez, Mark 2000 *The Origins of Multiculturalism in Australian Politics 1945–1975*. Victoria: Melbourne University Press.

Ngo, Bic 2010 *Unresolved Identities: Discourse, Ambivalence, and Urban Immigrant Students*.Albany: SUNY Press.
Novak, Michael 1972 *The Rise of the Unmeltable Ethnics: Politics and Culture in the Seventies*. New York: MacMillan Publishing Co. Inc.
Papastergiadis, Nicos 2000 *The Turbulence of Migration*. Cambridge: Polity Press.
Philips, Kevin 2006 *American Theocracy: The Peril and Politics of Radical Religion, Oil, and Borrowed Money in the 21st Century*. New York: Penguin Group Inc.
Portes, Alejandro 2003 "Conclusion: Theoretical Convergences and Empirical Evidence in the Study of Immigrant Transnationalism," *International Migration Review* 37(3): 874–892.
Sarroub, Loukia K. 2005 *All American Yemeni Girls*. Philadelphia: University of Pennsylvania Press.
Sinclair, John and Malcolm Coulthard 1975 *Towards an Analysis of Discourse*. Oxford: Oxford University Press.
Snel, Erik, Godfried Engbersen and Arjen Leerkes 2006 "Transnational Involvement and Social Integration," *Global Networks* 6(3): 285–308.
Soysal, Yasemin Nuhoglu 1994 *Limits of Citizenship: Migrants and Postnational Membership in Europe*. Chicago: University of Chicago Press.
Vertovec, Steven 2007 "Super-diversity and Its Implications," *Ethnic and Racial Studies* 30(6): 1024–1054.
Weber, Eugene 1976 *Peasants into Frenchmen: The Modernization of Rural France 1870–1914*. Stanford: Stanford University Press.
Wilkerson, Isabel 2010 *The Warmth of Other Suns: The Epic Story of America's Great Migration*. New York: Vintage Books.
Wolf, Eric R. 2010 *Europe and the People Without History*. Second edition. Berkeley: University of California Press.

Index

Page numbers in italics are figures; with 'n' are notes.

Act of Union 112, 113, 143n2
Amnesty International 80, 96–7
Anam, Tahmima 72
Angel Island 50–7, *51*, *55*; see also hospitality
Antin, Mary 39–43, 45; see also hospitality
Arbeely, Khawaja Najib 136–7
assimilation 16, 27, 34, 39, 41–2, 76, 134, 154, 179; transnationalism 18–20; the Irish 113–14, 116; translation services 69, 73–5; labor migrants 78
asylum seekers 10, 14, 31, 34 n1, 35 n15, 50, 72–3
Australia 6, 7, 16–17, 18, 179; Chinese immigrants during the Gold Rush 66 n3; Yasmine Gooneratne's *A Change of Skies* 132–5

Babels 32–3
Bailyn, Bernard 70
Bain, David Haward 128
balcony talks 91–2
Banksy 92, *93*
Benedict, Ruth 2–3
Bhabha, Homi 18, 20–1
Bible translation 49–50, 59–65, 139, 143n3
Blewett, Peter 115
Boas, Franz 22–3
'boat people' 9–11
bodegas 150–3, *151*, *152*
Bourhis, Richard Y. 154
Brian, Tara, 15
Bryant, William Cullen, 109–10
Butterick, George, 156, 172–3

Caminetti, Anthony 53–4
Canada multiculturalism 16, 179; Portuguese migrants 75–6; *yuhaksaeng* (Korean visa students) *and iminja* (multi-generational Korean immigrants) 169–72
canal building and Irish immigrants 111–16, 115, 116
Carleton, William, 117
Castro, Brian, 66n3, 145n18
Celestials 111, 123, 144n8
Chametzky, Jules 42
Childe, Cromwell 137–8
Chin, Frank 121–6, 128
China 6, 10, 29, 39, 51–2, 54, 119–20, 121, 144n6, n8, 178, 195, 197; internal migrant female factory workers 85–9, *86*
Chinese Exclusion Act of 1882 51–2, 54, 129, 144n10; see also Geary Act of 1892 and Extension Act of 1904
Chinese migrants in the US (nineteenth century) Angel Island 50–5, *51*; poems carved in detention barracks 55–7, *55*; transcontinental railroad 119–30, *126*, *130*, 141–3; see also Opium War
Choi, Roy 165–6
citizen/ship politics of 11–12, 15–16, 20, 26, 31, 40–1, 53–4, 57, 70, 72, 78, 95, 114, 129, 145n19, 176, 179, 198 see also statelessness
co-ethnic/ity 2, 171–2
Conklin, William E. 12–13
connectivity 6, 15, 19, 71, 72, 76, 134, 143, 149, 164, 169, 171, 173, 198, 203

Constable, Nicole 89, 94
cosmopolitan/ism 15, 16, 29–31, 74, 181, 198; religion Kublai Khan 28–9, 64–5; from below 28, 180, 203–5; Korean *yuhaksaeng* 169–72; *see also* hospitality, transnationalism
Creeley, Robert 155–6, 172–3
cultural geography 140–1
cultural translation 3, 30, 34, 134, 138–41, 203–5; in young migrant identities: Moroccans in Spain 181–5, Portuguese in France 185–90, Yemenis in the United States 190–3, Lao and Hmong in the United States 194–8, Koreans in the United States 198–203, and Koreans in Canada 169–172; *see also* landscape, linguistic landscapes
culture, anthropological definitions of 22–7

dagongmei 86–8
Daniell, David 61–2
Dashti, Abdulmohsen 90
Dearinger, Ryan 120, 121, 128
DeGaulle, Charles 24–6, 204
de Lange, Nicolas 58–9
Denison, T.S. 128–9
Derrida, Jacques 141
deterritorialization 18, 20
displacement 5, 166; permanent 11–16
diversity 16, 17, 20, 21, 23, 25, 28, 33, 34, 39, 67, 149, 156, 166, 177, 182, 185, 196
Dobkin, Jake 151–3
domestic workers 34 n1, 69, 72, 76, 77, 86, 88, 89–95; Domestic Workers Convention 76–7

ECOS (*Traductores e Intérpretes por la Solidaridad*) 32
effective nationality 12–13
Eliot, John 44–5
Ellis Island 45–50, 47, 49, 52; *see also* hospitality
Empower Foundation, Thailand 97–104
E pluribus unum 21–2
ethnics/ethnicity 2, 9–11, 13, 16–19, 22, 40, 43, 54, 69, 71–1, 75, 85, 88, 108, 118, 129, 138, 143, 145 n19, 153–4, 156, 165–8, 171–2, 174n4, 178, 180–2, 194–201
European Union 17, 176–7; refugees 7

Extension Act of 1904 51

Fabian, Johannes 30, 131, 145n20
faction fighting 117–18
Ferro, Edward 52
forced labor 76–7; Forced Migration Review 13; trafficking 82, translation 85
foreigner talk 90–1

Gambetta, Léon 177
García-Sánchez, Immaculada 181–5
Gardner, Andrew 79, 80, 81
Geary Act of 1892 51
Geertz, Clifford 23–7
global ethics 30, 57, 81, 172; *see also* translation ethics, hospitality
Global Initiative to Fight Human Trafficking (GIFT) 84
Global Voices (translator organization) 33
Goffman, Erving, 108
Gold, Jonathan 166
Golden Spike ceremony 122, *123*, 124, 125–6, *126*, 145 n16,
Gold Rush 51, 66 n3, 145 n18,
Goldstein, Tara 75
Gooneratne, Yasmine 132
Gordon, Avery F. 141
Gramsci, Antonio 21, 35n14
Great Famine effects on Irish Migration 112, 113, 118, 119, 143n2
Gulf States and male contract laborers 79–80
Guterres, Antonio 13

Hall, Stuart 18
Harb, Sirène 139
Harkness, Laura 79
Harney, Nicholas 19
Hassan, Waïl 139
Hit and Run report 98–101; *see also* Empower Foundation
Hmong 9–11; relations with Lao students 194–8
Hoerder, Dirk 70, 75
Homestead Act of 1862 111
hospitality global 7–15, and cosmopolitanism 27–31, 39; Kant's notion of 29–30; linguistic 31–2, 45, 65
Huang, Eddie 202; hip hop culture 202–3
hukou system, China 85, 87, 88, 89

210 Index

identity/identities 2–3, 11, 15–20, 24, 26, 28, 34, 46, 78, 85, 88, 91–2, 95, 108, 112, 129, 134, 140–1, 145 n18, 154, 166, *see also* young migrant identities
iminja 169–72
Immigration Act of 1917 40, 49, 66n1
indentured servitude 70–1
Indonesia 77, 95
Industrial Revolution 69, 111, 114, 177, 178
Ingold, Tim 4–6, 142–3
inter-ethnic relations 43; workers' rights in Koreatown, Los Angeles 168; Lao and Hmong students in the United States 194–8
inter-semiotic signs 150, *150*, 173 n1
interaction order Goffman's notion of 108–9, 143, 156, 172
internal migration Europe 176–178; Chinese female factory workers 85–9, *86*
international community 9, 12, 15, 31
International Labour Organization for Migration (IOM) 83
International Labour Organization (ILO) 76–7, 92–3; the *kafala* system 79; trafficking 82
interpreters 44, 83; Ellis Island 48, 52; Angel Island 52–3
intra-ethnic relations 169–72, 198
intra-lingual translations 176n1
Irish migrants in the United States (nineteenth century) canal workers 113–19, *115*, *116* (navvies in the U.K. 111–13); transcontinental railroad 128–9, 142–3

Jenolan Caves 134
Jerome, St. 62
Jewish refugees 1–2, 40, 153; *SS St. Louis* 9
Jordan, Miriam 165

kafala system 76, 79
Kalayaan 93
Kang, Kristy 166–7
Kang, M. Agnes 199–203
Kant, Immanuel 27, 29–30
Kenny, Kevin 118–19
Kogi Korean BBQ 165–6
Korean (language) Koreatown, Los Angeles 157–65, 167, 169; Toronto, Canada 169–72

Koreans migrants in the United States 198–204; Koreatown, Los Angeles 156–69, *158*, *162*, 173; *see also* Canada
Korean wave (*hallyu*) 171, 174n14, 199
Koser, Khalid 73
Koven, Michele 186–90
Kublai Khan 28–9, 64–5
'Kumjing' dolls 101–2, *101*; *see also* Empower Foundation
Kurasawa, Fuyuki 28
Kushner, Aviya 62

labor migrants 69–72, 103, 178; female domestic workers 89–95; female factory workers in China 85–9; overseas contract workers 76–81; sex workers 96–103; trafficking 82–5; *see also* indentured servitude 70–1
Laczko, Frank, 15
LaGuardia, Fiorello 47
Landry, Rodrigue 154
landscape translation of 3–6, 108; Chinese migrant railroad workers 119–30, *126*; invisible/visible specters 140–3; Irish and Chinese migrants 130; Irish migrant navvies and railroad workers 111–19, *115*, *116*; mound builders 109–11; Rihbany 135–40; Sri Lankan migrants 132–5, *133*; *see also* linguistic landscapes
language 2–3, 22–3, 25, 27–8, 31–3, 35n11; Angel Island 52–6; as form of control over domestic workers 90–2; Chinese factories 86–8; domestic worker activism 93–4; Ellis island 46, 49–50; inadequate interpreting for sex workers 99–100, 103; intra-ethnic relations 169–73; Irish migrants 112, 118; labor trafficking 83–5; Massachusett 44; migrant identity 181, 182–90, 196, 198, 200, 201–3, 205; migrant labor contracts 76–81, 104n1; Rihbany 136, 137, 139, 140; Satterlee's *Burning Wycliffe* 62–3; translated signs 149–55, 156–66; translation 57–9, 64–5, 73–6; Wycliffe and Tyndale Bible translations 59–62
Lao, relations with Hmong students 194–8
Last Rescue in Siam 102–3

Latin Americans 69; in Koreatown 156, 157, 165
Lee, Edwar 52–3
Lee, J.J. 113
Lee, Robert G. 128–9
Lee, Youngmin 167
Lepore, Jill 44
linguistic landscapes as translations 149–54; bodegas in New York City 150–4, *151*, *152*; inter-semiotic sign, British Museum 150, *150*; vs. multilingualism 155–6; public signage in Koreatown, Los Angeles 156–69, *158*, *159*, *160*, *161*, *162*
'Little Syria' New York City 135–40
Lo, Adrienne 199–203
loan words 154
Longhi, Vittorio 78–9
Low, Law Shee 54–5
Luban, David 57–8

McIvor, Liz 112
MacLochlainn, Alf 117–18
Majaj, Lisa Suhair 139
Malinowski, David 164
'Mida Tapestry' project 102, *102*; see also Empower Foundation
Migrante International 93
migration and social media 2, 8, 33, 94, 176; 'axes of differentiation' 178–80; diachronic 1, 114; human security 71–7; hybridity/postcolonial theory 18–22, 185; synchronic 1, 74–6, 114, 203; as 'wayfaring' (Ingold) 3–6, *4*, *5*; see also transnational/ism
Miller, Kirby 114
Mitra, Ananda 94
Modood, Tariq, 21
mound builders 109–10, 111
Murphy, Catherine 97
Muslims 13, 17, 26, 153, 179; Indonesian domestic workers 94–95; Yemeni migrants 190–3, 203, 204

naming 1–2, 11, 16, 88, 101, 120, 122, 123–4, 127, 134–5, 144n10, 144n18, 156, 164–5, 170, 174n4, 182, 195–6
Nast, Thomas 51–2, *51*
National Domestic Worker Alliance 93
nativism 23, 40, 42, 51, 54, 114, 117, 119, 127, 128, 129, 143n3, 145n19
navvies 111–13

Ngai, Pun 86–7
Ngo, Bic 194–8
Nichols, Mike 46
Nida, Eugene 60
Nyguen Huu Chung 10–11

O'Tuathaigh, Gearoid 117
Olson, Charles 155–6, 172–3
Opium War effects on Chinese migration 6, 119, 120, 144n6
'otherness' 1, 78, 135, 141, 149, 198

Palermo Protocols 82
Palestinians 13–14
paper sons 144n10
Park, Kyonghwan 167
Philip (Metacom) 44–5
pied noirs 24–6, 204
Polo, Marco 28–9
post-nationalist models of citizenship 179–80
praying towns 44
Project Lingua (translator organization) 33
Promontory Point, Utah 122, 141, 145n15
Puritans 43–5, 65

racial/ization 2, 16, 20, 30, 40, 66 n3, 125, 129, 130, 135, 140, 145 n19, 170, 172, 194, 201, 202
racism 22, 51, 66n3, 135, 140, 142, 145n19, 178, 196
Ranciere, Jacques 20
recognition 3, 17, 189–90; Clifford Geertz and 23–7; legal 13, 15, 73, 85; mutual 27–30, 156, 180–1; politics of 141–2, 178; as remembrance 130–5, *133*; and translation 39, 56, 59, 60, 164, 198; see also hospitality, cosmopolitanism
refugees 6, 31, 34 n1, 50, 72–3, 194–5; Palestinian 13–14; *pied noirs* and *harkis* 26; Syrian 7–9, 9–11; Vietnam and Cambodia 9–11; relations between Irish and Chinese migrants 128–9, 141–2, 144n7
remittance workers 72, 81, 92
reterritorialization 20
Ricoeur, Paul 31–32 see also linguistic hospitality
Rihbany, Rev. Abraham Mitrie 135–40, 141

Roediger, David 145n19
Rumbaut, Rubén 10
Russell, Andrew J. 122, *123*, 124–5, *126*

Sarroub, Loukia 190–3
Sassamon, John 43–5, 65
Satterlee, Thom, 62–4
Sawyer, John Birge 53
sex work/ers 96–104
Shakir, Evelyn 139
Sherman, August 40, *41*, *42*, 66n2
Shin, Hyunjung 169–72
signs given/given off 108–9, 114, 119, 125, 126–8, 141–3, 155, 165, 173; *see also* linguistic landscapes
Spain 177; Moroccan migrants 181–5, 203, 204
Spanish (language) Koreatown, Los Angeles 150–4, 157–60, 163, 165; Moroccans in Spain 183
Sri Lankan migrants (fictional) 132–5
SS *St. Louis* 9
statelessness 11–13
stick fighting 143n4
Syrians 7–9, 9–11; *see also* Rihbany, Rev. Abraham Mitrie

taskscape 143, 154, 173; Koreatown, Los Angeles 156–66
Tchen, John Kuo Wei 120, 128, 144n7
Tilly, Christopher 6
Tlaxcala (translator organization) 33
Traduttori per la Pace (translator organization) 33
transcontinental railroad Chinese immigrants 119–30, *123*, *126*, *127*, *130*, 145n16; Irish immigrants 128–9, 142–3
translation and mutual understanding 31–2; the absence or inadequacy of 84, 88, 91, 99–100, 103; and activism 32–4, 92–4, 97–104; and Angel Island 56 (*see also* interpreters); and the Bible 59–65, 143 n3; and Ellis Island 50 (*see also* interpreters); ethics and role morality 57–9, 65; and hospitality 45; and ideology 39; migrant labor contracts 76–80; as outreach tool 83–4, 93–4, 101; services 69, 73–5; *see also* cultural translation, language, linguistic landscapes

Translation for Progress (translator organization) 33
transnational/ism 6, 15, 18–20, 39, 69, 72, 74–5, 78, 81, 88–9, 114, 134, 138, 157, 166–71, 176, 179, 181, 189–90, 198–205; *see also* cosmopolitanism, hospitality, linguistic landscapes
Turki, Fawaz, 14
Tyndale, William 59–60, 62, 64, 65

United Nations Global Initiative to Fight Human Trafficking (GIFT) 84
United Nations High Commissioner for Refugee (UNHCR) 7, 8, 11, 12, 13
United Nations Relief and Works Agency for Palestine Refugees (UNRWA) 13–14
Urban Institute 84

Victims of Trafficking and Violence Protection Act 82

Walker's Fragments 112
Wampanoag tribe 43–5
Watts, Autumn 80, 81
Weber, Eugene 177
Werbner, Pnina 21
Werner, Louis 146n22
Williams, William H. 116–17, 118
Wolf, Eric R. 178, 180
Women in Informal Employment: Globalizing and Organizing (WIEGO) 93
Woodham-Smith, Cecil 143n2
Wycliffe, John 59–65
Wyse, Francis 113–14

xiangxiamei 88

young migrant identities 176–81; Koreans in the United States 198–203 and Canada 169–72; Lao and Hmong in the United States 194–8; Moroccans in Spain 181–5; Portuguese in France 185–90; Yemenis in the United States 190–3; *see also* identity/identities
Yu, Eui-Young 167
yuhaksaeng 169–72